IMAGE
AND
REALITY

Recent Titles in
Contributions in Military History

IMAGE
AND
REALITY
The Making of
the German Officer,
1921-1933

DAVID N. SPIRES

Contributions in Military History, Number 38

GREENWOOD PRESS
Westport, Connecticut • London, England

Library of Congress Cataloging in Publication Data

Spires, David N.
  Image and reality.

  (Contributions in military history, ISSN 0084-9251 ;
no. 38)
  Bibliography: p.
  Includes index.
  1. Germany. Heer—Officers—History—20th century.
2. Military education—Germany—History—20th century.
3. Sociology, Germany—History—20th century.   I. Title
II. Series.
UB415.G4S65   1984   355.3'3'0943   83-22560
ISBN 0-313-23722-0 (lib. bdg.)

Library of Congress Catalog Card Number: 83-22560
ISBN: 0-313-23722-0
ISSN: 0084-9251

First published in 1984

Greenwood Press
A division of Congressional Information Service, Inc.
88 Post Road West, Westport, Connecticut 06881

Printed in the United States of America

10 9 8 7 6 5 4 3 2 1

Contents

Preface

The Reichswehr, the German Army during the Weimar era, oc-
cupies a unique place in the annals of modern military history, for
it was "that rare phenomenon -- a truly professional army."[1] Not
since the days of Frederick the Great had Prussia-Germany fielded a
force consisting entirely of officers and enlisted men whose active
lives were devoted to soldiering. And even the Frederican standing
army was not professional in the contemporary sense of the word.[2]
The army of the Second Empire had by no means been a professional
one. It had a core of career officers and non-commissioned officers, but the vast majority of the troops were conscripts who saw
a short period of active service and then performed reserve duty.
The Wilhelmine Army, in fact, was a national army based on univer-
sal conscription -- a prototype of the "nation-in-arms" -- and not,
like the Reichswehr, an "all-volunteer," long-serving professional
army. Not only was the Reichswehr something new in German history,
it represented something special among other armed forces of the
post-World War I period. Both Great Britain and the United States
established professional armies at this time which suffered from
many problems similar to those that beset the Reichswehr. All
three were small armies that had to cope with meager budgets and
exiguous, fixed personnel allocations. For the typical officer in
the interwar professional army, life centered on the realities of
limited opportunities for career advancement and the endless
routine of peacetime training. But in the terms of size,
structure, and equipment, the interwar British and American armies
were tailored to meet the respective countries' defensive
requirements as defined by political and military leaders within a
framework of national autonomy. Although subsequent critics,
viewing events through the prism of later developments, might
harshly judge national preparedness at the time, planners were at
liberty to develop military forces according to their assessment

of potential threats to national security. Neither the British nor the Americans expected to participate again in a major continental conflict, for example, so their armed forces were shaped accordingly.

The situation of the Reichswehr was radically different. Its structure was imposed on a defeated nation by the fiat of the victors. Despite substantial agreement among competent objective observers that the Reichswehr was inadequate for Germany's defensive needs, it could not legally alter its structure. According to Article 160 of the Versailles Treaty, the size of the Reichswehr was set at 100,000 men, including 4,000 officers committed to twenty-five years of unbroken service. The Reichswehr was even numerically inferior to the Weimar police forces.[3]

Unlike most other professional armies, therefore, the Reichswehr was not organized and equipped by its own leaders to meet Germany's defensive needs. The obvious weaknesses of the Army and the fact that it was imposed on Germany contributed to its being viewed by Germans as an alien organization. Reichswehr officers would have preferred something similar to the conscript-based army of the empire. Even the Reichswehr's chief political critics, the socialists, if given the choice, would have accepted either the Imperial Army or some form of militia in place of the professional force. Like the Republic it served, the Reichswehr was unwanted and unloved. If the Versailles Treaty can be blamed for many of the Reichswehr's limitations, however, the objectives established by General Hans von Seeckt and continued by his successors compounded the Army's problems.

When Seeckt assumed command in 1920, he was sixty-four years old and in the twilight of a distinguished career. Although the son of a highly decorated Imperial Army general and himself Prussian to the core, he developed a breadth of vision unusual to his class. At an early age he was transferred to the General Staff, where he rapidly achieved a reputation for diligence and keen intelligence. Indeed, Seeckt was one of the few senior German officers to emerge from the Great War with an enhanced reputation. Significantly, he achieved his greatest fame as chief of staff to Field Marshal von Mackensen on the eastern front, where, in contrast to operations in the west, the concept of mobile warfare remained a reality. Later he served as Germany's key military diplomat in various posts. Seeckt came to the Reichswehr convinced that the new Army must reflect traditional Prussian virtues and learn from the experiences of modern warfare.

His task was especially taxing for two reasons. First of all, for many Germans, military defeat, demobilization, and economic distress led to widespread confusion and despair. Traditional values and standards of conduct seemed irrelevant in a society on the verge of disintegration. The Freikorps, the military vigilante groups that plagued defeated Germany for many months following the armistice, illustrated the turmoil that became endemic in the political life of the Weimar Republic. How could Seeckt uphold the old conservative Prussian virtues within a rapidly changing social order? Public hostility, moreover, placed the Reichswehr in a difficult position. The Army found that social groups it normally relied on were, at first, unwilling to help the armed forces that supported a government imposed by the Versailles Treaty powers. On the other hand, the traditional leftist opponents of the military could not be expected to curtail their criticism, especially in light of the experience of the right-wing Kapp Putsch in the spring of 1920. Seeckt thus faced a challenge of the highest order.

Although the Treaty restrictions and German wartime experiences on the western front might presuppose a defensive-minded army whose main task was maintaining internal order, Seeckt opted instead to create a viable military force capable of meeting external threats and a leadership cadre for the larger, national army of the post-Versailles future. But in establishing this dual mission, Seeckt created a dilemma for the Reichswehr.[4]

Under any circumstances, it would be extremely difficult for a professional army to perform successfully two missions with such divergent objectives. The mission of combat readiness requires continuous unit preparedness training at all organizational levels. It is designed to prepare the army to meet a present threat. But the mission of cadre training focuses on future contingencies and emphasized the individual rather than the unit. Officers and enlisted men who undergo such training are frequently drawn from their units to attend courses of instruction dealing with the most current developments in arms, equipment, and doctrine. Because such training lessens the army's ability to perform effective unit training, the small professional army faces the problem of achieving a balance between the missions of combat readiness and cadre training. For the Reichswehr, burdened with an artificial framework of imposed restrictions, the objective was next to impossible from the beginning. Throughout the Weimar period, the basic challenge facing the military authorities was the creation of a workable balance between the two missions.

My approach to the Reichswehr differs from the traditional view of the republican army. Because most scholars consider Weimar's military a transitory force without a dynamic of its own, they do not focus on the Reichswehr as a military institution in contemporary Weimar sciety. Instead, they view the army from the vantage point of the Third Reich by emphasizing political activities and its failure to support the Republic adequately or deal effectively with the threat of National Socialism. Early pioneering studies by Herbert Rosinski, John Wheeler-Bennett, Wolfgang Sauer, and Gordon Craig prepared the path of political indictment for others to follow.[5] Even when the political historians discuss the Reichswehr and politics.[6] On the other hand, military historians interested in the development of weapons and doctrine concentrate either on the early progress of the tank and airplane or, more commonly, on the Army's clandestine rearmament efforts.[7]

That traditional studies deal largely with Reichswehr's peripheral activities is not surprising. The average officer's day-to-day work focused on routine tasks of education, training, and career advancement. The historian seeking a subject naturally gravitates to the more stimulating fringes. For the early Weimar years, the subject has been the Freikorps and the so-called "Black Reichswehr." For the subsequent period, interest has centered on

illegal mobilization planning, flying training, and weapons development -- especially involving the Soviet connection. This view of
the Reichswehr distorts its nature and impact as a legitimate armed
force. Paradoxically, the general historian of Weimar grants the
Republic a life of its own, while the military historian sees the
Republic as a steppingstone to the Third Reich -- an interpretation, interesting enough, increasingly favored by both West and
East German historians.

The present study seeks to correct this imbalance and dis-
torted image of the Republic's armed forces by examining the
Reichswehr from within, as it attempted to perform its contradictory missions of combat readiness and cadre training. It com-
plements Michael Geyer's outstanding recent work, Aufrüstung oder
Sicherheit, which stresses the Reichswehr's growing integration
into German affairs.[8] Analysis of the Reichswehr officer's career
structure provides a firm base from which to evaluate the Army's
military and political role in the Weimar Republic. Historians
cannot concentrate solely on the Army leaders' political machinations to explain the decisions that were taken in the political
sphere. Equally important were the internal pressures and problems
that resulted from the Reichswehr's attempt to perform contradictory missions under severe handicaps. The German experience,
moreover, provides useful lessons for today's professional armed
forces because they confronted similar problems: the conflict between traditional values and the needs of the modern technolog-
ically-oriented institution, the issue of conformity as a barrier
to initiative and progress, and the tendency to emphasize training
promoting the narrow outlook of the specialist rather than the
broad view of the generalist.

Statistical evidence provides a major part of the story. I
have, however, tried to avoid a narrow technical analysis, and instead focused primarily on a specific segment of the Army and on
specific individuals -- the Bavarian Seventh Division and officers
such as Eduard Zorn and Ferdinand Jodl. Their experiences provide
a means of examining the advantages and disadvantages of the officer's career as well as the nature of the professional army under
its three commanders. Of the three men who served in the post of
commander-in-chief, Wilhelm Heye, heretofore the forgotten man of
the Reichswehr, emerges in a new light. Indeed, his role was fundamental to the development of the Reichswehr both as a combat-
ready force and as an army of leaders for the future Wehrmacht.

The present work is based on primarily on German documents
captured at the conclusion of the Second World War and retained on
microfilm at the National Archives in Washington, D.C. Perhaps it
is best at the outset to confront the question of this study's
heavy reliance on Bavarian sources. In view of Bavaria's
separatist inclinations, can the Bavarian Seventh Division
legitimately serve as a case study for the larger Reichswehr? The
answer is a definite "yes." For one thing, we must recognize that
the separatism of the Bavarian Reichswehr has been exaggerated.
Admittedly, relations between the Berlin High Command its Bavarian
subordinates were uneasy during the early Weimar period and nearly
reached the breaking point during the 1923 Hitler Putsch. After

General Kress von Kressenstein was appointed Division Commander in 1924, relations with Berlin improved markedly. Nevertheless, there is no indication from German or American sources that the Army leaders, either before or after the crisis year of 1923, tried either to bribe its Bavarian component or discriminate against it, in any way.[9] If, for example, one reviews the treatment of minorities in Warren L. Young's Minorities and the Military, it is clear that Bavarians do not meet the author's criterion of a minority group.[10] In Germany they were treated neither as a minority nor a special group.

In fact, the picture of the Berlin-Munich military relationship that emerges from the records is generally characterized by harmony rather than acrimony. In the field of senior-level divisional appointments, for instance, extensive correspondence for the years 1929 and 1930 between the division Chiefs of Staff and Colonel Gunther Hammerstein-Equord, Defense Ministry branch chief for division assignments, shows an unusual degree of cooperation.[11] And one is reminded of the statement by General Joachim von Stulpnagel, the brilliant, outspoken Chief of Personnel under General Heye, that "especially in the delicate area of personnel policy I never had serious difficulties with the Bavarians."[12]

Finally, it is important to remember that, if this study is based largely on Bavarian files, at least fifty percent of the documents in these files originated in the Berlin Defense Ministry. And Bavarian commentary and implementation directives make it clear that throughout the Weimar period Reichswehr policy rather than particularist Bavarian policy was being carried out at the local level. The text to follow will show that the Seventh Division serves as a legitimate case study for the Reichswehr as a whole.

Unfortunately, it was not possible to supplement my findings adequately with information from individual officer personnel folders. Although the latter are housed at the Bundesarchiv-Militararchiv in Freiburg, Germany, many are missing or incomplete and all are restricted from examination for a period of thirty years following the individual's death. Despite this difficulty, available evidence is sufficient to support this analysis of the making of the Reichswehr officer. In this age of high cost publishing, footnotes have been kept brief and to a minimum. They are designed to serve as guides to further investigation.

The picture that emerges is a comprehensive description of officer education and training and the nature of the professional army in the Weimar Republic. Contrary to conventional wisdom, the Army by and large fulfilled the military terms of the Versailles Treaty. Like most bureaucratic institutions, it tended to do in practice what it was expected to do according to legal fiat. In this story of the Reichswehr's determination to perform contradictory missions within a restricted framework are found lessons for any professional armed force as well as explanations for crucial political decisions taken by Reichswehr leaders in the twilight years of the Weimar Republic.

In the preparation of this study my obligations are many. The United States Air Force Academy sponsored my doctoral dissertation, upon which the present work is based. Thanks are also due the staffs of the National Archives, particularly the archivists in the Navy and Old Army Branch, Military Archives Division, and the inter-library loan departments of the University of Washington and the United States Air Force Academy. Their assistance is much appreciated. I must single out five individuals for special thanks. Professor Peter F. Sugar, who served as my Thesis Advisor at the University of Washington, provided invaluable criticism and constant encouragement. Professor Sugar is a Doktorvater in the traditional sense of the term, and for that I am deeply grateful. The late Professor Harold J. Gordon, Jr. offered generous assistance in developing the subject of this study, and he continued to put at my disposal a wealth of personal knowledge and the testimony of his many friends among former Reichswehr officers. The stylistic expertise of Professor Stanley E. Hilton helped purge the manuscript of many rough edges. I am especially grateful to my good friend, Professor Dennis E. Showlter, who willing provided expert criticism, valuable stimulus, and essential support when it was most needed. Finally, and above all, I owe a special debt of gratitude to my wife, Nancy Elaine Wallace-Spires, without whom this project could not have been completed.

Abbreviations

A	Training battalion
Abt.	Battalion
a.D.	Retired
Adj.	Adjutant
Art.	Artillery
II/A.R.2	2nd Battalion of the 2nd Artillery Regiment
2/A.R.2	2nd Battery of the 2nd Artillery Regiment
Art.Kdr.	Artillery commander (division)
Bad.	Baden
Battr.	Battery
Bav.	Bavaria
Br.	Branch
Brig.Gen.	Brigadier General
Btl.	Battalion
Capt.	Captain
CH	Chef der Heeresleitung (commander-in-chief)
ch.	Character (promotion on retirement) rank
C.PA	Chief (commander) of the Personnel Office
C.St.	Chief of staff
C.TA	Chief (commander) of the Truppenamt
Col.	Colonel
DIV./Div.	Division
Eng.	Engineer
Esk.	Squadron (cavalry)
F.A.	Supply battalion (horse-drawn)

Frhr.	Freiherr (baron)
Gen.	General
Gen.St.	General Staff
Gest.	Killed/died
GP.	Group command
Hq.	Headquarters
In1	Education and Training Inspectorate
In2	Infantry Inspectorate
In3	Cavalry Inspectorate
In4	Artillery Inspectorate
In5	Engineering and Garrison Inspectorate
In6	Supply Inspectorate
In7	Signals Inspectorate
Inf.	Infantry
Inf.Kdr.	Infantry commander (division)
I.R.	Infantry regiment
II/I.R.2	2nd Battalion of the 2nd Infantry Regiment
2/I.R.2	2nd Company of the 2nd Infantry Regiment
Jr.	Junior
K.A.	Motor transport battalion
Kav.	Cavalry
Kdr.	Commander
Kdt.	Commandant (garrison/training site)
Kdtr.	Commandant's office
Kp.	Company
Lt.	Lieutenant

M.A.	Military attache
Maj.	Major
M.G.	Machine-gun
MinA	Ministeramt
Mot.	Motorized
M.W.	Trench mortar
NA	National Archives (Washington, D.C.)
N.A.	Signals battalion
NCO	Noncommissioned officer
OER	Officer efficiency report
Offz.	Officer(s)
PA	Personnel Office
P.B.	Engineer battalion
Pr.	Prussia
R	Ritter (knight)
r.	Mounted (horse)
R.G.	Record Group (National Archives)
R.R.	Cavalry regiment
2/R.R.2	2nd Squadron of the 2nd Cavalry Regiment
R.St.	Regiment staff
R.St.O.	Regiment staff officer
RWM	Reichswehrministerium (Defense Ministry)
S.A.	Medical battalion
Sax.	Saxony
Sch.	School
Sig.	Signals

T1	Army Branch (Truppenamt)
T2	Organization Branch (Truppenamt)
T3	Statistical Branch (Truppenamt)
T7	Transportation Branch (Truppenamt)
TA	Truppenamt
Tech.	Technical (branch)
T.U.P.	Training site
v.	von
VH	Administrative Office (Defense Ministry)
W,WehrA.,Wehr-A	Wehramt (Defense Ministry)
(W)	Munitions officer
Wa	Weapons Office (Defense Ministry)
Wü	Württemburg

IMAGE
AND
REALITY

1.
Officer Candidate Selection

The future of any army depends on the quality of its officer corps, and that quality, in turn, is a direct result of the selection process. The Germany Army is an excellent example of the truth of this maxim. Most interested students give the Wehrmacht, particularly its officer corps, high marks for its performance in the Second World War and see the roots of German military excellence in the early years of the Weimar Republic and the miniature cadre army created and developed by its second commander-in-chief, General Hans von Seeckt. The conventional view of Seeckt's work is well-known.[1] Insulated from domestic political interference and permitted to operate within and around the strictures of the Versailles Treaty, he was able to hand-pick his officers for the Reichswehr and replenish his small officer corps with the best talent available from a sufficient reservoir of potential civilian recruits. By 1926, when he was forced into retirement, his work was largely accomplished. The system of officer selection he had established was already producing able young officers who would provide the core of the future German army. His successors only had to maintain the original Seecktian system of recruiting the best for its officer corps. This description, however, is much too superficial. It does not explain, for example, what the Army high command meant by the best talent available, or discuss the criteria and procedures it established to achieve its objective. Generally, previous studies of officer selection have been either too broad or exclusively narrow in focus.[2] What is required is a comprehensive analysis of the operation and effectiveness of the officer recruitment program in order to show how the Reichswehr developed a regular, routine method of choosing its future leaders.

*   *   *

The best way to begin is with Seeckt's famous message to the Army on New Year's Day, 1921. "Fellow officers," he declared, "the Reichswehr exists. A new chapter in Germany military history begins."[3] The new officer corps of 4,000 men had been culled from 24,000 wartime officers and Provisional Reichswehr officers -- a reduction in strength demanded by the peace treaty. Both General Walther Reinhardt, the first commander-in-chief, and Seeckt were determined to have only the best. On April 28, 1920, the very day of his appointemnt following the Kapp Putsch, Seeckt described the principles upon which he intended to build his officer corps. Characteristically, he turned to tradition for guidance and inspiration. The old ideals and principles had stood the test of war and defeat and would again serve to guide the Army in the future. "As in the past," he said, "the German officer will be chosen according to his ability and his character."[4] These two criteria became the cornerstones of officer selection for the initial formation of the Reichswehr, as well as for the regular officer candidate system.

Even before the final, legal formation of the Reichswehr on January 1, 1921, the high command issued the officer replacement regulation (Offizier-Ergänzungsbestimmungen), which remained in effect for seven years. While the general criteria that had served as the basis for designating the initial 4,000 were retained, requiring proven military ability was no longer possible. The new officer candidates normally had no military experience, which meant that the Reichswehr now had to focus on the individual's potential ability for the profession -- and the measure of such ability became his level of general education.

The policy-makers firmly believed that turning the small, professional Reichswehr into a combat effective organization would require the intelligent application of every form of modern technology. This in turn could only be realized by an educated officer corps, and no one was more aware of this than Seeckt himself. But a sound technical education, which could be gained during military service, was not sufficient. "The position of the officer in the life of the people," Seeckt asserted, "demands not only a good military education but a sound general education as well...."[5] "Even a soldier requires the schooling of the spirit and broad view if he does not intend to be superficial in his calling."[6] Seeckt, moreover, was aware that a professional army that failed to maintain close ties with society at large could easily degenerate into a mercenary force. His ideas on education also reflected his belief that the Reichswehr must become a national army rather than one of vigilantes divorced from the German people.

Seeckt's standard of education for the future officer was incorporated into the new regulation by requiring a diploma (Abitur) from a nine-class secondary school, the equivalent of the American high school.[7] Applicants with the Abitur entered a four-year training program leading to promotion to lieutenant. The Reichswehr, however, made available an alternative program to outstanding recruits who lacked the diploma at the time of enlistment. These men could earn the equivalent of the Abitur by passing a series of examinations spread over two years. Then they entered the regular four-year program.[8]

Even with the Abitur, however, an applicant had no hope of being accepted if he was found deficient in character attributes. Indeed, his integrity provided the ultimate test of eligibility, and, especially in questionable cases, always came first. Seeckt, in 1921, aptly described the close relationship between education and character:

> Knowledge should not be confined to military matters; it should serve to enhance education in general and make a soldier into a valuable, useful member of society for the remainder of his life. But what a man knows and what he can do are less important than what he is, and the strengthening of character takes precedence over improvement of the mind.[9]

The high command, of course, had to establish procedures to implement Seeckt's policy, and here, too, the Reichswehr turned to the past. When Seeckt confirmed that "the historic, traditional position and responsibility of regimental commanders should be maintained to the full under the guidance of their superior officers," the course ahead was clear.[10] As it had been in the Imperial Army, so it would be in the Reichswehr: regimental commanders would personally decide on an officer aspirant's character and general suitability for his regiment. In doing so, individual commanders would be responsible for preserving the officers corps' homogeneity.

The Reichswehr's emphasis on education and character may not appear remarkable at first sight. After all, both had been important criteria in the make-up of the military officer since the emergence of the French revolutionary armies. In Prussia-Germany, however, education had always taken second place to character, which was usually determined by social origins or professional background. Boyen, Scharnhorst, and their like-minded successors faced an uphill struggle throughout the nineteenth century to make entry into the officer profession subject to uniform standards of merit and education. By the turn of the century, the conflict over entry requirements had worsened under pressure from the new, complex industrial society. The debate centered on the types of schools and subjects considered suitable preparation for officership. It was generally assumed that sons of aristocrats and the wealthy bourgeoisie attended humanistic secondary schools (humanistische Gymnasia) for a broad, general education, whereas sons of lower middle class and working class families normally were sent to technical secondary schools (Realschulen) to secure a higher standard of living. Diehards were unwilling to accept the exclusive criterion of the Abitur, especially the diploma from the more vocational-oriented school, because too many candidates of "sound character" -- meaning aristocrats and sons of serving officers -- would be excluded. The aristocracy, as a rule, tended to shun professions associated with the new industrial-technological society. The problem became particularly acute on the eve of the First World War when the great 1913 expansion opened the officer corps to an unprecedented number of bourgeois with Abiturs from technical

schools. Faced with this problem, the Kaiser, William II, not surprisingly, vacilllated between both positions but ultimately could
be counted on to grant dispensations to sons of officers without
the Abitur.[11]
     In effect, the Army's dilemma was to maintain traditional
Prussian aristocratic values -- epitomized in the concept of character -- in the new age of the masses and modern military technology. The tension between the aristocratic and technocratic heri-
tages was personalized during the war in the intriguing partnership
of Hindenburg and Ludendorff. Here, in dramatic contrast, the old
Germany of the Prussian aristocrat and the new world of the ruthless bourgeois technocrat were united to conduct modern warfare.
Their performance has received mixed reviews. As Michael Geyer
points out in his latest study, Seeckt, for one, was very critical
of what he termed the Army's lack of preparedness for the challenges of modern war.[12] The so-called lessons of the war -- the tactical and technical in particular -- would soon comprise a major pil-
lar of the Reichswehr's training program.
     For Seeckt, however, the aristocratic heritage was even more
important. But how does a military leader ensure that his officers
demonstrate good character and the officer corps retain its homogeneity? Even during normal times, when one could rely for morals
education on support from traditional conservative institutions
like the family, church, and school, it was not easy to produce officers of good character with technical expertise. And conditions
in postwar Germany were far from normal. If the war had called
into question the traditional western liberal value system for all
countries, it led to a crisis in Germany of unusually severe proportions. Defeat in war and the shameful Versailles peace treaty precipitated civil war for five years after the armistice. In the
midst of this turmoil of social disintegration and political uncertainty, the stage was set for Seeckt's greatest challenge -- preserving the new, small, and crippled Reichswehr.
     Perhpas it was only natural that he turned to character educa-
tion as the key building block and the Abitur as the outward sign
of good moral fiber. In the aftermath of war, Seeckt required an
officer corps bright enough to handle the new technology. The Abitur would at least provide intelligent candidates with the general
education desired by Seeckt as a sound base for subsequent specialized technical training within the Army. But the technically-
trained officer could not be expected to act responsible and apply
his knowledge correctly if he were not a moral, thinking being -- a
man of good character. He also saw in the Abitur the practical way
of acquiring officers with the same set of traditional values --
loyalty, courage, honor, and obedience. But because the war had
questioned all traditional values, it was false to assume that sons
of aristocrats or wealthy bourgeoisie, even with the Abitur, rou-
tinely would exhibit the values of the Prussian gentleman. Perhaps
this helps to explain Seeckt's special zeal for character education
in the officer corps.
     To be sure, intellect can be defined relative to formal educa-
tion. But in practical terms, how does a military organization ensure sound character? The concept is, after all, imprecise, and

dictionary definitions offer litle beyond subjective generalities such as moral qualities, ethical standards, principles, and the like.   Is character an innate quality or one that can be learned and developed?   Are the attributes of character universally recognized, or do they vary depending on the relative state of social morality or other criteria?   Seeckt never really defined what he meant by character.   Of course, he had never been in a position where he had had to define it, and military leaders traditionally emphasize character without articulating what they mean.   One is reminded of Klaus Epstein's insight that conservatives are most convincing when they do not have to explain things.   When forced to define and defend their principles and beliefs, they often find that their arguments lose a great deal of their merit and appeal.[13]

For Seeckt the problem of definition was complicated by the heritage of war, with its enormous moral and technological challenge.   In effect, the question becomes: could a concept like character, in light of postwar conditions, be used effectively if not clearly and precisely defined?   And, ultimately, if it comes to mean blind loyalty and obedience, where then is there room for the officer of initiative and independent thinking in this much-heralded army of future leaders?   It is imperative to focus on the concept of character from the ouset of this study because, for Seeckt, it served as the bedrock of officer education and training.

On the surface, however, the conditions which gave birth to the Reichswehr appeared to provide an opportunity to achieve what the Imperial Army never could.   Now, for the first time in German history, the Army might reasonably expect to field an officer corps that displayed relatively high standards of both intellect and character.   The Reichswehr's officer recruitment system was designed and implemented with the purpose of attracting men who met these standards?   How well did it succeed?

            *   *   *

From the outset it was difficult to select recruits who met the high character standards.   The desire to achieve a balance between quality and quantity became the major goal for Reichswehr personnel planners.   In 1921 the problem was especially acute because the first officer class of that year would not complete officer training until 1924.   In the interim, therefore, the Army would have to find qualified lieutenants, and this was no easy task.   On hand, as Harold Gordon has pointed out, were several sources of replacements, including Imperial Army cadets, young enlisted men, non-commissioned officers (NCOs), and former officers.   All four sources were used to fill the vacancies.[14]   Any attempt to evaluate the quality of these new lieutenants is difficult because of insufficient documentation and unsatisfactory standards of measurement.   Most scholars agree that these officers were not up to the new standards by noting the failure of the new lieutenants to receive promotion on schedule and their early dismissal from the service.[15]   But if the early lieutenants were not exceptionally gifted, neither do they appear as deficient as their critics imply.   Furthermore, even during the early years, it seems that the Army was more concerned with selecting quality replacements than merely meeting its numberical quotas.

*   *   *

How did the selection process actually work? The example of Eduard Zorn, who was selected for the officer candidate training program in 1921, is instructive.[16]   In April 1921, Colonel Friedrich Ritter von Haack, Commander of the 19th Infantry Regiment, admitted Zorn as a volunteer for officer training. This was the culmination of the selection process that had begun the previous year when Zorn applied in writing directly to the regiment commander. He was required to furnish the following specific information: date of birth, citizenship, religious affiliation, educational level, professional status of his father, and personal life history. Records indicate that Zorn was a Bavarian Protestant, resident of Munich, preparing to take the Abitur -- and an Abitur from the Munich cadet school at that. He also satisfied the age requirement (between 17 and 21). Additionally, Zorn had to assure the commander of his parents' permission to enter the Army and provide at least two letters from prominent members of the community attesting to his character. Haack, for his part, conducted his own investigation of Zorn's character and general behavior.

While the commander was conducting his investigation, Zorn reported to a local military medical facility for a battery of physical tests. He was then ready for a personal interview with Haack, the final and most important stage in the selection process. Normally, the regimental commander was assisted by several senior officers in a searching examination which lasted from one to three days. After clearing this final hurdle, Zorn's name was added to the regimental roster and forwarded to district headquarters and then to Berlin for confirmation. Sometime prior to April 1, Zorn received instructions to report to the prestigious Munich battalion of the 19th Infantry Regiment for induction before being transferred to the training unit in Landshut.

Clearly Eduard Zorn possessed several assets which eased his ordeal considerably. As a candidate for the Abitur, he fulfilled the Reichswehr's educational prerequisite. Only by failing the examination would his application have been in jeopardy. In the event of the latter, he could have waited to retake the examination the following year or followed the example of fellow applicant, Friedrich Velhorn, who, because he lacked the Abitur, entered the six-year training program on April 1, 1921. As far as Zorn's character was concerned, Haack no doubt spent little time investigating because Zorn's father, who was killed during the war, had earlier commanded the Munich cadet corps. Armies usually give sons of deceased veterans special consideration, and the Reichswehr appears to have done the same.[17]

Eduard Zorn's experience illustrates a number of characteristics of the Reichswehr's selection system. First of all, the requirements for selection were reasonably comprehensive and discriminating. Second, the decision to accept or reject the applicant was entirely in the hands of the regimental commander. Zorn could have satisfied the educational and physical criteria, yet found himself rejected without explanation or recourse to outside authority. Finally, he seems to have represented the type of future officer the selection process was designed to certify. But if Zorn represented the ideal type of reichswehr cadet, the Army faced the problem of finding Zorns in sufficient number.

        *   *   *

By the summer of 1921, Seeckt faced disaster. After the spring figures of officer recruits were tabulated, it was clear that the Reichswehr had not attracted enough qualified applicants. Postwar public hostility to everything military seemed to be continuing. Seeckt was alarmed about the lack of support from families of former officers, higher officials, and aristocrats. Part of the solution was greater publicity. To inform both the public and the officer corps, leaflets describing the advantages of the officer career were published and distributed. Seeckt also reminded commanders that they alone were responsible for officer recruiting and suggested that they establish contacts with individuals and groups that had supported the old German Army.[18]

Most importantly, Seeckt provided yearly quotas for each branch of service, as well as the individual regiments and battalions (see appendix 1, table 1). His goal was a yearly figure of 250 officer recruits who possessed the Abitur. Since the Versailles Treaty prohibited the Army from admitting and eliminating more than 200 officers in any given year, the figure of 250 was not unreasonable. And if by the end of 1921 fewer than a hundred candidates had been selected, by the summer of 1922 Seeckt could afford to be more optimistic.[19]

During the intervening months, the climate of opinion among segments of German society traditionally inclined to support the military had slowly turned in the Reichswehr's favor. What part Seeckt's publicity program played in this turnabout is uncertain. Probably more significant was the apparent stability of the Army and the severe inflation and economic competition faced by the middle and upper classes. Although most authorities date the end of the applicant shortage and the Army's unpopularity sometime in 1923, it appears that the reversal began the previous year. In August 1922, Seeckt reported that the number of new officer recruits for the year, together with 96 non-Abitur candidates already in the Army, could possible reach a total of 259.[20] Looking ahead to 1926 (see appendix 1, table 2), however, the year in which the 1922 officer recruits would be expected to become lieutenants, the figure of 176 is far below the 259 officers projected by Seeckt. Only 26 of the 96 non-Abitur candidates, furthermore, progressed all the way through the training program.[21] The lower numbers illustrate not only the excessive optimism of the planners but also the difficulty of completing the program.

Other factors also contributed to the problem of an officer shortage, especially during the early years. Since the selection system was decentralized geographically orgnizationally, efforts by Berlin to adjust deficiencies were always difficult. In practice,

the local commander's prerogative was supreme and his was the responsibility for recruitment. If his regiment, for whatever reason, was unpopular, he likely could fill his quota only by settling
for less qualified applicants. This possibility was Seeckt's primary anxiety since he always considered the quality of recruits
more important than their numbers. Specifically, he singled out
the non-Abitur candidate for particular attention. "Non-Abiturs
must receive the most careful scrutiny," he emphasized in August
1922. "Not only must their military performance be judged excellent, but their personality and ... behavior must receive uncondi-
tional approval."[22]

For Seeckt, the Abitur was the mark of social maturity as
well as educational accomplishment, and candidates without it were
always suspect. Ten days after the August message, Seeckt cautioned over-zealous commanders to select only those non-Abiturs who
could be expected to pass the two stringent qualifying examinations
(Vorprüfung and Nachprüfung), which were required to bring them up
to the level of the Abiturs. "Our purpose," he continued, "is not
to get the largest possible number of recruits through the
Nachprüfung, but to assist only those who have proven themselves
qualified on the Vorprüfung and by their performance on and off
duty."[23]

Seeckt returned to the problem in his policy letter of
December 1922, in which he acknowledged that the number of volunteers without the diploma was relatively high. Because what he
perceived as their intellectual and emotional immaturity was impossible to overcome completely, he remonstrated that personality
judgements were of "decisive value."[24] To Seeckt, the non-Abiturs
represented a threat to the educational and social standards that
he had established for the Reichswehr officer, and he repeatedly
demanded that they receive the most rigorous examination. In this
instance, character was clearly more important than education for,
in reality, the basic objective was to preserve the officer corps'
homogeneity.

Obviously, the rapidly increasing number of applicants for officer training was a mixed blessing that the Reichswehr was uncertain how to handle. The planners wanted the best available talent,
but were unwilling to close the door to less educated, non-Abitur
applicants. In the late summer of 1923, Brigadier General von
Metzsch, Chief Inspector for Education and Training, confessed that
the Army was in a "transition" period, in which the whole problem
of officer recruitment was "in flux." He restated the need to
maintain the highest standards, but affirmed the practice of admitting non-Abiturs. Such a concession, he noted, would bring in
many "who had to leave school only because of their parents' economic need."[25] This argument, of course, had also been used in the
Imperial Army to justify exceptions to the educational standard.

By early 1924 the number of applicants had risen to the point
where the same Metzsch could declare that a figure of 500 well-
qualified recruits was not out of the question. But he did not
address the obvious issue of how the training program could be expected to absorb this number of officers. In any event, by this
time the shortages of the first year and a half had been largely

overcome for most units of the three main branches. Now the task facing the planners was to keep individual units from exceeding their quotas and, above all, to maintain the original high selection standards. Seeckt continued the battle for quality recruits until he left office.

       ★   ★   ★

    The Reichswehr's ceaseless efforts to keep educational requirements high raises the question of why the Army did not select its recruits exclusively from among Abitur applicants. With an estimated 19,000 of them facing a highly competitive civilian job market every year, the Army should have been able to attract its full quota.[26] Even considering those who failed to qualify or had no interest in a military career, there should have remained a sufficient number after 1922 who could meet the rigorous selection criteria. In fact, there is little doubt that such was the case for most units. Zorn's regimental commander admitted as much in early 1924, and it is unlikely that his was the only regiment so fortunate. If acceptance of non-Abitur recruits was, as he stated, limited to "special cases," the door was never closed to their entry.[27] Seeckt, despite his preference for Abitur recruits, demanded only that non-Abiturs earn the equivalent of the diploma because he seemed more concerned about the individual's character. Clearly the Army considered the alternate path to the officer career necessary and useful. But, like its Imperial predecessor, the Reichswehr found itself compromising between the objectives of education and upbringing.

    The Reichswehr's handling of the non-Abitur program also suggests that Army leaders were aware that problems could occur if the education standards were unrealistically high. Too many qualified replacements would mean unhealthy competition and disgruntled men, and would endanger morale. The Reichswehr, with progressively fewer available positions up the ladder of command and with promotions and dismissals a constant source of discontent, did not want the additional irritants certain to accompany an officer corps dominated by highly-qualifed, over-ambitious men. What it did require was a large number of moderately bright, moderately ambitious men who would be content to serve long years training recruits in isolated garrisons. This situation would enable the Army to recognize exceptionally gifted officers and help limit dissension. It appears that the Army's non-Abitur program contributed to this end without requiring too high a price in lowered educational standards.

       ★   ★   ★

    By the time Wilhelm Heye assumed command of the Army in October 1926, the regular officer candidate program had graduated three classes of new lieutenants, and the confusion and uncertainty of the early years seemed to have ended. Heye inherited a proven system and entertained no serious thoughts about making major changes. In the first few months of his stewardship, however, there was no guarantee that he or the Reichswehr officer candidate system would emerge unscathed from the attacks of its critics.

Organizations tend to be particularly susceptible to outside pressure during changes in leadership. For the Reichswehr, late 1926 was just such a vulnerable period. In October Seeckt had been forced to resign because he had allowed the Crown Prince to participate in the Army's annual autumn field maneuvers. Heye, who lacked Seeckt's personal authority, soon found himself besieged by critics who considered the time opportune for making major changes in the Reichswehr.

There were two major efforts to force reforms on the Army. One was made in a December 1926 Reichstag speech by the socialist leader Scheidemann, who accused the Army of illegal border activity and covert military supply and training operations with the Soviet Union. The second involved a series of articles written by the speaker of the Reichstag, Paul Löbe, who advocated reform of Reichswehr recruiting practices.[28] While the high command condemned both for their lack of patriotism, it was Löbe, not Scheidemann, who provoked the most anger and fear. The reason is quite apparent. Whereas Scheidemann had criticized peripheral illegal activities, Löbe had struck at the Army's heart by threatening the officer corps' social make-up. He proposed to reform the selection system in order to produce a different type of Reichswehr officer. His system would have been centralized and supervised by civilians demonstrably loyal to the Republic, and the local commander would have lost his traditional authority to judge the character of his recruits.

Löbe's charges dealt with the fundamental social composition of the German officer corps, and scholars ever since have been especially concerned with this aspect of the Reichswehr. Basically, critics charged the Army with deliberate inbreeding, designed to develop a distinct type of officer. Army officials, they said, recruited from among only those social classes that had strong ties to the Imperial Army. Individuals not among the chosen few had little or no hope of gaining admittance. The best visible evidence was the excessively high proportion of aristocrats in the military compared with German society as a whole. For these critics, the Reichswehr's test of charcter was the social origin of the recruit.[29]

Available statistics do indeed tend to support the charge that the Reichswehr officer more than likely was a product of families traditionally inclined to support the German Army. And the nobility clearly comprised a large segment of the officer corps throughout the Weimar period (see appendix 1, table 2). But is it really useful to focus on nobles' representation in the officer corps in order to draw conclusions about military social attitudes? Even F. L. Carsten, a severe critic, has admitted that no essential difference in basic attitudes existed between noble and non-noble officers.[30] An "old" bourgeois officer family, like the Heyes, moreover, which traditionally supplied officers to the Army, could be more significant than "new" noble families. What is needed are more studies like that by Nicholas von Preradovich, which shows that in 1932 only five of the forty-two generals were of the old,

Junker nobility. The majority were either bourgeois or only recently ennobled.[31]

Although the general conclusion that most officers came from
conservative social groups must be accepted, the real requirement
is to determine why this was the case and what it explains about
the Reichswehr officer. It should come as no surprise that the officer corps was made up of groups which traditionally had supported
the military. In fact, the real surprise would be if this were not
the case. Groups, whatever their composition, tend to reproduce
themselves, and non-revolutionary military organizations historically have drawn their officers from the conservative classes. The
Reichswehr, with its strong appeal to tradition, homogeneity, and
exclusiveness conformed to this pattern.

Yet, if members of the middle and upper classes predominated
in the officer corps, it is not necessarily correct to say that the
Army was guilty of deliberate inbreeding. True, the Reichswehr did
consciously appeal to the old classes for recruits, and did not encourage outsiders to enter the training program. But if the Army
appealed to the conservative elements, it really had very little
choice. During the early Weimar years, in particular, the military
could not attract officer recruits from the lower middle and working classes because they were either alienated from the military or
disintereted in the profession. The educational prerequisite, too,
served as a barrier -- seen by some as a deliberate one -- to most
at the lower end of the economic ladder, and this situation altered
very little during the later years of the Republic. As defenders
of the Army were and are quick to point out, the Reichswehr could
only recruit from among those who applied, and the majority of
applicants represented the upper and middle classes. If the
Reichswehr preferred not to admit candidates from certain social
groups, the latter's members for their part normally did not want
to join the Army.

Karl Demeter is certainly correct when he argues that the social composition of the Reichswehr office corps is best viewed as
reflecting a continuation of prewar trends.[32] Sons of officers and
noblemen were prominent in the Imperial Army. Because the
Reichswehr officer corps was much smaller, their presence would
tend to be especially noticeable. The fact that certain branches
and units listed more nobles than others can be accounted for in
the same manner. The traditionally pro-military groups would be
more inclined to heed the Reichswehr's appeal to elitism, tradition, and service rather than seek economically profitable careers
elsewhere. If this was the type of officer the Reichswehr wanted,
this was the kind of recruit most readily available.

In the final analysis, it is impossible to determine precisely
whether the Army deliberately excluded certain types of potential
recruits on the basis of social background because the selection
system was too decentralized and too dependent on the person of the
local commander and conditions.[33] Required are more studies like
Hermann Teske's detailed analysis of his former regiment and its
recruiting practices.[34] Until similar work becomes available for
other regiments, documentation permitting, one can only explain in
general terms why the Reichswehr officer tended to come from the

conservative segments of German society.

              *   *   *

Lobe's attempt to reform the Reichswehr's selection system proved fruitless in the end. In the revised recruiting regulations, published in December 1927, the only concession made by the Army was to prohibit the participation of certain patriotic associations in the selection process and to require a police report on the political activities of enlisted recruits. The authority of individual commanders to select their own men was upheld. As before, commanders would decide on the character of their recruits, and homogeneity would be preserved.

If the new replacement regulation conceded little to its critics, however, it included a significant addition to the selection system. After 1927, all officer candidate applicants were required to undergo a series of psychological tests designed to determine character and general aptitude for the officer profession.[35] It would be incorrect to state that political pressure was directly responsible for the introduction of comprehensive psychological testing. Such testing had been standard practice for enlisted men in the technical branches since 1920, and Seeckt, according to his first biographer, Friedrich von Rabenau, had begun rudimentary tests for officers in 1925 or 1926.[36] It was left to Heye, however, who was more inclined to experiment with new concepts and procedures, to apply comprehensive psychological methods experiment with new concepts and procedures, to apply comprehensive psychological methods to officer selection. This testing, so the Army believed, could serve as an initial screening mechanism for the large number of applicants.

The psychological examination (Psycho-technische Eignungsprufung) consisted of two parts and was administered twice each year in the individual districts. Under instructions from Berlin, each district formed a board of examiners, composed of at least one senior officer, one medical officer, and two psychologists. The examination covered general intelligence and personality and included electric shock treatments. By all accounts it was an extremely demanding, physically and mentally.

From its inception, the psychological test was a subject of heated debate in Army circles. The Militar-Wochenblatt, the semi-official military weekly, carried throughout the late 1920s and early 1930s articles by defenders and detractors of the examination. Some critics claimed that psychoanalysis was hardly a science and could not hope to become an objective method of measuring a man's character and personality. Others accused the Army psychologists of being too young, having no combat experience, and trying to create a conformist ideal officer (Einheitsoffizier). Typical was a field officer's criticism that "nobody knows anything definite about the thing [psychoanalysis], it remains black magic for most of us."[37] Most alarming of all, however, the opponents perceived in the test a threat to the regimental commander's authority and his independent judgment of an individual's character.

Former officer Kurt Hesse, on the other hand, author of several psychological studies himself, was one of the most able defenders of the new procedure. Arguing that critics of the examination did not really understand what it attempted to do, he explained each phase of the test and the purpose behind it. While the diversified nature of the examining board ensured a variety of viewpoints, he said, the military officer was the key decision-maker. Most importantly, the board's findings were only an additional aid to the commander, who in no way obligated to abide by the board's decision.[38]

On the whole, the psychological test appears to have been a positive addition to the Reichswehr selection process. Regardless of its claim to be scientific, it provided the Army with a more uniform method of determining aptitude and character because only about 450 of the 1600 applicants, or a little more than twice the yearly requirement, were passed from the first to the second stage of the test. Indeed, the Reichswehr leaders never seem to have doubted the usefulness of the psychological test.

The psychological test was the last addition to the officer selection system after 1927. On the surface, the program appeared to be functioning efficiently and producing quality candidates. Heye was reaping the benefits of the Seeckt period, as recruits of 1924 and after were promoted to lieutenants during his tenure. In 1928, for example, the Army promoted 252 cadets to lieutenant, the highest figure in the Reichswehr's brief history (see appendix 1, table 2). Applications for officer candidate training were generally high, and the Army believed that the psychological test improved the quality of the officer training classes.

But beneath the surface there were signs that all was not right. It is well-known that senior officers criticized Heye's handling of the political problems in 1926 and 1927.[39] What normally has been overlooked is the growing internal discord resulting from Heye's refinement of various aspects of the Seeckt system. The debate surrounding the psychological test is a case in point because to many it appeared to threaten traditional authority. Heye also seems to have taken a special interest in rewarding qualified NCOs with admission to officer candidate training, and this was considered by some an unwarranted concession to democracy and a threat to the Army's educational standards.[40]

For the most part, criticism remained muted, and the selection system functioned relatively smoothly during the period of reorganization and experimentation after 1928. Even when, during the summer of 1932, the Personnel Office announced the higher officer candidate recruiting requirements for the fall and the following spring, the leaders refused to compromise on standards of selection. Significantly, only Abitur applicants were to be considered for the supplemental classes.[41] The planners were determined to prevent the officer corps of the expanded army they envisioned from being deluged with future lieutenants possessing less than the highest qualifications.

*   *   *

It is clear that quality was the overriding objective of the cadet selection program. In this area, the Reichswehr reaped the mixed blessings of being a small, professional army. As much as the officer corps hated the Versailles Treaty, it had forced the Army to be far more selective than the conscript Imperial Army was able to be. Generally the high command responded by admitting only officer recruits who could meet the high standards of education and character. To its credit, it was willing to modify its numerical goals in order to preserve its standards of quality.

The procedures that were employed demonstrate an effective blend of traditional practices, like the regimental commander's authority, and progressive techniques, most notably the psychological aptitude test. As Eduard Zorn's experience indicates, applicants underwent a rigorous evaulation process in which the criteria were applied with very little compromise or favoritism.

This is not to suggest that personal influence and the individual's social or professional background were unimportant. Indeed, both the wide latitude accorded the local commander and the importance of the character evaluation meant that selection was based partly on subjective factors. The issue of social origins, however, -- especially the distinction between noble and non-noble -- is largely bogus. No professional military organization is prepared to seek as cadets individuals who fail to display aptitude for or interest in the profession. Because those segments of German society which had traditionally avoided the military career were also alienated from the Reichswehr, the Army had little need deliberately to exclude them. Consequently, the applicants who were motivated to serve were those more likely to come from classes that had always supplied the bulk of the officer replacements.

If the Reichswehr's selection system exhibited sound criteria and procedures and attracted motivated people, it does not follow that it was entirely successful. In fact, if the focus is only on the problem areas -- the inital shortage of applicants, the imbalanced force structure, the excessive optimism of the planners, and the constant attention to quality -- the conclusion might readily be drawn that the system was a failure. That this is not the case is evident from the fact that these problems were eventually overcome.

Analysis of the officer candidate selection system does raise several disturbing questions. For one thing, it is a bit alarming to note the dissension that developed when Heye introduced psychological aptitude testing. Although conservatism and resistance to change are common characteristics of military institutions, it is somewhat disquieting to observe such strong opposition to tests that the leaders and independent authorities considered progressive and beneficial to the system. Although it took Seeckt at least until the end of 1924, when Zorn's class graduated, to institutionalize completely the officer candiate program, Heye inherited a proven system which he was not inclined to alter significantly. His only major addition was the aptitude test, and this generated substantial unrest. It almost appears as though the opposition was less concerned with the merits of the case than with Heye's unwillingness to preserve the Seeckt system intact. This form of discontent is dangerous in any officer corps, but especially one considered to be progressive. Although one might argue that the psychological test is only a minor reform, subsequent chapters will show that a number of Heye's major reforms produced widespread discontent and threatened to destroy his attempt to make the professional army a vital partner in the Republic's future.

This analysis of the selection system also raises an important question regarding the criteria of education and character. Seeckt continuously faced a dilemma when considering non-Abitur applicants. His standard of education was the Abitur certificate, which to him implied a sound general educational background and the requisite character to serve as an officer. It is highly questionable, however, whether such a qualification guaranteed intelligence and ability and insured that such men would not become alienated from the "life of the people." And there always seemed to be a sizeable number of applicants without the Abitur who were considered excellent officer material. But, if they lacked the Abitur, what was to be their test of character? Was it a certain type of social background or, where applicable, past military performance? In the end, if Seeckt considered character the basic test of an applicant's suitabaility for selection, his use of this imprecise concept only served to confuse the situation.

The officer candidate selection program certainly played a key role in determining the quality of the future officer corps. The real test of the program's effectiveness, however, -- and of Seeckt's method of character education -- came during the course of the four years of training that cadets, like Eduard Zorn, underwent to become officers in the Reichswehr.

2.
Officer Candidate Training

From the very day of enlistment, the Reichswehr officer candidate was destined to be a leader. Every aspect of his training was designed with this objective in mind. Leadership, in the Reichswehr lexicon, meant three things: exercising authority through personal example; extracting maximum performance from men and equipment through thorough knowledge and application of regulations; and demonstrating the ability to imbue subordinates with the aim of continuing the Army's historic mission of serving Germany as the "school of the nation."[1] Officer candidate training reflected the Reichswehr's determination to develop these skills. The training period for the officer recruit was long and difficult for a number of reasons. In one sense, the Army had little choice in the matter because it was legally prohibited from replacing its officers rapidly. More significant, however, were the effects of the lost war and the new challenge of military technology, which convinced Reichswehr leaders that "scientific" or theoretical training was esssential for officer candidates. The war also stimulated a new relationship between officer and enlisted man, which the Army sought to encourage by having the cadet experience the life of the enlisted man from raw recruit to senior NCO. Furthermore, what the Army considered to be the Republic seemed to call for long-term and systemic character education.[2] How well did the Army train its future leaders? What was it like for cadets to pass through the training cycle? What were they expected to learn, and how well did they profit from the instruction? Are any hallmarks of the future Wehrmacht identifiable in this early stage of training? Finally, what kind of problems did the Army experience with officer training, and what impact did they have? Eduard Zorn's career as an officer candidate illustrates the nature of the program and the problems associated with its implementation.

*   *   *

The responsibility for officer candidate training, which was centered at the regimental level, was accorded the highest priority by Seeckt.   Indeed, in his opinion, officer education took "precedence over all other training goals."[3] For guidance, regimental commanders relied on the officer replacement regulation.   Yet, because much of the regulation was general in nature and the Army's command structure decentralized, their prerogatives in training matters were extensive.   At the local level they had to show only that their programs would meet established goals.   In Zorn's case, Colonel Ritter von Haack delegated authority for the formation and execution of his cadet training program to his chief staff officer, Lieutenant Colonel Karl Ritter von Prager.   The latter relied on several experienced officers to conduct the program on a day-to-day basis.

After Zorn was sworn in as a volunteer in April 1921, he was assigned to Lieutenant Colonel Nickolaus Schemmel's training battalion in Landshut, where he served until shortly before Christmas.   The length of time recruits spent in the training battalion varied considerably from division to division. Volunteers such as Zorn received no special consideration.   "They will be trained and assigned...like other recruits," Schemmel was instructed.   "They will not be quartered in the same room, but divided among the other enlisted men in order to experience the life of the enlisted men."[4]   The principal objective of the training at Landshut was to transform the recruits into fully competent riflemen.   Zorn's duties thus consisted of basic military training common to infantry units: closed and open order drill, use of the rifle, grenade, and light machine-gun, and target practice.   It may have appeared to Zorn that combat instruction took second place to work details, which included everything from guard duty to the cleaning of barracks and horse stalls.   During his free time, he was expected to study infantry regulations.   At this stage in his training, Zorn's contact with officers outside his immediate training environment was kept to a minimum, and throughout the period, he was carefully supervised both on and off duty.

In December, at the conclusion of basic training, Zorn was transferred to Captain Eduard Dietl's company in Munich, where he remained until late March 1922, undergoing theoretical and practical training for the purpose of developing group leadership abilities.   Dietl and Major Hans Schonharl divided the subject material, which included military affairs, weapons science, field service, terrain study, and calisthenics.   In addition, specialists from the technical branches were called in to lecture on their particular arm and the concept of combined arms training.   Oral and written examinations were given monthly on each subject.   During April and May, Zorn was assigned to the machine-gun and trench mortar companies for familiarization training, and then in June he returned to Dietl's company to prepare for the Officer Candidate Examination (OCE), scheduled for the following month, and to continue his training for group leadership. Assisting him in preparation for the examination was a specially-appointed cadet.[5]

While Zorn was readying himself for the examination, he was joined by non-Abitur officer candidates who had reached this stage of training by following a different and more demanding route. Technically, the Reichswehr did not recognize non-Abiturs as candidates until after they had passed the Vorprüfung. Considered the equivalent of the Imperial Army's "Einjährige" examination, the Vorprüfung was devised in Berlin and administered at division level every April. The subjects tested included German, history, mathematics, geography, physics, chemistry, and foreign language. Except for specific questions, the examination changed little during the period. If the individual failed on his first attempt, he could repeat the test the following year. To be eligible for the Vorprüfung, non-Abiturs had to have served at least two years enlisted duty and received from their superiors a positive recommendation based on "military performance, character traits, personality, and potential for improvement." Those who passed the first test entered a training program leading to the Nachprüfung, which was the Reichswehr's equivalent of the Abitur examination of the nine-class high school. It tested the same type of subjects required on the first examination, but was considerably more difficult.[6]

Although at this time the non-Abitur's duties were similar to those of Zorn, he was trained separately from the Abitur cadets. This was partly because the non-Abitur's military schedule was supplemented by a special preparatory program. They were relieved of work details, quartered in separate enlisted barracks, provided with civilian tutors, and their activities were carefully monitored. Throughout the year they were evaluated for character development and general officer potential. Those who passed the second test and received the required favorable character evaluation joined the Abiturs who, like Zorn, were preparing for that year's OCE.

Zorn and approximately twenty other cadets gathered at division headquarters in Munich in early July 1922 to take the examination, which tested both general knowledge and understanding of specific service branches, i.e., the subjects studied during the winter training program. Group leadership, physical training, and the final oral examination were most important. Interestingly enough, the cadets were discouraged from attempting to conform to some type of pre-set or "school" solution. The OCE also changed little from year to year. Comprehensive figures are not available to determine the number who passed each year, but in 1924 only twelve of twenty-four cadets graduated to the first year Infantry School course. This suggests that the examination was reasonably difficult.[7]

After passing the OCE, Zorn was promoted to Lance Corporal (Gefreiter) and returned to field duty. For the next three months, he was trained in the various responsibilities of the senior NCO, and, for the first time, was accepted into the life of the officer corps. Then in September 1922, he and approximately 140 other cadets entered the first ten and one-half months' course at the Infantry School in Munich.

All officer candidates, regardless of their ultimate branch of service, attended the basic course at the Infantry School, where training focused primarily but not exclusively on the infantry. The course emphasized theory during the first seven months and practical applications for the remainder of the time, concluding with several field exercises and a written and oral examination.[8] The service school, however, was intended to do much more than instruct the cadets in technical military subjects: "The service schools serve to instruct and train the officer aspirants....The future of the Army depends not only on the professional ability of the future officers, but to a greater extent upon their spirit and character."[9] Instruction was designed to generate enthusiasm for the profession, encourage leadership development, and nourish patriotism and espirit de corps. Caste haughtiness and branch conceit had no place in the new Army, which must demonstrate that the "military profession has lost none of its old idealism." The experiences of the World War, furthermore, must be studied and evaluated and due attention given to the psychology of war and the welfare of the troops. Although the peacetime soldier requires comprehensive, scientific training, "instruction is designed not to pile up knowledge but to train leaders."

The school's organization and method of instruction, like that of today's military academies, were planned to encourage maximum student involvement. The basic instructional unit was the section, which normally was made up of fifteen to twenty cadets. Class size was purposely small to promote better interaction between instructor and cadet. On the average, the school day lasted from 7 a.m. to 7 p.m. every day except Wednesday and Saturday afternoons. Wednesdays were usually reserved for terrain exercises in the Munich environs. Although lecturing was the normal instructional method during the first course, both courses stressed classroom discussion, in which the cadets were expected to give extemporaneous reports on the subjects under review.

The study plan for the first course (see appendix, table 1) shows that the curriculum was extremely comprehensive and that theoretical instruction took precedence. Although tactics, which averaged six hours per week, was the most important subject taught at the school, the plan does not indicate fully the dominating role it played. As the subject description points out, "tactics is the principle subject of military scientific instruction and the instructor of tactics heads the scientific portion of the course. The study plans of the technical subjects should be made to comply with the study plan for tactics."[10] In fact, all individual courses emphasized tactical principles as well, and examination questions dealing with tactics always carried the most weight in scoring. Tactics, by implication, means the cooperation of all arms, so the curriculum stressed the inter-relationship of all service branches.

When the course ended in the summer of 1923, Zorn was promoted to Ensign (Fähnrich) and briefly reassigned to the 19th Infantry Regiment before returning to the Infantry School for the second course in September. Only cadets from the infantry branch took this course. Although the subject matter was largely the same as presented in the first course, the emphasis was reversed. Now, practical instruction took precedence (see appendix 2, table 2). Again, tactics held first place in the curriculum. Even military history was taught primarily from a tactical perspective. During the second course, Zorn was challenged more extensively to develop his imagination and teaching abilities, especially in the terrain exercises and instructional trips. The examinations covered every subject taught during the course year. Before each final examination, a written evaluation was submitted on every cadet for subject studied during the year. These were compared with scores from the written tests, and, in cases of disparity or failure, the cadet was examined orally by the school's board of examiners.

What conclusions can be drawn about the service schools? First of all, the curriculum was reasonably comprehensive and reflected the high command's desire to profit from wartime experiences and new technical developments. The academic arrangements and methods of instruction, moreover, promoted individual initiative and clearly challenged the cadets, who wereencouraged to reach decisions within a prescribed format, but not to seek a standard solution. It is obvious, too, that instruction was expected to develop character and leadership qualities as well as technical knowledge.

Were any characteristics of the future Wehrmacht present? To be sure, 1923 is too early to expect to see blitzkrieg doctrine being studied at the schools. The subject of aircraft was taught primarily from the standpoint of air defense. Yet cadets began early in their careers to master tactics and the art of making rapid, accurate decisions and issuing simple, direct orders. Tactical instruction always conformed to a prescribed format. The student was presented with a "Friend-Foe" problem, and then required to evaluate the situation, make a quick decision, and give appropriate commands. Emphasis was always on combined arms concepts and situations calling for solutions based on principles of mobil warfare. This basic tactical format served as the cornerstone for all levels of Reichswehr training and played the same crucial role during the Wehrmacht years.

After Zorn completed the second Infantry School course, he returned to the field for summer duty and the autumn maneuvers and then took the Officer Examination. As a result of his performance, he was promoted to Senior Ensign (Oberfähnrich) and reassigned to his regiment. All that remained now was for Zorn to pass his final and most important evaluation as a cadet -- acceptance by the entire regimental officer corps. In his case, the officers of his battalion voted to approve him for promotion, then the other battalions of I.R. 19 followed suit. The required paperwork, including the document obligating Zorn to serve twenty-five years as an officer, was sent forward for Berlin's approval. His promotion was subsequently granted and he received a date of rank (Patent) of December 1, 1924, which included an order of merit number for his promotion group.[11]

When Lieutenant Eduard Zorn took his place in the officer

corps at the end of 1924, he could look back on four years of intensive preparation as an enlisted man. As a result of his training in the regiment and at the service schools, he was expected to be thoroughly familiar with the problems of the troops he would command. As an infantry lieutenant, he now supposedly possessed thorough knowledge of his infantry arm and an appreciation of all other branches of the Army. Along with his technical knowledge, he embodied the high ideals and strength of character Seeckt required of his Reichswehr officers -- or so Army leaders thought. In effect, after four years' training of mind and spirit, Lieutenant Eduard Zorn was assumed to fit the mold of the officer who was leader, instructor, and educator.

                    *   *   *

     Zorn's experience reveals what the cadet training program was intended to achieve. How well did it succeed? If Seeckt was correct, the training program always was in difficulty. Some of this dissatisfaction concerned normal criticism of weak areas, but the record does indicate legitimate, major problems.
     The Army was most interested in the eighteen months of cadet training preceding the first service school course. This period was crucial because the cadets here were most impressionable and susceptible to fundamental instruction. Despite the difference in degree of training and objectives for Abitur and non-Abitur cadets during this period, the Reichswehr tended to focus primarily on the character development of both Abitur and non-Abitur cadet. The concepts of character and character education in the context of Reichswehr training were all-encompassing, including such elements as discipline, bearing and behavior, as well as ethical and moral integrity. From the Reichswehr's viewpoint, cadets were expected to show a high level of Erziehung, or schooling in general terms.
     From this general standpoint, Seeckt and his commanders were never satisfied with the quality of non-Abitur cadets who, being less educated, were regarded as less mature. Because of this, these cadets required a longer period of time for their military and theoretical training and their character education. Proof of this was seen in the results of the Vorprüfung and Nachprüfung -- especially the latter -- which were never considered satisfactory. Particularly during the early years, usually less than half of the cadets taking the examinations passed. In Bavaria, for example, this was the norm for the years 1921-1924. Seeckt believed that poor test performances not only indicated a weak educational foundation for future technical study at the service schools, but also deficiencies in those character attributes required of the future officer. He consequently gave repeated instructions to his commanders to "evaluate as carefully as possible the non-Abitur's on and off-duty activity and his relations were enlisted men in order to form a realistic impression of his character and personality."[12]
     Even high test scores, however, did not satisfy Seeckt, who still insisted on character evaluations of cadets by unit commanders. The examination score, he reminded them in August 1922, was only one "contributing factor" to future success as an officer.[13]

Indeed, he wrote seven months later, experience had demonstrated that oftentimes "good test-takers were, in terms of personality and character, weaker soldiers or lacked the capability of being leaders conscious of their responsibilities."[14]   He attempted to solve this problem by making the Vorprüfung more difficult to pass and thereby force an early decision, which, he declared, would be in the best interests of the Army and the individual.   Now non-Abiturs had to distinguish rather than merely prove themselves.

Seeckt, however, was never able to solve the problem to his satisfaction.   Periodically he received reports from the Infantry School which described the sub-standard performance of many cadets, who arrived with unequal levels of training, which meant that many had to be sent back to their units because of deficiencies.   Seeckt saw in all this a failure of character and he placed blame squarely on the commanders, who, he said, were not taking their training responsibilities seriously and were submitting evaluation certificates that failed to provide a clear description of the cadet's character and general ability.[15]   For Seeckt, in other words, the fault lay not in the content of the training program, but in its ineffective application, particularly in the area of character building and evaluation.

Clearly, it was the weak performance of non-Abiturs that convinced Reichswehr officials to refuse the numerous requests from the field to shorten the two-year prerequisite and make the examinations easier.   In 1923, for example, the Chief of Military Education and Training conducted a thorough review of the requests for changes -- the main problem involved non-Abiturs who had almost as much formal education as the Abiturs -- but declined to reduce or eliminate the two-year prerequisite for that type of non-Abitur. Neither did Seeckt act on such requests later, contending that the non-Abitur required a longer period in which to demonstrate his character and general potential for the officer profession.   He apparently did like, however, a proposal advanced by the commandant of the Infantry School.   Alarmed at unequal standards of training and the growing dismissal rate, he suggested the eighteen-month period be divided into six phases, each having specific, limited training objectives.   In this way, all cadets would receive progressive training designed to make them qualified to enter the Infantry School's first course at the same level of proficiency.[16]

Seeckt attached the problem directly in a decree of January 1923.   Citing a long list of abuses involving character deficiencies of students who had entered the school with Eduard Zorn the previous September, he said the fault lay with the troop units. The solution was a more unified approach to training, and he promised new guidelines.   Two months later the Army promulgated the "Guidelines for the Training of Officer Candidates" to cover the eighteen months preceding the first weapons school course.   Justifying the move, Seeckt said flatly that fully one third of the cadets at the Infantry School were not up to standards.   To correct this situation, the directive, following closely the Infantry School commander's proposal, divided the eighteen months into six periods with detailed training descriptions for each.[17]

The "Guidelines" reflected the high command's concern about

three basic problems related, in one form or another, to the issue
of character.   First, Army leaders now questioned one of the
cardinal features of the cadet training program: the relationship
between officer candidate and enlisted man.   Although the Army
believed that it must continue to train the officer candidates with
the enlisted recruits, the latter's different social background
threatened the character standards Seeckt had set for his future
officers.   Seeckt in January had admitted that intimate association
between the two seemed to have produced an "unhealthy influence" on
the officer recruits.[18] The issue, in practical terms, centered on
the question of quarters. Should cadets be quartered with the enlisted men and NCOs, as Zorn had been, or should they be housed
separately? The latter solution ran the risk of creating resent-
ment among the enlisted men. Seeckt's answer was something of a
compromise. Cadets should live with the enlisted men for at least
part of the training period, but their education from the date they
entered the Army must be conducted by officers.[19]

The second problem, and one that Seeckt never was able to
eliminate, concerned the timeless custom of work details. This duty included everything from normal care and cleaning of equipment
and barracks to personal favors demanded by NCOs and officers. Not
only were such tasks often personally demeaning to the cadets, they
also squandered valuable "soldierly" training time. In any event,
abuses of this custom did not reflect well on the character of the
officers and NCOs involved.   Seeckt prescribed that in certain
phases of the general training period cadets be entirely exempt
from work details and in others that such details be permitted only
in cases where they would be of definite value to the future officer. The latter qualification, of course, left the door wide open
to abuse.[20]

The third area of concern involved the off-duty activities.
Disciplinary infractions by cadets outside the garrison could be
eliminated, Seeckt believed, by closer supervision. He consequently now charged the company commanders and officers specifically assigned to recruits with this responsibility. He also prescribed
the type of off-duty privileges that cadets were to enjoy.[21]

None of these problems, of course, involved the technical or
military side of officer candidate training. Seeckt seems to have
been confident that unit training was turning the officer cadet into a reasonably competent soldier. In many cases, however, the cadet appeared to lack a good character foundation, and this, too, he
said, was the responsibility of the units.

                *   *   *

Clearly, Seeckt faced an uphill battle in his efforts to promote high standards of character in a time of postwar permissive-
ness and political turmoil. One event in particular during this
turbulent era threatened the very foundations of the cadet training
program. Indeed, if Seeckt had any doubts about the wisdom of his
overriding emphasis on character education, they were silenced by
the Hitler Putsch of November 1923.[22]

Seeckt's problems with the Infantry School were a part of the larger issue of Reich-Bavarian relations. When the authority of Imperial Germany collapsed in 1918, Munich became the center of the left-wing revolutionary movement. Even though the Munich-based communist government was suppressed rapidly the following spring, the excessive violence and intensity of feeling left Bavarians with a deep hatred of left-wing extremism. The city subsequently became the center for the most radical groups of the political right -- the so-called "patriotic" associations. From the beginning the Reichswehr maintained close ties with the paramilitary separatist movement, whose rallying cry was the "march on Berlin."

This intense Bavarian feeling now blended with the more traditional antipathy toward Prussia and the German national government which predated the Weimar period. Now, in republican Germany, Bavarian particularists saw in Berlin a leftist, socialist government bent on political centralization at their expense. The uneasy federalist compromise between Berlin and Munich worsened in the face of the growing economic and political emergency. The crisis came to a head in the fall of 1923, when the Bavarians declared a state of emergency in September and appointed a state commissioner with dictatorial powers. Berlin responded by declaring martial law and entrusting the fate of the country to Seeckt and the Army. The next month Bavaria assumed control of the local Reichswehr division and ordered its members to take a new oath of allegiance to the Bavarian state. Now Reichswehr officers and Infantry School cadets were confronted with a conflict of loyalties that went to the heart of the military system. It was in this tumultuous atmosphere that the Hitler Putsch occurred. Here, in the participation by Infantry School cadets in direct disobedience of orders, Seeckt saw proof that the Reichswehr cadet training program was far from successful.[23]

Although the chief culprits were commissioned officer students, the cadets freely took part in the proceedings. From the diary notes of one Cadet F. Schraml, a student in the first course, it is evident that the instructors at the school failed to exert the leadership and discipline expected of them. On October 22, for example, the commandant told the students to "think about" Seeckt's order of the 20th, which demanded that the officers and students remain loyal to Berlin, and decide for themselves whether to support the central government. The commandant was followed by a local colonel, who defended the Bavarian position and attempted to convince the students to follow his course of action. Schraml's control officer, furthermore, made little or no effort to restrain his charges.[24]

Seeckt's response to what he called "mutiny" and its effects on the officer candidate training program was sharp, but he followed military custom by keeping the whole affair largely within the Army. The day after the putsch, he closed the school and ordered the students back to their units, enjoining commanders to investigate individual degrees of involvement. From the beginning, however, Seeckt held the school officer corps and the officer student ringleaders responsible. He concluded that the vast majority of the students had been led astray and believed their actions had the approval of their superiors, so he ended up counseling unit commanders to be lenient in judging cadets.

If school officials were responsible, Seeckt saw the source of the indiscipline in the field units' failure to instil proper training principles in their cadets before releasing them to the school. "A few school weeks cannot create what has been neglected during many years in the field," he observed, "especially when the mass of the students are of a disposition that does not deserve to be called patriotic but must be designated as militarily insubordinate."[25]   To Seeckt, then, the problem was simply a question of military discipline.

The effects of the affair were unquestionably detrimental to the training program. The Infantry School was transferred to the Ohrdruf training grounds in Thuringia, and the move created hardship for both instructors and students. When the school reopened in the spring of 1924, furthermore, the duration of courses for both first and second-year students had to be cut in half in order not to disrupt ensuing classes. In October, following the conclusion of the courses, General von Haack, Zorn's former regimental commander, who was now Seeckt's chief of staff, issued a report that confirmed the detrimental effect on cadet training resulting from the move and the compressed instructional period. Second-year students, like Zorn, who had been trained in the first course at Munich prior to the putsch, demonstrated on the Officer Examination that they were adequately prepared for promotion to lieutenant. The first year students, however, were still deficient in fundamentals and were not expected to pass the examination in 1925 without more intensive basic training. Not until the Infantry School was transferred permanently to Dresden in 1926 did the training cycle resume its normal routine.[26]

Seeckt's decrees over the next three years indicate that, while the training program had improved, many of the old defects continued. Although progress had been generally satisfactory, he said in March 1926, many commanders were still not taking their responsibilities seriously enough, especially regarding monitoring of off-duty activities. Once again, he cited specific abuses that reflected low standards of character and threatened the ideals of young cadets. The latter still arrived at the Infantry School without a uniform training background, and too many had to be sent back to their units. Commanders were responsible for the ultimate performance of their cadets, he admonished, and they should make it a point of honor to see that their cadets remained at school.[27]

Two months later the Reichswehr leader took up again the matter of work details which, the Infantry School had reported, were probably responsible for many training deficiencies. Seeckt was seriously concerned, since he suspected that cadets, out of fear of punishment, did not report many instances of abuse. The thing to do, he decided, was to eliminate purposeless work details from field training altogether -- and he so ordered in May 1926. Time at the Infantry School was too valuable to waste correcting deficiencies that might not have occurred had cadets not squandered time on non-essential tasks, he explained. Seeckt also admonished officers about the proper discharge of their responsibilities. Only by properly educating the cadets, he remonstrated, could the

Army avoid the embarrassment that had befallen one regiment, which had four of its cadets rejected from the school. Further abuse, he warned, would affect the efficiency ratings of the commanders concerned.[28]

Seeckt continued his battle against the problems in the officer candidate training program until he left office. It is significant that he always viewed both the problems and their solutions in terms of the "education" of the officer cadets. He seldom dwelled on technical, military deficiencies and never referred to weaknesses in the weapons school curricula or methods of instruction. It was not the program that was at fault but its implementation. The technical side of training appeared well in hand and would take care of itself, he thought, if the officer corps carried out its responsibility to develop the character of its replacements through proper education.

*   *   *

The Reichswehr officer candidate training program, in its structure and content, remained largely unchanged after Seeckt's forced retirement in late 1926. General Heye, who was determined to continue and refine the Seectk programs, was not the kind to tamper unless the need was urgent. Together with Defense Minister Wilhelm Groener, he also continued Seeckt's practice of insisting on character development in the officer corps. To be sure, the courses at the weapons schools were adjusted periodically to accommodate new developments in the various branches of the Army. Seeckt's 1923 regulation, however, remained in effect until 1931, when General von Hammerstein had it amended to include some special (sonder) training.

This does not mean that all parties in the Reichswehr were content with the cadet training program. Particularly during the period of Heye's leadership, sharp opposition to the program began to emerge. This group of critics was led by the Chief of Military Education and Training, Brigadier General Hilmar Ritter von Mittelberger, who circulated within the Defense Ministry in April 1930 a proposal for sweeping changes in military education. Although Mittelbeger, a Bavarian, admitted that the present training program had served the Army well in the past, he urged reform in several areas. For one thing, he argued, there was too little emphasis on ledership training at the troop level. The eighteen-month period prior to the first weapons school course was too short to develop practical leadership with the small units. Instruction at the schools, moreover, was too difficult for young soldiers, and the two years spent there created a gap in their practical training that could not be bridged. When the cadets returned to their units after the second course, he concluded, they had too little authority and experience to deal properly with the troops.

Mittelberger proposed a reorganization plan that admittedly would generate some turmoil for several years. According to his scheme, the cadets initially would serve two and one-half years in the field before attending the first course. The second course would be eliminated altogether and included in the general officer training program.   In this manner, junior officer would do their branch training after gaining extensive practical experience in the field.[29]

Despite the apparent early support of Heye and several of his chief subordinates, no major changes occurred in cadet training until 1932. The adjustments that were made prior to that time were minor, involving recruits who entered special, accelerated programs in the fall instead of spring. Most were cadets assigned to a preliminary flight course, and the Reichswehr experimented with various methods of coordinating the training activity of the regular and special cadets without sacrificing standards. In 1932, however, Reichswehr planners were required to produce an effective new program to accomodate larger classes of cadets expected the following spring. At the end of 1932, field units were required to submit suggested plans that would encompass a twelve rather than an eighteen-month training period in the field units before attendance at the Infantry School. Unlike Mittelberger's plan, which called for a two and one-half year assignement with troops as prerequisite, the effort in late 1932 was to get the cadets to the Infantry School as soon as possible. Most units believed that the new twelve-month plan could be implemented without sacrificing the basic objectives of cadet training.[30]

      *   *   *

How successful was the leadership in meeting its objectives?' Clearly Seeckt must receive high marks for developing the technical military proficiency of his cadets. Generally, he spent very little time worrying about the technical and tactical side of training, and it is in this area that the Reichswehr is perhaps most admired. Significantly, at this early stage of training, the Reichswehr attempted to develop cadet initiative in response to tactical problems. But this objective proved difficult to achieve. Tactical training can only develop initiative within very narrow limits, and the Reichswehr's ability to do this effectively at this level must be questioned.

Given the formalized problem-solving method used in working tactical problems, it was not a simple matter to exhibit flexibility and initiative. Perhaps more significantly, young men who had only recently entered the Army would hardly be prepared to take excessive risks which could result in failure and displease their superiors. Seeckt, moreover, emphasized the attributes of discipline and obedience, and the cadet, above all else, was instructed to do his duty and obey the orders of his superiors. This type of direction is more conducive to conformist thinking and not the reverse. If, in theory, the Reichswehr promoted independent thinking in working military problems, the result in practice seems certain to have fallen short of the objective. The recruits, nevertheless, did have four years in which to learn their trade, and if they demonstrated little genuine initiative at this early period, they nevertheless attained a relatively high level of technical proficiency.

But military expertise was only one objective of cadet train-

ing.   There can be no question that character, or character
education, was the most vital element in Seeckt's program.   In
effect, he attempted to institutionalize character in his future
officers and demanded that future leaders demonstrate, above all,
the highest standards of character and personal integrity.   Here,
too, the Reichswehr fell short of its goal, and the problem lies in
the way in which the concept was used.   Seeckt criticized all sorts
of problems in the cadet training program.   Some, like the failure
to arrive at the Infantry School with the proper equipment, appear
minor.   Others clearly were major problems that concerned deficient
performance, unethical conduct, and illegal political activity.
Although he viewed all abuses as flaws of character and a result of
ineffective character education, he never defined the concept carefully.   Because all problems were considered character problems,
character became a catch-all concept shorn of much of its effectiveness.   The result was utter confusion for cadets undergoing
training during the Weimar years.

It is not coincidental that Seeckt was preoccupied with both
character and the Abitur qualification.   Because he associated
character, as well as social standing and maturity, with the Abitur, he was overly concerned with the progress of cadets who lacked
the diploma.   On the other hand, there is no evidence to show that
the abuses he described applied only to cadets who entered training
without the Abitur.   Seeckt really wanted the motivated cadet who
exhibited a love of the service and unquestioned loyalty.   These
were the virtues of the old-fashioned Prussian gentleman, and
Seeckt assumed that these attributes somehow were demonstrated in
the Abitur, as if it inherently signified the quality of gentleman.

Considering the war's negative effects on traditional values,
it is doubtful whether Seeckt could produce his kind of gentleman
in the postwar years.   At this time the Reichswehr needed education
and training that stressed carefully defined concepts of proper and
improper conduct and ethical values.   Society at large, by Army
standards, was not providing this training.   Unfortunately, Reichswehr cadets received an all-encompassing concept of character that
for many offered little guidance about moral conduct.   In the end,
Seeckt's character education foundered on the rock of personal integrity and loyalty that was such an important part of the program.   Significantly, cadets received very little formal political
or civics education.   It was espcially in this field, however, that
clear thinking was needed because Reichswehr members pledged their
loyalty to a very unpopular government.   Furthermore, loyalty to
the republican government, as Seeckt defined it, was always conditional and subordinated to the higher concept of the state.   This
meant that an officer's relationship to etablished authority was
never clearly established and amounted to moral or ethical relativ-
ism.[31]

Actually, Seeckt was merely perpetuating the historic role of
the German officer corps as a "state within the state" into the
postwar era.   The major difference, however, was that now for the
first time the Army was serving a government it despised.   For many
officers disloyalty to the Weimar was something akin to a patriotic
duty, as was shown during the 1923 Munich revolt.   And who is to

say that in their own minds the Infantry School cadets were not demonstrating "good character."   How could Seeckt's character education ultimately succeed when an officer's loyalty was always conditional?   Understandably, critics of the Reichswehr label it one of the "gravediggers" of the Republic.

In the final analysis, character, rather than serving a meaningful educational function, came to mean simply discipline and obedience -- to Seeckt.   Indeed, the test of character in the Reichswehr seemed to be less the social origins or educational accomplishments of the individual than obedience.   The issue of character that first appears during the recruiting and training of officer cadets is a constant theme throughtout all areas of officer education and training.   It is of special importance in the selection and training of officers for the General Staff.

3.
General Staff Candidate Selection

The general staff is the brain of an army, and no army can function without one. The Germany Army was the pioneer in the development of the modern, professional general staff. As a result of its performance in Germany's wars of unification in the mid-nineteenth century, the German General Staff earned a reputation at home and abroad for exceptional military professionalism. This reputation had not diminished in the eyes of Germany's World War one opponents who initially were determined to prevent the new postwar German Army from maintaining a general staff. Indeed, Article 160 of the Versailles Treaty prohibited the "Great German General Staff and all similar organizations."[1] Despite this restriction, however, the General Staff emerged in different form to function as the vital element of the Reichswehr. Its survival during the Weimar years can be attributed to ambiguous Treaty language and the acknowledgement that staff officers are necessary for the proper functioning of any army. Not only did the treaty specifically authorize "superior" staff officers at all headquarters units, it was silent on the prospect of a Reichswehr General Staff substantially different from the "Great German General Staff." When Seeckt reformed the General Staff under the new, innocuously-named Truppenamt (Troops Office) and removed its historic political prerogatives, the Allies approved the new organization and later, when unfavorable publicity surfaced, made only token protests. In any event, the General Staff and its replacement program were well-known to the Inter-Allied Control Commission from the Reichswehr's inception. Historians have paid considerable attention to the General Staff's influence on German political life and its performance in military situations -- a recent study attributes

German military success in World War Two to the "institutionalizing of military excellence" in the General Staff?[2] But what about the General Staff as an institution? How were staff officers recruited and what was the nature of their training? What were they expected to learn? These are the questions that have not been addressed satisfactorily. They can best be answered by an examination of the experience of a typical officer.

     *   *   *

For the sake of continuity, it would be useful to continue with Lieutenant Eduard Zorn as our reprsentative officer, but this is not possible. Zorn, it will be remembered, was among the very first group of officers promoted to lieutenant through the regular officer candidate training program. He was not eleigible to stand for the necessary entrance examination, however, until the spring of 1933. In other words, none of the men who had entered the regular officer candidate training program during the Weimar period even began General Staff training until the advent of the Third Reich. Careers like Zorn's make it clear that we are dealing with a very brief period of time during which an army had to establish and regularize its institutions. More specifically, it means that the vast majority of trainees in the Reichswehr period had ties to the Imperial Army and the experience of combat. The Reichswehr, in selecting an elite element from an army of leaders, was determined to maintain traditional ties and ensure that future General Staff officers were thoroughly grounded in field experience. In this way, General Staff officers continued to be a very small, elite group during the Weimar period.

One officer whose career does shed light on the established program during a period of transition in military and political affairs -- and whose training file survived the war largely intact -- was Ferdinand Jodl, younger brother of Alfred Jodl, Hitler's wartime Chief of the O.K.W. Operations Staff. Jodl's experience demonstrates the Reichswehr's careful attention to training procedures at all organizational levels. He had begun active duty as a cadet during the first month of the World War. Although he was promoted to lieutenant in September 1914, he, like many Bavarian junior officers, did not receive a Reich commission until a year later when the Bavarian army was absorbed into the Reichswehr. It is indicative of the depressing promotion situation in the new professional Reichswehr that almost a decade passed before he was promoted to first lieutenant.[3]

Jodl's General Staff selection experience began with the Defense Ministry's order of July 1926, which officially announced the entrance or District Examination (Wehrkreisprüfung) and described the eligibility parameters and test conditions. The selection process was first established by regulation in October 1920. Only after the officers had completed a four to five-month preparatory course, which was given in conjunction with regularly assigned duties, could they be admitted to the examination. Every junior officer was required to take the District Examination (DE), which was administered by the Truppenamt's Training Branch (T4) through the division chiefs of staff. Final selection was determined by the test result and the character report submitted by the individual's commander.[4]

Eligible with Jodl in 1926 were first lieutenants commissioned not later that April 1, 1925 and officers scheduled for promotion to captain who had not taken the test previously. The announcement that Jodl read also mentioned non-military subject areas to be tested and recommended reference works for study. Ten days later the 7th Artilllery Regiment nominated twelve of its officers, including Jodl. When the final list of eligible officers was published later in the summer, Jodl was among thirty-two Bavarian officers scheduled for the October preparatory course.[5]

Although the division chief of staff was responsible for the preparatory training, the course itself, which was conducted by correspondence from Munich and administered by a retired colonel named Ludwig Schrott, consisted of five military subjects taught at the level of the reinforced infantry regiment. Applied tactics, with nine lessons, was the key subject. The other four subjects required two lessons each. Basically, the instructional method first noted with the tactics course at the Infantry School was continued in the General Staff preparatory course. The officerswere required to estimate the situation presented, make a decision, and then formulate and issue the orders necessary for deployment of forces. The primary regulation for all problems, Leadership and Combat of the Combined Arms, was familiar throughout the officer corps.[6]

Schrott, who taught both in the courses on applied tactics and formal tactics, used this method which tested the application of command and combat regulations to specific tactical situations. The third subject, arms and equipment, tested comprehensive knowledge of the officer's own branch of service. Here the officer also had to solve tactical problems involving the proper method of employing the weapon and its effect on the other branches of the Reichswehr. Schrott, who devised the tactical lessons himself, normally relied on branch specialists with General Staff training for the more technical subjects such as field reconnaissance and engineering.

From early October to mid-February 1927, Jodl worked an average of one problem a week, normally on a different subject. Schrott's procedures were similar for all five subjects. He would issue a copy of the problems and his solution to each student. The solution was reviewed after the problem had been turned in. Once Schrott had received and scored all test papers, he published a general critique which evaluated the content and format of the student answers. The student retained his corrected paper and the critique for further reference.

In January, the first of two three-day oral evaluations was held in Munich and Nürnberg for all participants who could be spared from their regular duties. During this examination, Jodl was given a more difficult tactical problem, as well as instruction in non-military subjects. In February, after the second oral problem was presented, the Reichswehr published the examination schedule (see appendix 3, table 1).

Jodl took the District Examination, which was administered by Bavarian officers, during the third week of February at the Engineer School in Munich. With the exception of mathematics, physics, and chemistry, he was tested in all of the subjects listed on the schedule. Had Jodl chosen not to take the language section he would have had to take mathematics and one of the two science tests. Usually the latter three subjects were taken by officers competing for the technical General Staff candidate program. Immediately following the conclusion of the four-day final examination, all test materials were forwarded to Berlin, where they were graded by a team of General Staff officers in a procedure that maximized anonymity and security. At this point, Jodl's unit commander submitted the necessary evaluation of Jodl's character and potential for General Staff work. In late June, Jodl was notified that he was among thirty-seven officers out of a total of 270 examined who were selected for General Staff candidate training.[7]

*   *   *

Jodl's selection process illustrates the key role of the district officials and unit commanders. In an decentralized system, the weakest links are likely to be at the lower levels. In the General Staff candidate selection system, the Army always faced the problem of ensuring administrative uniformity, which is why it attempted in every way possible to promote common programs and create common procedures.

Every July the Army established the parameters for the subsequent DE by outlining the criteria for eligibility and likely contents of the examination. The preparatory program was described in a separate regulation, which set up common guidelines for all districts and enjoined the division chiefs of staff to appoint only well-qualified senior General Staff officers to implement the program. Furthermore, the program was intentionally designed to be administered concurrently with the regular winter training cycle of October to April, the period most suitable for theoretical training.

The Reichswehr also endeavored to equalize selection opportunities for all officers by publishing copies of the previous year's examination questions and solutions. In a related effort, it promoted semi-official publications like the Militär-Wochenblatt which, it addition to carrying numerous columns suggesting good study methods, issued a series of tactical problems and language lessons during every winter training cycle. The Reichswehr at the same time encouraged publication of studies by active officers like Colonel Friedrich Cochenhausen, whose work on troop leadership contained a useful chapter on preparation for the DE.[8]

The Reichswehr seldom altered the essential content and procedures of the DE. The examination was given at the same time in all districts, and elaborate precautions were taken to ensure that test security was not violated. On balance, the Army made every effort to standardize the process and equalize the opportunities for officers to prepare and pass the test.

Nevertheless, the decentralized nature of the selection system

was one potential problem that has been criticized.[9] Officers who
had to prepare for the examination and also perform regular duties
were clearly overburdened, and this situation was worse for officers whose commanders might not allow for sufficient individual
study time.   Furthermore, since the district instructors like
Schrott were allowed to develop their own lesson problems, unsatisfactory variations in course content could occur.   But did these
things seriously weaken the selection system?   The failure to meet
quotas and the high command's efforts to maintain standards of
quality suggest a negative answer.
     The total figures for the years 1927-1932, which are far below
the original figure of seventy, illustrate the overconfidence of
the planners (see appendix 3, table 2).   Furthermore, the Army in
this period limited the number of officers eligible to stand for
the DE.   During the first three years, the total number of eligible
officers had been well above 300, but for the 1924 examination, the
Defense Ministry announced that, since the earlier numbers were too
high, a limit of 300 would be enforced.   As indicated in Jodl's
case, 270 officers took the examination in 1927, but after that the
number of eligible officers dropped considerably.   In 1928, for example, only 118 officers took the examination, and the average figure for the following years was 150.[10]
     The Reichswehr also did more than limit the number of officers
eligible and selected by raising the required passing score from
150 points to 183 beginning in 1927.   Presumably, a factor that had
some bearing on this issue was the inordinately large group of 685
first lieutenants who, along with Jodl, were promoted on April 1,
1925, which meant that some of them were still standing for the DE
for the first time in 1931.[11]   In view of this, it is little wonder
that Zorn had to wait until 1933 for his turn.   More importantly,
the fact that the Reichswehr was dealing with the lower half of
this group after 1927 suggests that the passing score may have been
raised to ensure that the quality standards would not be jeopardized.   Although there is little to show that these officers were,
on the average, less qualified, Reichswehr leaders during the Heye
era were far more concerning with the quality of the officer corps
than their predecessors.   As soon as Heye became commander-in-chief
in late 1926, he began making changes in the General Staff selection system designed to create more stability in the program and to
increase the standards of quality.
     Gone was the inconsistency of the Seeckt years (see appendix
3, table 2).   The eligibility figure was continually maintained at
the lower figure of 150, and the yearly number of selectees was
stabilized at between thirty and forty.   There is also evidence to
suggest that the leaders were determined to ensure that proficiency
standards would not be compromised.   The Chief of the Truppenamt,
General Werner von Blomberg, for instance, issued a scathing five-
page critique of the papers submitted on the 1928 DE.   His comments
show that many of the weaknesses Schrott found in the work of his
charges were widespread among offices standing for the 1928 examination.
     The poor performance on tactical questions supplied Blomberg
with most of his ammunition.   The test papers showed little evi-

dence of logical thought, he argued, and often dealt with only one possible solution to the problem at hand. Command technique, furthermore, was too structured and the orders issued often unclear. On the formal tactics problems the students got bogged down in details, while the results of the field reconnaissance portion showed that many lacked the ability to evaluate the terrain correctly. Blomberg's comments on the non-military subjects were hardly more complimentary. The critique is significant for showing the high command's emphasis on quality standards and its displeasure that so many officers exhibited conformity of thought as well as conformity in method.[12]

Also suggestive of the Army's preoccupation with improving the quality of its General Staff selectees was the fact that in 1928 Bavarian authorities for the first time required unit commanders to indicate in character reports whether or not candidates for the DE possessed the Abitur certificate.[13] In early 1929, furthermore, the Reichswehr announced that beginning in October all participants in the correspondence course would be permitted to study course material two afternoons each week, and that the oral evaluations would be administered to all officers in one rather than two locations -- both changes that contributed to greater uniformity in the program. All of this indicates that Heye's modifications of the General Staff candidate selection system resulted in increased stability and greater selectivity after 1927. Now the important question is: what kind of officer was selected by this process?

                 *   *   *

The typical candidate has been described by others: he was a first lieutenant between twenty-five and thirty years of age, who had from three to nine years service in the officer corps behind him and who also possessed a reasonable high level of general education. Personal favoritism played no role in his selection nor did his specific branch of service, duty assignment and location. Performance on the DE was the key, and this examination was primarily a test of the officer's level of general education.[14] How well did Jodl conform to this ideal officer?

Fortunately, his scores are available for each of the subjects tested on his DE (see appendix 3, table 1). The multipliers listed for the individual subjects show quite clearly that the military topics were considered most important. Of these, the key tactical ones, applied and formal tactics and field reconnaissance carried the most weight, and the officer would be expected to score high in these fields in order to do well on the examination.

It is not surprising to see Jodl register a strong performance in these areas because his scores in the preparatory course were excellent. Schrott's marginal comments on Jodl's papers indicate that he was very satisfied with the work of the young lieutenant, who had to meet two objectives in the solution of tactical problems. The Army demanded, first, that the student rigidly conform to the established method of solving tactical problems, and also required him to demonstrate, within the rigid structural framework, great flexibility and initiative.[15]

Whether Jodl had to deal with the simple advance of a combined arms detachment, as in the first applied tactics problem, or the complex deployment of a cavalry brigade, as in the ninth, the problem-solving method never varied. He was presented first with a detailed situation and then asked to evaluate this situation by beginning with what he wanted his forces to do. Only then would he examine the enemy's intentions. By testing his various options against possible enemy counteractions, the best course of action would become evident and he would make the right decision. The final step involved issuing the orders for deployment of his personnel and equipment within the framework of the combined arms concept.

Equally important, however, was the manner in which the solution was expressed. Clarity, conciseness, and the use of correct terminology were required virtues. Above all, the students were taught to avoid the "chancellery" (ornate) style and superfluous phrases. Even where no time limit was involved, students were urged to practice speed as well as thoroughness. All tactical problems were expected to be worked according to established procedures, and every move had to be supported by the appropriate regulation.

At the same time, there is ample evidence that within this rigid format Schrott expected his students to be more than blind copiers of the regulations. The problems were intentionally designed to challenge the officer by presenting difficult situations and requiring the employment of the most modern equipment. Tactical air forces, for example, were always included in the order of battle; Jodl also had to deal with the tank in both offensive and defensive roles. The tactical tests were based largely on actual maneuver situations from the 1926 autumn exercise.

Along with demanding subject material, the instructors always sought to present the students with exercises that required difficult decisions. Many situations stressed the "frictions" of combat and uncertainity of events. In these cses, officers were told to be flexible and avoid the single-solution approach. As Schrott cautioned the students,

> there are many views on tactics. In reality, success determines whether you were correct. But with theoretical work, it is often difficult to say whether something was unconditionally right or wrong. Therefore, I do not want my solution in any way to be considered the single, correct, official solution.[16]

Certain problems specifically required deviation from orders. Students in these cases were told to use their own judgment and improvise, but only after thorough consideration of the overall situation. The goal of instruction was thus to teach a model for a pattern of thought (Gedankengang), while at the same time avoiding a patterned response to a given situation.

Although the Reichswehr evidently took pains to develop initiative, the problem of achieving a good balance between conformity and improvisation is nonetheless a difficult one. Too much stress

on improvisation can create disorder, while too much attention to
method can produce regimentation and the danger of thinking along
set lines.   Although it is important to establish a common method
for solving tactical problems, there also exists the very real possibility that rigid conformity in method will produce a rigid men-
tality, one in which it is never questioned why things should be
done, only how they can be done.   And the consequences of such
thinking can have a dangerous impact in areas outside the narrow
world of tactical instruction.

Indeed, the tactical training that Jodl and other General
Staff candidates received appears to have been somewhat unique.
All armies want officers who follow procedures but also show some
flexibility.   No army wants or needs officers, especially staff officers, who go rigidly by the book.   The American military attache,
however, in his evaluation of the 1924 DE, correctly noted that the
Reichswehr's concern for imaginative responses and individual initiative seemed far less evident in other armies.[17]

It is clear that the instruction in the preparatory course demanded that the officer thoroughly master tactics, and Jodl did
quite well in the most important tactical subjects on the examination.   His scores on the general education subjects were no less
impressive, and this suggests another facet in the make-up of the
General Staff candidate.   The successful officers needed to possess
a great deal of energy and motivation.   To be sure, the general education questions do not appear exceptionally difficult in themselves.   The civics test, for instance, required the students to
compare the constitutional prerogatives of the Reichstag under the
charters of 1871 and 1919.   The history question concerned Anglo-
German efforts at rapprochement before the war, and the question
on economic geography required a description and evaluation of
Germany's brown coal industry.[18]   The Reichswehr, in its July
announcement, had provided the general areas from which questions
would be drawn, but none of these subjects was included in the correspondence course.   Indeed, the entire preparatory program was
largely a matter of self-study and was undertaken in conjunction
with regular duties.   The candidate, therefore, had to display a
high degree of motivation and self-discipline in order to prepare
for the examination.

It has been argued that the major goal of the DE was to test
the "general educational level" (Bildungsniveau) of the candidates,
but Jodl's experience on the examination points up the inaccuracy
of that claim.[19]   If the Reichswehr intended to test general knowledge, this goal was at least seriously compromised during the
phase of preparatory study.   The examination questions were neither
challenging intellectually nor accorded a multiplier equal to that
established for the military questions.   In fact, the examination
appears to have been more a test of technical, tactical military
knowledge and physical endurance than of general education.   At
this point in the career of a future General Staff officer, the
Reichswehr was looking for the technical specialist rather than the
generalist.

The DE was officially supplemented by the unit commander's
character report.   With the evidence at hand, however, there is no

way to determine how it was used or how effective it was in providing an accurate image of the individual.   According to former
General Staff officer Hermann Teske, "the character evaluation only
played the roll of a negative factor in selection."   He went on to
explain that in his experience such cases were extremely rare.[20]
Although Teske is supported by another former officer, Kurt Weckmann, the latter seems to imply that the evaluation played a more
positive, decisive part in the selection process by providing the
field units a voice in the matter.[21]

In Jodl's case, however, there are other factors that help to
explain why his chances for selection were particularly good.   For
one thing, his candidacy certainly was not hurt by the fact that
his older brother Alfred was already recognized as a promising
young General Staff officer.   Brother combinations were not uncommon in the Reichswehr, and could often prove profitable to an officer's career.   A change of assignment in September 1926 also created useful opportunities for young Jodl.   Transferred from Landsberg
to a supply battalion in Munich, he became its adjutant in the following spring.   In the Bavarian capital Jodl clearly enjoyed advantages that were normally unavailabe to officer stationed in small
garrison towns.   Not only did he have access to Schrott and other
senior General Staff officers who could offer personal assistance,
he was also near a university environment -- and Schrott specifically recommended that all officers based in Munich attend a series
of lectures on foreign policy at the local university.   The Army,
in fact, obtained special permission for its officers to attend.[22]
This combination of factors ensured Jodl of success on the DE,
which he passed in the spring of 1927.   Jodl was obviously a fine
young officer -- but how typical was he?

Twelve of the other thirty-six officers who passed the examination in 1927 were, like Jodl, natives of Bavaria (see appendix 3,
table 3).   All of them had more than ten years service in the officer corps and thus satisfied the Reichswehr's criterion of proven
experience in the field.   None of them were nobles, which is not
unusual because, in contrast to many Prussian contingents, they
were not prominent in the Bavarian units.   In fact, only one
Bavarian aristocrat was eligible for the examination in 1927.
Interestingly enough, six of the thirteen were assigned as adjutants in 1927, and most of the others had probably served in that
capacity earlier.   In the Reichswehr, the positions of adjutant and
staff officer were frequently reserved for officers who were considered particularly compenent.[23]   Also, eleven of the thirteen were
stationed in major Bavarian cities, where they were offered the
kind of opportunities available to Jodl.   Here again, officers assigned to major garrisons and headquarters units were generally
those who showed special promise.

Analysis of Ferdinand Jodl and his fellow Bavarian selectees
suggests that, from the Reichswehr's point of view, the officers
chosen for General Staff training were tactically proficient combat
veterans, field-tested in the peacetime army, and capable of handling the rigorous duties ahead of them as candidates.   In a sense,
they had already demonstrated outstanding ability in their careers.   Statistics based on yearly listings of all General Staff

selectees during the period 1928-1932 indicate, furthermore, that the Bavarian officers were representative of the entire body (see appendix 3, tables 4 and 5).

For one thing, the vast majority, like those in Jodl's group, consisted of experienced field officers with ten or more years of service. Representatives of the technical branches, moreover, were consistently in the minority, probably because such officers usually chose to attend the technical colleges rather than enter the regular General Staff training program. The infantry, on the other hand, invariably led the way with double the number of candidates from rival branches -- the artillery and cavalry. In addition, a rather high number of the officers had been assigned to adjutant staff positions. Several officers when selected were instructors at service schools, an assignment that demanded general professional ability, outstanding potential, and special skills with a particular weapon. The relatively high number of machine-gun officers represented among infantry selectees indicates, parenthetically, that the wartime prestige and importance of the machine-gunner had not diminished in the Reichswehr. It is clear, also, that a substantial number of officers had been stationed, as candidates, in larger garrison towns -- Munich, Nürnberg, Würzburg, and the like -- where they presumably had been able to take advantage of broader educational opportunities.

*   *   *

On balance, the system of selecting General Staff candidates functioned well. By 1927, when Ferdinand Jodl went through the process, most of the problems that plagued Reichswehr leaders in the early years had been solved, and the remaining difficulties were inherent in the decentralized nature of the program. Army administrators could make some structural or procedural changes, like those Heye introduced in 1928 and 1929, but these were largely refinements made in an already proven institution. More important were the policy changes that produced stability in the program during the later Weimar period, and these changes seem to have been effected without a sacrifice in quality. Those who criticize the system for its lack of uniformity and unequal opportunities are correct. The case of Jodl and the other selectees has shown that they were more fortunate in certain areas than other officers. Analysis here perforce has only alluded to the issue of preferential treatment. Favoritism exists in all personal relationships and in all military organizations, but the important thing is that the Reichswehr apparently attempted to limit its impact as much as possible. Any other course of action would have created dissension and unhealthy rivalries in an already highly competitive system. The only way to alleviate the problems identified in the preparatory course was to concentrate all phases of selection -- initial screening, preparatory course, DE -- in one locale. A major step in this direction ws taken in 1932, when the entire General Staff candidate program was reorganized into Officer Classes (Offizierlehrgänge) which were held in Berlin.[24] Yet the preparatory course remained at division level because, as the critics are quick to forget, any centrally-operated course would have removed too many officers from their field units -- a perennially severe problem in any case for a small professional army that attempted to fulfill two missions, and certainly the reason that the preliminary training course was made an additional duty in the first place. By and large, the high command was satisfied that, as long as General Staff officers were involved in the program at key levels, the system would produce the candidates it wanted.

What is clear, is this type of candidate does not conform in all particulars to the conventional image. This is not to imply that the General Staff candidate was less competent than he had been made out to be. If anything, he appears to have been more experienced, more proficient, and more motivated than previous research has indicated. While exceptionally able, however, he was not a generalist, but above all a technical specialist who was expected to be highly proficient in tactics. There were, however, possible inconsistencies noted between method and initiative in the Reichswehr's tactical training objectives and the potential for rigid thought and conformity -- problems that are even more evident in the General Staff candidate training program.

4.
General Staff Candidate Training

On April 1, 1932, Captain Ferdinand Jodl was officially authorized to wear the carmine trouser stripes of the German Staff officer. As he took his place among the elite of the Reichswehr, he could look back on five and one-half years of the most rigorous training in the German Army. Although many scholars have described the General Staff training program, few have done more than outline its organization or list the subjects studied.[1] Clearly the program requires further investigation, which must be done in the context of the Reichswehr's position as a small, professional army faced with unique difficulties in the pursuit of its military objectives. Jodl's experience will again serve as an effective means of evaluating the operation and nature of the program, comparing the roles of Seeckt and Heye, and constructing a general profile of the individual most likely to become a General Staff officer. Most importantly, the experience of Jodl and his fellow candidates showed that the Reichswehr's General Staff program tended to produce the type of officer whose technical military brilliance was often marred by rigid patterns of thought and conformist thinking -- deficiencies that posed grave problems for the future.

*   *   *

Jodl was notified of his selection for General Staff candidate training in the spring of 1927. Although formal, theoretical training was not scheduled until October 1927, his initiation actually began that summer with a field assignment in a branch of the service other than his own. In Jodl's case, he served in the Munich-based First Battalion of the 19th Infantry Regiment. During

July and August he was assigned as a platoon leader (Zugführer) to
the third and fourth companies in order to "better understand the
combat requirements expected of infantry troops after a hard
march."[2] In early September Jodl was transferred to the battalion
staff where he could participate in the fall maneuvers as an infantry staff officer. Following his summer duty and a brief holiday,
Jodl joined the staff of Division VI in the famous cathedral city
of Münster. There, together with nine other candiates, he spent
the next two years taking a variety of theoretical and practical
courses. His training program, which was supervised by two General
Staff officers assigned by Berlin expressly for this purpose, emphasized tactical training at all levels.[3]
     During the first-year course (D1), Jodl's class was required
to demonstrate proficiency in several different types of tactical
situations, first at the infantry regiment level and then the division (see appendix 4, table 1). Study focused on a series of
twenty-eight textbook tactical lessons which were spread throughout
the eight months of academic training. Students solved the problems in two parts. In the first, the situation was evaluated according to the standard method. After correction by the instructor, orders were written for the deployment of forces. This requirement was supplemented by five major tactical studies prepared
by senior officers of the division including the Chief of Staff,
Colonel Walther von Brauchitsch. Each task was based on the 1927
fall maneuver and included several variations on the main theme.
After the papers were scored, the responsible senior officer published a general critique of the class' performance. After Christmas, the students planned their own tactical problems in which they
acted as exercise leaders and assumed specific command and staff
roles. In addition to the regular tactics requirements, a number
of special lessons concerning tactical employment of particular
weapons were assigned. Jodl, for example, worked on six lengthy
artillery assignments prepared by the Inspector of Artillery in
1923.
     Among the other military subjects in the curriculum, military
history, which involved lectures and student projects dealing with
important battles, was the most important. Logistics and related
subjects were normally handled in conjunction with assigned tactical problems. Even when they were presented as separate lessons,
they always required solutions which stressed tactics and the combined arms concept. Non-military subjects received little if any
attention during the first-year course.
     Jodl's first year of theoretical instruction was supplemented
by two instructional staff "rides" in the spring.[4] This was his
first encounter with the tactical ride, which was central to German
staff training. The first of these exercises took place in Meck-
lenburg-Holstein over a six-day period in March 1928 under the supervision of instructors who worked division-level tactical problems suitable for that particular geographic area. In this manner,
the students were prepared for the second and more important ride
in May. The latter required them to solve the problems independently and served as a screening process to select the most qualified officers for the second year of instruction. Jodl success-

fully passed his first-year tests and was assigned to summer duty with the Fourth Signals Battalion at Dresden. After the fall exercise, he returned to Münster for course D2, the second year of General Staff training.

This course involved division-size forces and, like the D1 course, it included a series of basic tactical lessons, a number of problems focusing on the specific branches, and several instructional rides (see appendix 4, table 2). It differed from the first year only in the addition of several tactics-related subjects and a more challenging series of tactical problems. Among the latter were three new types of theoretical combat exercises: the map planning exercise (Planübung), the war game (Kriegsspiel), and the terrain evaluation (Geländesprechung). Military subjects again dominated the course curriculum. In all phases of instruction, whether in the seminar room or on the exercise grounds, the students were expected to assume more responsibility than they had during the first-year course.

The D2 course concluded with two important rides that were used to select officers for the final year of training. In May all trainees in Jodl's class participated in Übungsreise Erzgebirge, which was led by Division VI General Staff instructors. Afterwards, the chief instructor and the division chief of staff prepared a list of the participants in order of merit. Significantly, the criteria for ranking the officers were character, personality, and performance in that order.[5] From this list, which was forwarded to Berlin, the Reichswehr's Training Section chose the officers it wanted to examine in its own selection tactical ride in June. On both rides, all trainees were required to perform as leader and team member in the daily tactical exercises. As a result of these rides, Jodl was one of twelve officers selected to attend the third year of training (1929-1930) in Berlin. Four officers were chosen from each of three division staffs, and three were assigned to the third year class directly from field units (see appendix 4, table 4).

The third-year couse, referred to as Lehrgang R, was administered by Major Hans Reinhardt and Captain Walther Model, who were assigned to Group III of the Army's training section (see appendix 4, table 3). Both officers would later reach the highest echelons of the Wehrmacht. They frequently called on specialists from the Defense Ministry to help them in difficult technical areas. Contrary to the previous courses, Lehrgang R was far better organized and structured. At the start of the course, Major Reinhardt issued a syllabus describing administrative duties and information and the schedule of academic lesson requirements. Each of the fifteen officers was expected to prepare four major tactical problems: a terrain evaluation, a war game, a maneuver plan (Manöveranlage), and a military history lecture (Kriegsgeschichtlicher Vortrag). All four assignments focused on tactical operations. For example, even Jodl's military history question, "how could the strategy of annihilation have been achieved in the battle of Gumbinnen in 1914?", was primarily one of the tactics.[6]

Although Jodl was familiar with the first two assignments from his experience at Münster, the requirements now were far more

challenging. The most important difference was the level of instruction -- the reinforced infantry division operating within the
framework of corps and army forces. Probably his most difficult
assignment was to plan an actual maneuver of the reinforced Fourth
Division scheduled for September 1930.

For these lessons, Jodl was given the particulars of the problems four weeks in advance and had the services of an army civilian
"official" assigned to the Training Section. Prior to presenta-
tion, he had to brief the Chief of the Training Section, Lieutenant
Colonel Wilhelm List, and other Defense Ministry officers. Although these four projects comprised the major academic tactical
requirements, Lehrgang R continued the practice of having the students work on a series of textbook lessons. These were designed by
senior officers in the Ministry and stressed realistic combat conditions, challenging the students to respond to as many different
types of tactical situations as possible. Although supply and logistics needs had to be considered in all tactical problems, they
were often made the subjects of specific war games. In this way,
the officers could assume the roles of specialists in logistics or
communications at division staff level.

Emphasis throughout the course was on student involvement and
participation. Jodl's seminar classroom instruction normally lasted from 0900 to 1300 hours, with Wednesdays reserved for terrain
exercises and Thursday afternoons set aside for war games. Instruction in the so-called non-military or general education subjects was usually carried out in the lecture hall. All officers
were required to attend the famous Thursday morning lecture series
initiated in 1923 by Seeckt.[7] These talks were given by both military and civilian officials on major topics of the day. However,
since the curriculum included only two non-military subjects, "Economic Situation" and "External and Internal Political Situation,"
it is clear that military considerations also dominated the third-
year program.

Lehrgang R also continued to supplement theoretical instruction with instructional staff rides. The first occurred at the
start of the term when the officers were taken on the five-day
"welcome" ride. Additional rides included a winter exercise in the
Erzgebirge and staff visits to naval facilities in March and industrial sites in March and May. The final staff ride, Übungsreise
Rhön, took place from May 7-17, 1930, and was led by Brauchitsch,
the newly-appointed Chief of the Training Section and Jodl's former
superior. The exercise included representatives of the Training
Section and the Personnel Office, who used the staff rides as an
important means of judging officers at first hand. The Übungsreise
Rhön was the climax of Jodl's three years of General Staff training. His performance would determine whether he would be appointed
to the General Staff, and he did indeed pass this final hurdle. He
did not, however, join the General Staff immediately. Instead, he
was assigned to the Training Section of the Truppenamt for two
years of probationary training. On April 1, 1932, he was officially posted to the Truppenamt as a General Staff officer.

                *   *   *

That Jodl is representative of General Staff candidates can be confirmed by comparing him with other officers in his 1927-1929 class (see appendix 4, table 4). By this time the composition of the class had already changed. Of the original thirty-seven officers who passed the 1927 District Examination, seven left training during the first year. Captains Otto Beutler and Willi Schneckenburger, and First Lieutenant Hans Spelder, however, were added to Jodl's third-year class.

An analysis of this group indicates that all but one of the thirty-three officers were war veterans with at least ten years of active duty. All had served a considerable amount of time in field units before entering staff training. It is clear that even at the junior officer level the Army continued its traditional policy of rotating promising officers between field and staff duties, and still adhered to Seeckt's policy of requiring General Staff officers to prove themselves first in the field. At least twenty-six of the thirty-three men represented the combat arms of the Reichswehr. To be sure, these branches were granted higher eligibility quotas, and one would expect such officers to be more experienced in tactics than those in the technical branches. Nevertheless, it is curious that only one cavalry officer, First Lieutenant von Wagner, was included. Likewise, it is not surprising that Prussia, the largest state, supplied the majority of the candidates.

Especially in terms of previous assignments, the careers of the officers substantiate the composite developed in the last chapter. Not only had ten of the eighteen infantry officers served as machine-gunners, at least nineteen of the thirty-three had been assigned, like Jodl, as adjutants or unit staff officers at some point in the Reichswehr careers. Staff-type duty, furthermore, was important for lieutenants and first lieutenants because normally they were considered too junior for field command assignments.

Jodl's group presents a record of outstanding military performance. Only two factors suggest that these officers may not have owed their success entirely to their own abilities. A majority were stationed in major garrison and headquarters units, which provided broad opportunities for studying both military and general education subjects. Secondly, nine of the thirty-three appear to have had family members serving in the Army at the same time.[8] The importance of character evaluations and the close personal ties among officers in the small professional Army are reminders that personal impressions were quite influential in this as in other forms of selection. On the other hand, only two nobles are included in Jodl's class, and one, Wagner, was eliminated after the second year. Clearly, in the competition for General Staff service, the aristocratic pedigree was unimportant.

Jodl's experience does not raise several questions. For instance, his first Lehrgang R superior was Lieutenant Colonel List, a Bavarian, the second was Brauchitsch, his chief of staff at Munster. Obviously, Jodl was well-known to both officers. Also, it is curious that from Jodl's D2 class, four officers from each Reichswehr division were chosen for Lehrgang R. Such uniformity suggests that the high command may have consciously resorted to equal representation among the divisions. It also indicates that

the selection may have been made prior to the D2 selection staff
ride because twenty officers is a large group to judge effectively
on the basis of one brief tactical ride. Nevertheless, the evidence indicates that Jodl is representative of his group and that
the class itself is an adequate cross-section of the Reichswehr.

As for Jodl's Lehrgang R class, this group of officers can be
compared usefully with others in the late Weimar period who progressed at least as far as the third year of training (see appendix
4, tables 5 and 6). A composite of their career profiles shows
that the 1930-1931 and 1931-1932 groups differ from Jodl's class in
several respects. Unlike Jodl's group, nobles are more prominent,
the technical branches are not well-represented, and Prussian officers are more predominant. All three classes, furthermore, include
officers who had been partially trained earlier, which suggests
that during the Seeckt period the Reichswehr faced the problem of
an over-crowded system. Evidence from the Seeckt era confirms that
Jodl's group is somewhat exceptional in terms of geographic area
and branch of service (see appendix 4, table 7). The typical General Staff officer was likely to be Prussian, non-noble, and related to at least one other officer in the Army. As a rule, he represented the combat arms but not necessarily the cavalry.

This analysis indicates that from the Reichswehr's viewpoint,
the officers selected for General Staff candidate training were
tactically-proficient combat veterans, field-tested in the peacetime army and fully capable of handling the rigorous duties ahead
of them as General Staff officers. They had already demonstrated
outstanding ability and potential for future leadership in their
careers prior to their selection. In this sense, Ferdinand Jodl is
certainly representative of this group. Nevertheless, although
Jodl and his peers appear to represent the best of the junior officers, the nature of the education and training they underwent to
become General Staff officers poses serious questions about their
preparation for future responsibilities as well as the nature of
the military profession.

*   *   *

It is clear from Ferdinand Jodl's experience that he was primarily expected to display a command of tactical operations involving division-level forces. In terms of both time and emphasis,
tactics dominated the curriculum in all three years of training.
In its objectives, however, Jodl's tactical training differed very
little from the type of training he first encountered during his
preparations for the DE. To be sure, the kinds of problems were
different and the size of forces involved greater. But if Jodl
found the lessons more complex and challenging, the combat situations still stressed tactics and had to be worked according to the
standard problem-solving method first underscored by Schrott. Indeed, every tactical problem worked during his training followed
the same format: first, a rapid and critical evaluation of the
situation based on all possible contingencies as prescribed in regulations; second, an unqualified decision resulting from this process of elimination; finally, brief, clear, and precise orders.

The tactical instruction of a General Staff candidate continually attempted to balance conformity of method with flexibility of response. This problem-solving method is also referred to by the unique German expression, Auftragstaktik, according to which any subordinate staff officer was expected to react in a prescribed manner but was free to solve the problem as he thought best.[9] As retired General Heinz Guderian later observed, "from this basic uniformity of reaction it was hoped to create a wide conformity of decision."[10] But this method was potentially flawed because a set method could result in a rigid pattern of thought producing unrealistic, textbook responses to combat situations.

The chief difficulty facing the instructors was precisely how to train General Staff selectees to respond flexibly to tactical problems within the established format. Critiques and marginal comments on student papers, for example, reflect this concern. To cite one illustration, Major Reinhardt criticized Jodl's Lehrgang R maneuver study becuse it wa "too static." Significantly, Jodl's logistics portion of the maneuver, which demanded less improvisation, received high praise for its thoroughness and attention to detail. Such tactical problems were to be prepared so that the planners could resort to more than a single course of action. As Reinhardt consistently emphasized, the primary necessity in all tactical work must be a situation which allowed individual commanders and staff officers enough flexibility to make realistic decisions.

Because General Staff instructors believed that textbook instruction alone could not achieve the objective of flexible response, training stressed certain personal attributes -- responsibility, imagination, initiative -- which normally did not appear in the course syllabus and instructional materials. Candidates were expected to accept responsibility for their actions willingly, to use their imaginations, and to take the initiative.Instructors always challenged the officers to apply their knowledge to practical situations. Clearly trainees were also required to possess a certain kind of stamina because the program was such that only officers who were willing and able to spend long and tedious hours mastering a variety of difficult subjects could succeed.

Although at all times the pressure to perform was intense and the workload enormous, the subjects which lay outside the realm of tactics demanded far less from the trainees. This was especially so of the non-military topics, most of which were taught in the third year. Most were presented in lecture form by specialists in the particular fields. It seems, however, that Jodl was only required to be familiar with the general nature of the material. And the most intriguing of these subjects, "Foreign and Domestic Politics," was intentionally presented in a noncontroversial manner. The value of such instruction obviously is questionable.[11]

Yet how was it possible to develop the characteristics of responsibility, imagination, and initiative in a meaningful, practical way? The answer was never very clear. More often than not the leaders resorted to stressing the even more elusive quality of character, as if it could produce flexible response to tactical problems. As future standard bearers of a proud tradition, General

Staff candidates were expected to demonstrate integrity and impeccable personal behavior above all other attributes. Although the third-year curriculum included a subject dealing with General Staff duties, there was no formal course on character building as such because character development was expected to result from the personal examples set by the instructors, the camaraderie among the General Staff candidates themselves, and the extremely high standards demanded in course work and personal behavior.

If the Reichswehr's emphasis on character appears excessive, it is nevertheless true that such has always been an important part of military education and training. Reichswehr officers were well aware of the importance of character because it had been drummed into their heads throughout their careers. Although this is not necessarily detrimental to officer education, the same problems developed here that were evident in the officer career structure discussed earlier. Character, rather than serving an educational function, came to mean discipline and obedience, and tended to generate conformity and conformist thinking rather than initiative and independence. Indeed, for General Staff instructors, character education was a two-edged sword in their crusade to develop flexible response.

*   *   *

Jodl, of course, went through training after Seeckt had left office. How does his experience differ from those of officers who were trained during the formative years of the Seeckt era? It is generally assumed that the system functioned without major changes throughout the Weimar period, but in Jodl's case several officers from field units were added to his third-year class and the final staff ride. This alone suggests that the conventional view of an uninterrupted three-year program was not standard for all General Staff candidates. On the contrary, these field officers were not simply line officers whose outstanding performance with the troops had drawn the attention of higher authorities. Rather, all were officers who had completed part of their General Staff course as much as six years earlier.[12] There is, moreover, the so-called Year of Practice to consider.[13] From career information on a number of Bavarian officers, it is known that the Year of Practice did not replace the first or second year of training but was a supplement to the second year. Officers in the Year of Practice who completed the entire General Staff program were, therefore, required to train for four years instead of three.

In addition, officers in the D1 course in 1923 and 1924 took what amounted to a correspondence course directed by General Staff officers from Munich. Except for three or four meetings in the Bavarian capital, they remained with their field units, where, with the exception of riding and physical training, they were relieved of all unit duties. Only for the D2 course were the officers assigned to the division staff for regularly supervised academic training. After the second-year course, however, the successful officers entered the Practical Year which consisted of a full twelve-month tour of duty with their former regiment.

The Practical Year remains something of a mystery because it is unclear whether the assignment was designed to require officers to renew links with field troops, to provide the Reichswehr with a reserve for future training, or to give the Army General Staff a means of testing further those officers whose performance was questionable. All of these explanations are plausible, and the official training directive of 1922 offers no rationale for the additional year. The practice resulted in a reserve of officers for the future as the addition of the officers to Jodl's class indicates. And clearly it allowed the Reichswehr to expand the evluation process for weaker officers.

Nevertheless, the Army seems to have instituted the Practical Year for another reason as well -- the problems inherent in the structure of the small professional army. For example, the number of officers who entered the Year of Practice in 1924 totaled thirty-seven and, considering the extremely limited requirement for new General Staff officers, this figure is very high for any such reserve. Furthermore, during that same year the Army announced that eleven officers had just been appointed to the General Staff itself, forty-two to the second year course, and eleven officers were projected for Lehrgang R sometime in the future.[14] The Reichswehr planners seem to have seriously overestimated the requirements of officers eligible for training. Indeed, by 1924 it appears that Army leaders realized that the General Staff program had encountered severe problems, and used the Practical Year as a means of relieving the overcrowded system.

If the first-year course invited deviations from training objectives by reason of its location in the field units, the Year of Practice, which resulted in a four-year program, considerably slowed the pace of General Staff appointments. With the large number of potential selectees available every year, there was little need to maintain a reserve of trainees for the Reichswehr. Furthermore, there were already too many fully-qualified officers who were unable to obtain General Staff assignments because the positions were filled. Reichswehr records indicate that the Army at no time intended to create an excessively large number of fully-qualified General Staff officers as a reserve for a future expanded army. This seems to have been the case despite the fact that the partially-trained officers could serve that purpose to some extent. From the Army's point of view, the path to a career as a General Staff officer was becoming increasingly and dangerously blocked. This explanation, as well as disatisfaction about the issue of conformity, accounts for the drastic modification of the original selection projections and the major overhaul in the training program that had occurred when Jodl went through it.

*   *   *

Far more than Seeckt, Wilhelm Heye recognized the danger that conformity posed to the professional army. He viewed the problem of conformity in General Staff training as part of the larger question of an officer corps afflicted by widespread conformism and careerism. On September 22, 1927, in what was certainly his most im-

portant address to the Reichswehr, Heye extolled the virtues of
character, integrity, and non-conformist thinking, and criticized
the Army's tendency to produce officers with "the debilitating
character of lackeys."[15] This was the first time that any Reichswehr leader directly confronted the issue of conformity as a threat
to the high quality and performance of the officer corps. The very
fact that Heye felt compelled to attack the problem so vigorously
indicates the seriousness of the situation.

For Heye, conformism was a by-product of the professional
army. As he often warned, "insecurity was inherent in the nature
of the officer profession."[16] Reichswehr officers who at best
faced limited promotion opportunities, keen competition in every
area, and the threat of a forced selection-out program were unlikely to allow themselves to become identified as troublemakers. One
false step could mean the end of an officer's career. Under these
conditions, most officers were more inclined to conform than to
demonstrate independent thinking. Or they became ruthless career-
ists driven to advance rapidly and caring little for the welfare of
subordinates and fellow officers. Both types of officers were ana-
thema to Heye.

And if Heye, like Seeckt before him, advocated character education as one answer to this dilemma, he at least faced the question directly. He also realized that the ultimate solution could
only be achieved by altering the very structure of the professional
Reichswehr. This was illegal as long as the Versailles Treaty was
enforced. It should be recognized at this point, however, that under Heye clandestine evasions of the Treaty were never widespread.
Indeed, Heye more than any other military figure attempted to make
the Reichswehr work as a professional force.

While a new structure might be the panacea for the ills of
the Army, Heye was not content to let the General Staff candidate
training program continue unreformed. In fact, he made a number of
changes in the system that did more than merely modify a program
inherited from Seeckt. Heye's objective was to rationalize and
stabilize the program. In late 1926, he eliminated the Year of
Practice and established the standard three-year course most authors cite. Heye realized that if the original intent was to foster thoroughness in training, the practical result was to produce
too many potential replacements for the Reichswehr's framework to
handle. Then in 1927 the D1 course was shifted from field units to
division staffs. This had the effect of promoting uniformity of
training procedures and instruction while reducing the friction
that had developed from assigning General Staff candidates to regular line units. On the other hand, it is not clear that the units
affected received replacements, and without replacements the always
short-handed situation would worsen.[17]

Then, the divisions were divided into two groups which alternated training responsibilities every year. In odd-numbered years
selectees were assigned to Divisions I, V, and Vi for two years,
and in even years to Divisions II, III, IV, and VII. Division
staffs, therefore, like Jodl's Division VI in Münster, would train
the same class of officers for two years before receiving a new
one. Along with encouraging more uniformity and stability, this

change provided needed relief to the divisions because they could
now concentrate one one goup of trainees at a time. Furthermore,
since Berlin attempted to equalize the burden of traiing, officers
were, like Jodl, often assigned to divisions other than their own,
which served to combat the effects of parochialism. In this regard, too, Berlin now required that at least one of the two General
Staff instructors assigned to the particular division be from a
different one. During the Seeckt years these instructors ususlly
were General Staff officers from the same division to which they
were assigned. For example, in 1924 the two Division VII instructors, Lieutenant Colonel List and Captain Emil Leeb, were Bavarians. During the Heye years, however, while the second instructor,
Captain Alfred Jodl, was Bavarian, the first, Major Hans Felber,
was not. This does not appear to have been an isolated case because all four of Jodl's teachers at Munster were assigned from
outside the Division VI area. This procedure suggests that the
Reichswehr attempted to avoid regional inbreeding.[18]
       An additional organizational change occurred in 1927, when the
Training Section was transferred from the jurisdiction of the
commander-in-chief and subordinated directly to the Truppenamt. In
this way, the dynamic Brigadier General Werner von Blomberg -- future War Minister during the Third Reich -- who was more directly
involved with the entire Army's training program as Chief of The
Truppenamt, could give closer supervision to General Staff training.
       An interesting change in terminology also took place under
Heye, which seemed to threaten traditioal values. In an order of
March 1927, Heye announced that, because of insistence by the
Inter-Allied Military Control Commission, the terms General Staff
and General Staff Officer were being abandoned in favor of Führer-
stab and Führerstabsoffizier. Considering the prestige and tradition behind the German General Staff and the fact that Heye appeared to act under foreign pressure, it is easier to appreciate the
opposition such a change would create. Seeckt's biographer, Friedrich von Rabenau, an officer in the Reichswehr, showed nothing but
contempt for such a "colorless expression" to describe the General
Staff. Seeckt, he implied, would never have agreed to such a concession.[19] Official documents mask the friction created by this
change, but it cannot be ignored. Coming as it did shortly after a
strong leader was replaced by a weaker successor who was inclined
to make conciliatory moves toward political opponents, the new terminology was not universally welcome. Earlier it was noted that
scholars have generally overlooked the internal discord in the Army
that appears to have resulted from a number of changes or reforms
in the Seeckt system that were made by Heye. Although Carsten, for
example, discusses the opposition that developed within the Army
after Heye assumed command, he attributes the discontent to Heye's
political policies only.[20] Clearly, Heye's assault on tradition,
if made only to relieve foreign pressure, contributed to the discord.
       Taken as a whole, Heye's efforts to regularize and stabilize
the program represented significant improvement. Organizational
changes were only one part of Heye's impact on General Staff train-

ing objectives. This development is seen best by focusing on Lehr-gang R. It is well-known that the third-year course was begun in Berlin in the fall of 1923.[21] What has been over-looked are signs that this training was not confined to technical military instruction. In fact, Bavarian records indicate that in 1923, for example, the officers selected for the third year course were requested to choose from among four Hochschulen in Berlin: the university, the oriental seminar, the technical college, and the Hochschule für Politik.[22] Furthermore, as the American attache in Berlin commented, in the third year of training "no military instruction is given, but one purely of general culture."[23] During the Heye period, however, tactical-technical General Staff instruction replaced the emphasis on more general education. Indeed, there is no doubt that the Reichswehr after 1927 became increasingly technically and tactically oriented in all areas of military training. Despite Heye's organizational improvements in the General Staff training program, therefore, it is likely that the increased emphasis on tactics only served to compound the problem of rigidity of method and conformist, inflexible responses.

         *   *   *

Ferdinand Jodl's experience in General Staff training has provided a good means of examining the system: its operation, its objectives, and the the type of officer desired for General Staff duty. In many ways, the program merits the high praise it has traditionally received because it functioned efficiently and was well-organized, highly competitive, and challenging.

This success is largely attributable to the nature of the Army as a small professional force that had special problems. The restrictions imposed by the Versailles Treaty forced the Reichswehr to stress quality rather than quantity, and this was reflected in General Staff training. If the program historically had been elitist and extremely selective, it became more so in the Reichswehr because the reduced Army was not able to absorb a large number of General Staff replacements, and it had no intention of creating a reserve for some imaginary, if hoped for, future.

The size of the Reichswehr officer corps also meant that in General Staff training class size was small, candidates could receive more individual attention, and instructors and other officers in the evaluation process could base their judgments on extensive personal knowledge of the students. Indeed, the General Staff candidate program, like the General Staff corps itself, was a very personal system in which most of the officers and students knew each other well.

Nevertheless, the professional nature of the Reichswehr also created severe problems that have normally been overlooked in studies of General Staff achievements. The General Staff training program was, for example, more competitive than any other in the the Army. Available positions were few, and failure could result in a mediocre career. Under such intense pressure to perform superbly, one should expect to find a greater degree of conformity among the candidates rgardless of the effort to develop flexibility and inde-

pendent thinking in tactical work.   Surely, nonconformity would
hardly be fashionable considering the importance of character and
character reports which emphasized discipline, obedience, and loyalty.   Walter Goerlitz is certainly correct in observing that the
personal nature of the system "made the chances of efficient and
independent-minded outsiders somewhat slim in comparison with those
of highly qualified men who were sufficiently humble and adaptable
to fit themselves into the system."[24]   Indeed, the personal factor
could work for and against the objectives of the program.

Likewise, the organization of General Staff training was
strongly affected by the Reichswehr's special limitations.   The
Allies at Versailles had abolished the central institutions of the
Imperial Army's General Staff training program and forced the
Reichswehr to establish a decentralized system.   If the small size
of the Army enabled it to create an effective balance between central direction and local initiative, even the reliance on General
Staff officers at every stage of training could not prevent variations in emphasis and approach.   Uniform training could only have
been achieved by administering all training in Berlin in a manner
similar to that done in Lehrgang R.   It is significant that only in
1932, after the decision to expand the Army had already been made,
was such a step taken.   Had this been done at any earlier time, it
is unlikely that the field units could have borne the burden of the
losses in officer strength.

Heye achieved the most effective results in the organizational
area of the system.   By alternating division responsibilities for
the first two years of training, he provided the divisions more relief and promoted greater uniformity in training.   On the whole,
the Heye program was far more stable than Seeckt's, and this
achievement should be recognized by those who assume that the system functioned unchanged throughout the Weimar period.

To its credit, Reichswehr General Staff officers recognized
that overemphasis on tactics could result in the development of a
narrow outlook and rigid patterns of thinking.   Instructors were
fond of quoting Scharnhorst's maxim that the "study of detail must
never be allowed to cloud the picture as a whole,"[25] and in Jodl's
case his instructors repeatedly condemned absorption in detail and
the tendency to become too inflexible.   Nevertheless, at no time do
Reichswehr General Staff officers appear to have considered de-
emphasizing tactics.   Just the reverse occurred.   Tactical training, which by its nature means absorption in detail, was not bal-
anced sufficiently by study of strategic concepts and the broader
factors that affect warfare.   As the American military attache reported after visiting a second year General Staff training class,

> The course in strategy is very weak and is really not
> strategy at all but rather 'grand tactics' and the subjects
> considered under this head are rather the tactical consi-
> derations connected with the movements...armies in the the-
> ater of war rather than the underlying political, psycho-
> logical and economic grounds which must always be taken
> into account.[26]

Even in Jodl's Lehrgang R curriculum, in which one would expect to find a better balance between technical and general subjects, the emphasis remained on tactics and technical knowledge.

Part of the explanation for this faith in tactics can be attributed to tradition combined with the experience of the First World War. Since the elder Moltke, tactical instruction had become increasingly important in the Army's training programs. During the war the new technological developments and the significance of combined arms operations served to convince many that tactical instruction must remain the cornerstone of military success.[27]

It should also be noted that General Staff education and training reflected not only the difficult position of the Reichswehr, but the increasingly technically-oriented postwar world. It is significant that in Clausewitz' era, seventy percent of the War Academy's curriculum consisted of non-military subjects. By 1914, however, the relationship had been reversed, and this trend continued after the war. Seeckt, according to Rabenau, was aware that the imbalance between technical and non-technical subjects did not promote the wider outlook among General Staff officers that he favored, and that he worked to reduce the emphasis on specialized, technical instruction.[28] The evidence about a more non-technical Lehrgang R curriculum during his tenure suggests that he was working in this direction. So, too, does the criticism voiced by key officers like Blomberg, who maintained that Seeckt was unprogressive and unwilling to adapt himself to modern technologicl developments as rapidly as the Reichswehr required. Nevertheless, under Heye, when Jodl went through training, the entire three-year program had become predominantly military-technical in orientation.

The main factor in understanding the importance of tactical instruction in the postwar Army is the nature of the Reichswehr. According to the Treaty, the small Army was only expected to maintain internal order and protect the frontiers. Its ability to do even this was always questionable. It is not surprising that nearly every problem worked by Jodl during his training called for tactical responses to enemy offensive operations. This was the most realistic type of training the Reichswehr could practice. The size of the forces Jodl had to work with never exceeded the reinforced infantry division, and this force was the largest fielded by the Army during its annual autumn maneuvers. For success, the Reichswehr had to rely on speed, mobility, and the cooperation of the different branches, and this demanded complete mastery of tactical techniques and operations. In view of its special problems, the small Army could best perform as a tactical, rather than a strategic, offensive force.

It is often overlooked that problems in military education and training can affect areas outside the confines of the military. In the present case, the problems associated with General Staff candidate training were potentially dangerous for interests beyond the concern of tactics and strategy. Officers whose efforts are limited to the small world of tactics and technology are in danger of isolating themselves and failing to appreciate the larger issues affecting their society. It is well-known that John Wheeler-Bennettt and F. L. Carsten, among others, see a major problem in the Army's alienation from the Republic it served. They point to Seeckt's policy of the "non-political" Reichswehr, which in effect isolated the Army by encouraging officers to avoid politics and concentrate on the tools of the profession. This was especially true in the case of General Staff officers and candidates.[29]

Yet it is not correct to blame political attitudes alone for the failure of the officer corps to exhibit a better understanding of the issues affecting their society. Much of the problem must be seen in the tactical-technical orientation of the military profession and the structural limitations of the professional army. General Staff candidates were educated to devote themselves to the work of becoming proficient tactical operations specialists. Although the effort to promote flexibility in tactical training was admirable, the highly competitive program and the type of training encouraged conformity rather than independent thinking. Indeed, the whole nature of the General Staff candidate system militated against developing independent, aggressive officers who would be prepared to say "no" when faced with military or political situations they knew to be questionable. In this regard, the historian is tempted to speculate that the Reichswehr's training program and the inherent problems of the professional army facilitated Hitler's ability to dominate an officer corps unable to say "no" when confronted with the reality of the Third Reich.

If the General Staff training program produced remarkable results, it was nevertheless always restricted in its accomplishments by the very nature of the Army. In the final analysis, the achievements and the problems associated with the program must be understood in the context of the Reichswehr's unique position as a small professional army that was burdened with special problems.

5.
Officer Assignments

> I served in this beautiful garrison [Lötzen, in East Prussia] with the same battalion for 9 1/2 years, 7 1/2 as commander of the eleventh company, to which I was appointed on February 1, 1927. I consider the years as company commander my most enjoyable military experience during peacetime.[1]

But were the assignment experiences of other Reichswehr officers as rewarding as that of Herman Ramcke, the future Wehrmacht general of parachute troops? Was this type of lengthy company-level duty considered beneficial for career advancement? Perhaps more to the point, what were the "good" or "right" Reichswehr assignments, and how did the leaders place, as they said, the "right officer in the right assignment"? This question of assignments is critical to both the individual officer and the army: to the former, assignments are a matter of self-esteem and status, for the latter they serve to reward officer performance and recognize future leadership potential. The issue, furthermore, is obviously linked to the vital matter of morale -- a particularly sensitive question in the troubled environment of postwar Germany. The challenge facing Reichswehr planners in the assignment program was complicated by the professional nature of the Reichswehr and the missions it attempted to perform. In a small officer corps whose members faced a lengthy service commitment, assignment opportunities were necessarily limited. The training objectives pursued by the leaders, moreover, served to complicate the picture. While it was important to move the most competent officers through the different assignments as rapidly as possible, too much haste could result in deficiencies in the training of individual officers and endanger the Army's ability to maintain combat readiness. On balance, the Reichswehr never was able to overcome these problems, as is demonstrated in an examination of field (line) and staff assignments during the Reichswehr era.

*   *   *

The career profiles of Eduard Zorn and Ferdinand Jodl indicate that assignment opportunities for junior officers were severely limited in number and variety. The assignments of both as lieutenants and first lieutenants were restricted largely to duty in the basic field unit of their particular branch.[2] Zorn, for example, spent nearly his entire Reichswehr career as a platoon leader in two different companies. As a lieutenant and junior first lieutenant, he had, by 1932, yet to lead a company, the first important field command assignment. Furthermore, even though the Rangliste for that year carries him as a regimental staff officer in the 19th Infantry Regiment, his selection for General Staff training the following year suggests that his 1932 posting to the Munich regimental staff was made primarily to improve his chances for success on the District Examination.

Jodl's experience was similar. From 1923 through 1926, he served as one of six officers in the Landsberg artillery battery. As a junior first lieutenant in 1926, he was assigned to the horse-drawn supply battalion in Munich where, like Zorn, he could best prepare for the DE. Jodl's General Staff training assignments have been described earlier. Following his three-year course and his probationary training in early 1932, he was posted to the Truppenamt's Foreign Armies Section. Like most armies, the Reichswehr was concerned that its junior officers receive sufficient troop training experience in the lower-level units before assignment to more responsible staff and field positions. The careers of Zorn and Jodl conformed to that policy. Certainly for them the key development in their early careers was their selection for General Staff training, which opened the door to better career opportunities fn the future.

The majority of other Bavarian junior officers also held assignments as company, battery, or squadron officers (see appendix 5, tables 1 and 2). Generally, commanders of these units were captains, although during the Seeckt years senior first lieutenants were frequently assigned as company commanders. This situation was most prevalent in machine-gun companies, which had a smaller number of experienced officers from which to choose. Staff positions held by junior officers in the regiments and detachments were few and normally reserved for senior first lieutenants and captains.

Among officers in the grade of major and above, whom the Reichswehr termed Stabsoffiziere (not to be confused with officers of different ranks assigned to various staffs), the field command post of battalion commander in the infantry and artillery regiments was generally a lieutenant colonel's post, while regimental commanders were colonels. Not surprisingly, Stabsoffiziere filled the few available senior staff positions in these regiments. Assignments were more restricted for the cavalry regiment, which had no battalion-level assignment and only four squadrons. Normally the commander, a lieutenant colonel or colonel, and the regimental staff officer, a major or lieutenant colonel, were the only staff officers in the cavalry regiment. In the technical branch units, only the commander was a Stabsoffizier.

The division headquarters table of organization (TO) for 1932 shows that eleven of the eighteen officers assigned to the division staff were junior officers (see appendix 5, table 2). Like Jodl, most were assigned to the division staff for General Staff training. The divisional chief of staff, a General Staff officer, was the only colonel on the staff, while the divisions's sole general was its commander. The TOs for the remaining six infantry divisions show a similar correlation between an officer's grade and his assignment, and this pattern is reflected in earlier Rangliste. This survey shows that the division's very organizational structure limited the opportunity for many officers to hold field command and key staff assignments.

The experiences of 250 different Bavarian officers who were assigned to key command and staff positions in the field units during the Weimar period confirm that grade-assignment correlation (see appendix 5, table 3). Company commander and equivalent positions were normally held by captains, and battalion commander posts by lieutenant colonels. As a rule, company commanders served three years in the assignment and battalion commanders two. The forty-four General Staff officers among them show no significant deviation from the standard pattern. For the technical branch officers, published information shows that variations in their tour lengths were more common. This is probably because their units underwent more frequent organizational, personnel, and equipment changes. Although the technical officers present a somewhat special case, it is also evident that, even in the main branches, exceptions to the two and three-year tour lengths were not uncommon.

Captain von Schacky, for example, served uninterruptedly as Chief of the Third Company in the 19th Infantry Regiment from October 1921 until April 1928 (see appendix 5, table 3). On the other hand, Captain Gollwitzer spent less than a year as a company chief in 1926. Usually, General Staff officer careers reveal a greater emphasis on frequent rotation between field and staff duty. Their assignments were the most irregular because their actual assignment was sometimes different from their officially-published posting. Captain Maier is a case in point. Although officially he is listed as Chief of Company 15 in the 19th Infantry Regiment in 1930, he was in fact detached to the 9th Infantry Regiment in Berlin undergoing General Staff training. It should not be assumed that the Reichswehr resorted to deception in order to conceal General Staff training activities from the Versailles Treaty enforces. Rather, frequently it was normal procedure to keep the officer assigned to his permanent unit for administrative purposes if his transfer was to be temporary. This presented affected units with real hardship because they were prohibited from replacing the detached officers.

These deviations from the norm indicate that the goal of stability in the troop command assignments was difficult if not impossible to achieve, and was a major problem for Reichswehr planners.

In cases where the length varied from the prescribed standard, furthermore, an officer generally could not be considered to be in an
advantageous position in his career pattern. This would be particularly true where the length of the assignment was excessive. In
the latter case, not only would his career potential appear questionable, but he would be restricting the opportunity of other eligible officers to hold his assignment.

For the sixty-eight senior command staff officers at the division level during the Weimar period, assignments generally varied
from two to three, and the grade-assignment correlation conforms to
the 1932 pattern (see appendix 5, table 4). Yet exceptions to the
rule are frequent, and these are evident during both the early and
late Weimar era. Senior officers seem to have moved through the
assignments more rapidly than their junior counterparts, and it is
also apparent that in Division VIII the lower-level field command
positions were stepping stones to the senior assignments. The case
of Ritter von Leeb is typical. Beginning in 1921, his career shows
the following assignment pattern: division chief of staff, regimental battalion commander, regiment commander, divisional artillery commander, and finally division commander. As Leeb's history
indicates, officers did not become regiment or division commanders
without having first completed their training as company and battalion commanders and, for the most part, as senior staff officers. General Staff officers do not appear as exceptions to this
pattern; their careers show a clear pattern of rotation between
field and staff assignments.

It is especially instructive to examine the career histories
of officers who, in 1932, held responsible or senior command and
staff positions at the Bavarian regimental and division levels (see
appendix 5, table 5). In the 19th Regiment, for instance, all
three battalion commanders rotated regularly between important line
(field) and staff positions. Two of the three, Lieutenant Colonels
Joseph Kübler and Franz Müller, had served in the Defense Ministry
early in their Reichswehr careers. Both were General Staff officers, and Müller was a non-Bavarian. At the company level, four
commanders show an assignment pattern significantly different from
the others. Captains Günther Blumentritt, Edmund Hoffmeister,
Rudolf Hofmann, and Emil Vogel were General Staff officers whose
assignments alternated more regularly between line and higher staff
posts. Blumentritt and Hoffmeister were non-Bavarians who earlier
had cross-trained in a branch of service other than the infantry.

It appears that General Staff officers like Hoffmeister and
Blumentritt frequently were assigned to divisions other than their
"home" division. This resulted from Army policy and a shortage of
assignments in the particular home division when these officers
were eligible for them. If the variations in tour lengths suggest
that availability of assignments was a problem, assignment to a
"foreign" division also would have the advantage of broadening the
individual's experience and attacking the problem of divisional
parochialism. Although non-Bavarians were not numerous in the Seventh Division, they usually served in key field command assignments.

In the case of these four company commanders, it is clear that

the Reichswehr had identified them early for higher leadership positions because all four had received important staff assignments
as senior first lieutenants or junior captains. Significantly, all
four became general rank officers in the Wehrmacht. Most of the
remaining twelve company commanders had, like Hermann Ramcke, spent
their entire careers as company officers and company commanders.
The Reichswehr needed this type of perhaps less ambitious junior
officer who was both a good field commander and was willing to
serve many years training troops, frequently in isolated garrisons. Their Reichswehr careers, however, do not appear particularly promising, and such officers would not usually reach the general ranks even in the expanded Wehrmacht.[3]

It is unnecessary to examine the cavalry and artillery officers in detail. Their career patterns exhibit the dichotomy between officers who spent the majority of their careers in the regiment and those who rotated between regimental field assignments and
staff posts in the regiment and at higher headquarters (see appendix 5, table 5). Most of the second group appear to have been General Staff Officers targeted for rapid career advancement. While
it was essential for all officers to serve their training time in
the basic field units, those identified for future leadership re-
sponbilities were assigned to the key staff positions as well.

The officers assigned to important division-level posts in
1932 as well as the unit commanders and key staff officers demonstrate the same general assignment patterns. Many were General
Staff officers, including the three non-Bavarians serving with division. Rotation between line and staff assignments was the norm,
and eight of the officers had earlier served in a different branch
of the service. Once again, the technical branch officers show
significant variations.

The officers who served as commandants of garrisons or training sites are the most difficult of all to assess. In 1932 the
three divisions assignments were filled by non-General Staff officers. It is not entirely clear whether this type of assignment was
advantageous for career progression. For many officers, the kind
of assignment is less important than the point in their careers at
which they receive the post. Many Bavarian officers, for example,
served in the Ingolstadt or Munich garrisons or at Grafenwöhr early
in their careers and went on to positions of greater responsibility. On the other hand, senior officers who served as garrison
commandants, especially in the early Weimar period, often seemed to
terminate their careers in this assignment with a character rank
promotion (promotion on retirement), or what was often referred to
as a "golden handshake." Lieutenant Colonel Heinrich Aschenbrandt,
for one, preferred not to accept the Ingolstadt assignment in 1931
if this meant forfeiting the opportunity to reach the rank of colonel. Aschenbrandt was reassured that his career would not suffer,
and indeed he was promoted to colonel while serving at Ingolstadt.

It also should not be assumed that an assignment to the Munich
garrison was considered unimportant. The records show that great
care was taken in selecting officers for this duty because of its
political and ceremonial responsibilities. Rather, such a post
does not appear to be in the mainstream of operational line and

staff assignments that every army considers most important for career advancement. Most generals had by-passed garrison and training site assignments.[4]

The Bavarian officer careers described above show a number of common factors that are directly related to the Reichswehr's mission of developing a cadre of leaders for the national army of the future. For most officers, rotation between line and staff assignments beyond the company level was the rule. Even many company commanders experienced this rotation, if only within the battalion or regiment. Clearly the Reichswehr was concerned that all officers, but especially the most promising, did not become alienated from conditions in the field by serving too often and too long in staff positions. The General Staff officers, in particular, were rotated regularly between line and General Staff assignments.

Furthermore, the training objective of frequent cross-posting is evident in the assignment patterns. While this is not always clear in the case of junior officers, many, in fact, do show a history of duty in another branch of the service. The examples of cross-training are not accidental or due entirely to shortages in one or the other branches. Appendix 5, table 6 depicts the career profiles of officers who, in 1932, were assigned as infantry division commanders and infantry division chiefs of staff. Many of these officers had been assigned to a branch other than the infantry prior to their 1932 assignments. Indeed, it was not unusual for an infantry officer to command a cavalry division and for a cavalryman to command an infantry division.

The career history of Major General Gerd von Rundstedt is particularly illustrative of the Reichswehr's cross-training policy. Although Rundstedt was an infantry officer, he had served as a cavalry division commander and chief of staff before being assigned to command the Third Infantry Division. If Rundstedt and other senior officers are the most prominent examples, it should be noted that even officers who remained in the same branch throughout their careers were trained extensively in the weapons and tactics of the different arms.

*   *   *

The service records of the Bavarian and non-Bavarian officers described above make it possible to construct a representative career from lieutenant to general and to describe the various types of assignments the officer could expect along the way. Appendix 5, table 7 depicts the career opportunities for a Reichswehr infantry officer like Eduard Zorn. While an artillery officer could expect similar advancement, the cavalry and technical branch officers had a more difficult time because of the fewer number of field command positions available in their units. At the higher organizational levels, many cavalry officers served in other branches or in the Defense Ministry, while most senior technical officers served in one of the weapons inspectorates or the Weapons Office. It should also be remembered that, because assignments depended on many factors, the officer could not always expect to progress regularly through the various assignments in the established pattern.

As a lieutenant, the infantry officer could only look forward to several years as a platoon leader because of the Army's emphasis on thorough training at this level. For the first lieutenant, it apparently was advisable to serve in one of the regiment's staff positions which could facilitate early recognition and the beginning of a regular rotation between line and staff assignments. The ambitious infantry captain should have completed a full three-year tour as company commander. As a senior captain or junior major, he might have tried to secure an assignment on the division staff or, better yet, in the Defense Ministry. Other, perhaps slightly less favorable positions would include division garrison officer, regimental adjutant, Infantry School instructor, or group level staff officer.

An infantry officer should plan to serve in every line command position from company commander to division commander, with the possible exception of divisional infantry commander. The latter post was bypassed by many division commanders. Normally completion of the field assignment was the basic prerequisite for duty in one of the available staff positions. Command of troops, or "Front" service, was always the ultimate test of an officer's suitability for advancement.[5] On the other hand, the staff assignments offered the most variety and room to maneuver. Since the majority were at the various headquarters levels, they also provided the officer with good recognition by senior officers who would be best able to further his career. Clearly, early recognition was important, and a post on the division staff or in the Defense Ministry as a junior officer would prove beneficial.

On the staff side of the ladder, the most important assignment was division chief of staff, which required an officer of lieutenant colonel rank. All the division commanders in 1932 had served as division chiefs of staff. This post also called for a General Staff officer, meaning that few non-General Staff officers could hope to serve as division commanders unless waivers were granted. In the Reichswehr this was not often done.

It is difficult to determine the single most prestigious or important assignment on the infantry officer's career path. Certainly the post of regiment commander had lost none of the prestige it had acquired in the Imperial Army. Yet regiment commander was only one of several field assignments that had to be filled if the officer expected to become a division commander. On the staff side, however, there is little doubt that division chief of staff was the key post on the road to significant general rank assignments, and this was the case for senior officers from all branches of the service.

The career histories of the senior officers listed in appendix 5, table 6 indicate that those officers who managed to rotate their line and staff assignments in the manner described above were the ones most often advanced to the general ranks. They also show that, because rapid progression is extremely important, an officer should remain in his assignment, particularly the line assignment, the minimum amount of time necessary for training. Not surprisingly, it was the General Staff officer, whose career was carefully monitored, who had the best prospect of surmounting the inherent problems of the professional army.

On the other hand, decisions concerning the officer's career were only partially his own to make. To be sure, his performance was always the main factor, and, despite an understandable reluctance to do so, he could always make his assignment preferences known. Nevertheless, the decisions were usually reserved for others involved in the complex area of personnel management. Included on the broadest level would be every officer at every level who took part in the evaluation process. The objective at all times was to place the right man in the right assignment without creating instability in the unit's TO.

In a general sense, the procedures for recommending and assigning officers to available positions were similar to those for promotions and eliminations because the Officer Efficiency Report (OER) provided the basic means of performance evaluation. But most useful to the planners were so-called Recommendation Lists, which were completed by the rating officer and reviewed by the division commander for compatibility between officer qualifications and assignment criteria.

Seven lists were available to rating officers, and each list was accorded a general assignment category (see appendix 5, table 8). Individual subheadings enabled the rater to recommend his officer for a specific assignment. For example, Recommendation List VI, Weapons Schools, contained the subheading 1c for riding instructors at the Cavalry School. In the Seeckt period, the Army used an additional list to propose officers for a year of detached duty with another branch of the service. This list, which was for first lieutenants only, remained in effect until 1928, at which time Heye discontinued it because the long absences threatened unit stability and training. The Reichswehr, however, continued the practice of twelve-month cross-training assignments on an irregular basis.[6]

The Recommendation Lists included only staff assignments because it was assumed that the officer would be considered for line posts in normal sequence. Indeed, the prerequisite for every staff position, apart from date-of-rank (DOR) eligibility, was satisfactory completion of a full tour of duty at the "Front." That the Army seldom deviated from this policy is evident from the Seventh Division commander's review of the Recommendation Lists during the three-year period, 1925-1927. Major General Friedrich Freiherr Kress von Kressenstein reviewed every OER and Recommendation List submitted and often removed an officer he determined ineligible for the suggested assignment. In some cases, he judged the officer unfit or better suited for another post; in others he removed officers because the Personnel Office already had these officers identified for another assignment outside the division. Most officers were declared ineligible, however, because they had not served their full terms as company or battalion commanders. In the Seventh Division, field command received the highest priority, and there is no reason to assume that the other divisions or higher headquarters operated differently.

If the OER and the Recommendation Lists served to propose officers for specific assignments, the actual decisions were usually

made by a few officers in the division and the Berlin Personnel Office. Officially, the division's personnel officer, designated
IIa, was responsible for management of the division's TO, but assignment of officers down to the battalion level was the prerogative of the chief of staff, designated Ia. It was he who often
corresponded with officers in Section P1 of the Personnel Office
regarding assignments in the division. For the years of 1929 and
1930, extensive correspondence is available between Colonel Gunther
von Hammerstein-Equord, P1 Leader, and the Bavarian Chiefs of
Staff, Colonels Hans von Hosslin and Friedrich Dollmann concerning
the assignment of senior captains and Stabsoffiziere to posts in
and outside the division's area of responsibility.[7]

Their correspondence is very instructive. First of all, it is
clear that in this area the relationship between Berlin and Munich
was a good one. The problem of balancing the interests of the individual officer and the needs of the Army was difficult, requiring
considerable attention several months in advance of the normal fall
and winter assignment rotations. The decision-making process was
subtle, with Berlin both suggesting officers for specific assignments and requesting the Seventh Division's preferences. Seldom
did the Personnel Office refuse to agree with the Division's pro-
posals. Only in cases where a Bavarian officer was to be assigned
outside the Division and where the prerequisite of "Front" duty was
not completed did Berlin remain firm in the face of Bavarian requests. In the latter case, for instance, the Division wanted to
assign Lieutenant Colonel Alfred Wager to the post of Division
chief of staff in 1929 to succeed Colonel von Hosslin. Wager, however, despite admittedly outstanding credentials for the assignment, had not completed his tour as battalion commander, and, in
spite of repeated appeals from Munich, the Personnel Office would
not agree to violate the criteria of "Front" time. In the end,
Colonel Dollmann assumed the post for a year until Wager could complete his field assignment.

Other cases make it clear that the personnel planners made
every effort to satisfy individual preferences. One officer, Captain Rudolf Konrad, was initially scheduled to assume duties as a
defensive warfare specialist in the Defense Ministry's intelligence
department that the Division VII chief of staff considered unsuited
to Konrad's particular abilities and desires. After the exchange
of several messages between Berlin and Munich, Konrad was reassigned, as recommended by the division chief of staff, as a specialist
on offensive enemy capabilities. The two-year correspondence, furthermore, yields no sign that favoritism outweighed merit in the
decision-making process.

Despite the appearance of good personnel management practices
in assigning Bavarian officers, it is apparent that this was not
always the case in other Reichswehr divisions. The problem of
matching officers with available assignments was always difficult,
and units were known to violate the TO in their efforts to put the
"right man in the right position." Especially in the early years,
there were instances where officers were assigned to posts for
which they were ineligible. For example, captains were assigned as
platoon leaders, while in the same battalion first lieutenants, who

were two years away from promotion to captain, were assigned as company commanders.[8]   And as late as 1925 and 1926 the Personnel Office expressed alarm at the number of <u>Stabsoffiziere</u> in the regiments.[9] Not only was this considered bad policy in terms of an individual's career pattern and unit efficienty. The International Military Control Commission, moreover, threatened to use the violations as a sign of Germany's non-compliance with Treaty provisions. Only during the Heye administration under Brigadier General von Stulpnagel's vigorous leadership was the Personnel Office successful in its efforts to force all units to comply with their TOs.

Apart from the issue of non-compliance with the table, every unit experienced problems with normal personnel turnover and absences. For any number of reasons, a unit could suddenly find itself short of officers. Consequently, transfers among and between the regiments were frequent, although the ever-present shortage of money restricted the transfer policy primarily to unmarried officers.[10]

Transfers also occurred among the different branches. Because of the Reichswehr's emphasis on cross-training, officers were periodically detached for duty with another branch. In cases where the transfer was made permanent, the officer had to have completed four years of service in his original arm. The policy of cross-training, however, was not the only reason for branch transfers. During Seeckt's stewardship, widespread shortages made the transfer policy a necessity. Infantry officers, who were in the majority, were the most affected. In late 1922, for instance, some were transferred to the cavalry and artillery, while beginning with 1923 many were assigned to the technical branches, a practice that continued during the Heye years because of the organizational equiment changes that occurred in these arms.[11]

*   *   *

It is evident from the Bavarian experience that General Staff officers, especially those in the higher ranks, received special consideration. More often than not, they show a record of what appear to have been good assignments. But of course, there is more to an assignment than simply the position. The question of timing may also be professionally crucial. An assignment could damage an officer's career if he held it longer or shorter than the prescribed period, or if he happened to experience a personality conflict with his superior. These circumstances occur in all armies, and the Reichswehr was no exception. One can only refer to the established career opportunities (see appendix 5, table 7) and note that the senior officers in prominent assignments in 1932 got there by means of regular rotation between the line and staff assignments described.

Certainly for a junior officer like Zorn or Jodl, the path of General Staff service offered the best means to advance rapidly in circumstances made more difficult by the restrictions of the professional army.   However, despite these restrictions and the Reichswehr's demonstrated concern for General Staff officers, good assignments and favorable careers were not closed to the non-

General Staff officers. For example, the Rangliste shows that most troop commanders, at least up to and including battalion commanders, were not General Staff officers, and the majority of staff officers at all levels were not General Staff officers.

That the Reichswehr offered a good career to the competent officer without General Staff training was the very point that headquarters personnel officer Captain Friedrich Hossbach, future military adjutant to Adolf Hitler and author of the controversial Hossbach Memorandum, made in his lecture to officers of the 17th Infantry Regiment's Second Battalion in early 1932.[12] His audience consisted mainly of junior officers, and it was to them that he directed his comments. Although Hossbach admitted that the best careers could be expected by officers who completed regular General Staff training or its technical counterpart, he described a number of special assignments that were available to officers without this training. He recommended four in particular. The first was duty in the Defense Ministry and subordinate echelons like the weapons inspectorates. He noted that of the 216 authorized positions in the Defense Ministry, over half were held by non-General Staff officers. Second were assignments for so-called assistants (Hilfsoffiziere) in the division and group staffs and for officers who had not finished the three-year General Staff training program. The latter officers were most often assigned to upper echelon intelligence and transportation posts. Finally, Hossbach emphasized that good assignments were available in the adjutant service and at the weapons schools.

Most officers probably disagreed with him about the weapons school assignment. The post involved was that of control officer (Aufsichtsoffizier), who monitored officer candidate activities. This assignment in most armies is considered lacking in prestige, and the situation was no different in the Reichswehr. Despite Hossbach's contention that it was a good post, the Army could never fill the vacancies, and had to make a special effort, including appeals to patriotism and sense of duty, to recruit officers for the position.[13] But Hossbach's argument that officers could make their mark without the carmine stripes of the General Staff officer is confirmed by Rangliste information. If such officers could not always expect to reach the general ranks, they could, despite the restrictions imposed by the Reichswehr's organizational structure, hold good staff and field assignments on their way to completion of a successful career. The key to ensuring these opportunities was good personnel management, and, on the whole, the Reichswehr must be given high marks in this vital if uninspiring area.

On the other hand, the variations in tour lengths of the officers surveyed in this study underscore the monumental difficulties faced by the personnel planners. Although three-year assignments for company commanders and two-year posts for battalion commanders were standard policy, this rule was violated often. Despite the Army's intention to rotate all officers between line and staff positions, it seems that in junior ranks a combination of limited opportunities and the fact that not all offices were interested in or capable of assuming higher posts, particularly of the staff variety, meant that the policy of field-staff rotation applied most

consistently to Stabsoffiziere.   Yet the Reichswehr favored the
junior officer who was recognized as having potential with good
staff and field assignments at least above the rank of first lieutenant.   Here, selection for General Staff training was the key to
a favorable future.   Although most assignments, even at the higher
levels, were held by non-General Staff officers, the General Staff
corps, precisely because it was so small, could expect its officers
to receive the better staff and line assignments.

Certainly individual circumstances contributed to the variations in the tour lengths. Nevertheless, the problem of instability was more the result of the Reichswehr's competing, if not contradictory objectives.   On the one hand were the training objectives for the individual officer.   To produce the kind of leader
the Reichswehr desired, the officer had to be trained in a wide
variety of subjects and moved up the career path as rapidly as possible.   Yet, in accomplishing this objective, the broader goal of
unit training efficiency was threatened. Individual training required officers to be absent from their field units for extended
time periods, while rapid career progression often produced frequent turnover of key people in the field units.   In both cases,
the result was unit instability. From the leadership's point of
view, the problem of instability seriously endangered the Reichswehr's ability to perform its training mission of combat readiness.

Table of organization management problems reflect this contra-
diction between individual and unit objectives in the small professional army. Variations in tour length are evident merely from a
perusal of the Rangliste.   But, unseen are the frequent absences
from the units occasioned by individual training courses and other
forms of detached duty. It should come as no surprise to find that
friction resulting from officer absences runs like an undercurrent
throughout the history of the Reichswehr.   As will be seen in the
chapter dealing with operational training, the Heye team made a major effort to solve this problem.   The nature of the Reichswehr,
however, argued strongly against its success.

On balance, the problem of putting the "right man in the right
position" was compounded by the reality of the small professional
army's mission.   In order to train qualified leaders for both the
Reichswehr and the projected expanded army of a post-Versailles future, the leaders were forced to adopt a policy of rapid career
progression and broad comprehensive individual training.   At the
same time, this threatened to destabilize conditions in the units
and endanger the training mission of the Army.   To be sure, all
armies tend to pursue competing objectives. However, in the small
professional force, the multiplicity of goals is a severe handicap
for planners determined to assign the "right man to the right position."

6.
Officer Promotions

> One put up with the slow rate of promotion in view of the
> generally distressed economic condition of Germany. Above
> all, one knew that not the German government or the high
> command was at fault, but the Versailles Dictate [Diktat].[1]

To General Heinz Guderian, and many other former Reichswehr officers, the problems associated with the system of officer promotion
can be attributed to the Versailles Treaty restrictions on the
state and the Germany Army. But is the answer really this simple?
Indeed, a much more thorough investigation is required to understand the challenging problems faced by the planners and the solutions they sought within the framework of the small professional
army. Available studies of this subject offer little more than a
broad outline of its operation and effectiveness. The general conclusion is that, despite the fact that promotion opportunities were
not good, the system functioned without great difficulty, and individual discontent was limited. Even the best work published on the
topic seldom moves beyond a description of criteria and procedures
to an analysis of promotion opportunities for specific grades of
officers during the course of the Weimar Republic.[2] The effectiveness of the Reichswehr's promotion system can only be tested in
terms of objectives, criteria, procedures, and, most importantly,
career prospects for officers in the separate grades -- junior
(lieutenants, first lieutenants, captains), senior or field grade
officers (majors, lieutenant colonels, colonels) and generals. For
example, it is necessary to determine how an officer got promoted
in the Reichswehr and what his prospects were for advancement during the twelve-year history of the Army. Also, what type of of-

ficer, if any, benefited most under such a system, and how prevalent was favoritism in the promotion process? Who made the decisions and on what were they based? What kind of problems did the personnel planners face, and how did they attempt to solve them? Who received the preferential or early promotions, and what effect did this have on the Army as a whole? Finally, the problem of conformity must be confronted. In general, was the promotion system able to handle the problems of a professional military organization as well as those peculiar to the Germany Army during a turbulent period in history?

Throughout the Weimar period the officer effeciency report (OER) remained the primary means of evaluating officers for promotion -- as it did for assignments. The first regulation which governed the preparation of the reports (July 30, 1921) clearly established that promotion was to be based on the principle of seniority. Every spring the Personnel Office issued lists by grade of those officers who, according to date-of-rank (DOR), were eligible for consideration for promotion to the next higher grade. Unlike the Imperial Army, the Reichswehr did not introduce a separate promotion system for each branch of the service. By implementing a common system for all officers of a particular rank, the Reichswehr, from the outset, improved upon the system of promotion in the old army. Seniority alone, however, was insufficient for promotion. In addition to the required DOR, the officer had to have demonstrated potential for command expected of officers of the next higher rank. First lieutenants eligible for promotion to captain, for example, were evaluated according to their potential for the position of company commander, a post reserved for captains. Here we see the close connection between seniority and merit and between the officer's rank and assignment that was characteristic of the professional army. The evaluation process was designed to identify the "best" officers after four years of service in the officer corps.

As the 1921 regulation specified, the OER should reflect "first and foremost" the officer's qualities of character and then his intelligence, military proficiency, and physical capabilities. Consequently, character was at the core of the concept of merit. Character attributes included devotion to duty, subordination of personal interests to the higher goals of the Army, the willingness to make decisions and accept responsibility for them, and comradeship and concern for the welfare of subordinates. In effect, the Reichswehr was more concerned with an officer's character than with his objective military performance, and throughout the Reichswehr's history, character remained the key criterion in determining an officer's suitability for promotion.

*   *   *

The experiences of Eduard Zorn and Ferdinand Jodl, or rather the history of their promotion groups, provide an interesting commentary on procedures, criteria, and prospects for junior officers during the early and late years of the Weimar Republic.

Eduard Zorn first appeared as a new lieutenant in the 1925

Rangliste with a DOR of December 1, 1924(2). His sequence number
reflected the fact that he was the second highest ranking officer
among the eighty-four officers in his group (see appendix 6, table
1). Unlike other officers, lieutenants were awarded sequence numbers on the basis of their performance on the Officer Examination.
In subsequent years, Zorn's group underwent a number of changes.
For one, Wolfdietrich Ritter von Xylander, a future Wehrmacht general, was added to the group but ahead of Zorn. Apparently Xylander had completed officer candidate training with Zorn's class but
was not commissioned on schedule because he had supported the Hitler Putsch, thereby violating the Rechswehr's prohibition against
political activity. Two other officers were dismissed from the
service and two were placed at the bottom of the group. Such frequent changes are characteristic of most Reichswehr promotion group
histories.[3]
     In March of 1927, the Personnel Office, as was its policy,
circulated the eligibility figures for the next series of promotions for all grades. Eligible for consideration for promotion to
first lieutenant were all lieutenants with DORs of December 1, 1925
and earlier. Of the 220 lieutenants who qualified, the most senior
had served five years as a lieutenant. Because Zorn was eligible
for promotion at this time, he received an OER that was prepared by
his battalion commander and endorsed by his regiment commander.
Before November 15, the date by which the report had to arrive at
the Personnel Office, it had to be reviewed by the division infantry commander and the division commander. Once the Personnel Office had received all the reports, officers in Personnel Section 1
(P1) studied them to determine which officers met the criteria for
promotion to first lieutenant. Zorn experienced no difficulty at
this stage in his career and received a first lieutenant DOR of
March 1, 1928(2).[4]
     Two observations are in order regarding the promotion of Zorn
and other lieutenants in the late Weimar period. First of all, the
principle of seniority was followed very closely at this level. Of
the ten other first lieutenants in Zorn's group, all were promoted
according to their lieutenant DOR sequence numbers. On the other
hand, it is clear that even at this early date the Reichswehr had
identified Xylander for special consideration because he was included not in Zorn's first lieutenant group but the one preceding
it. In the case of Xylander, it appears that the Army had recognized one of the "best" officers within the four year period of
service in the officer corps.
     Secondly, Zorn's four years and four months time-in-grade
prior to his promotion to first lieutenant was not abnormal for
lieutenants whose entire period of officer training occurred after
the Reichswehr's official formation in 1921. But for other junior
officers, those who were promoted to first lieutenant prior to
1928, for instance, the promotion experience could be very different.
     Indeed, Ferdinand Jodl's case was much more typical of the ma-
jority of junior officers. It is not that the promotion criteria
and procedures were substantially different for Jodl; the operation
of the system for junior and senior ranking officers actually var-

ied little throughout the Weimar period. The striking fact about Jodl is that he had been a wartime lieutenant, and this made a great deal of difference to him, to his contemporaries, and to the career prospects of junior officers in general.

Jodl was a member of the largest single promotion group of any grade in the history of the Reichswehr and had spent twice the amount of time-in-grade than did Zorn. An examination of this group shows that, as in Zorn's case, they were promoted to first lieutenant in order of their lieutenant DOR sequence numbers. None of the officers were promoted out of sequence (see appendix 6, table 2), confirming the Army's dedication to the principle of seniority for junior officer promotions. Not surprisingly, a number of changes occurred in Jodl's promotion group after 1926 (see appendix 6, table 3). Fourteen officers, for example, were added to the group out of sequence and after the original list of 685 officers first appeared in the Rangliste. This is not necessarily unusual because it is well known that the Reichswehr frequently adjusted Patents to account for differences in age, education, and previous military service. In this instance, at least four of the fourteen (indicated by an asterisk) were dropped from the Reichswehr but later "reactivated" and given backdated Patents.[5] Although the promotion histories of the fourteen clearly are irregular and inconsistent with the principle of seniority, it must be remembered that fourteen violations of this type during a seven-year period is a very small figure.[6]

In addition to the fourteen officers added after 1926, a larger number was eliminated each year prior to 1930, the first year in which Jodl's group was officially eligible for promotion to captain. Although most of these officers suffered the fate of "normal" attrition, such as death or dismissal, a few were promoted early in violation of the seniority principle. Especially interesting are nine officers who were officially dismissed but reappear in a later Rangliste. This particular example seems to involve a part of the Reichswehr's clandestine activity because all nine officers appear on the top secret 1930 list of flying officers.[7] Even at that time, several of the officers were officially listed as dismissed from the service. Nevertheless, despite these exceptional cases, the vast majority of first lieutenants were promoted to captain on the basis of seniority.

This conclusion is further substantiated in the instance of Jodl's promotion to captain in 1931. The fifty officers in Jodl's captain group appear in the 1931 Rangliste sequentially according to their first lieutenant DOR sequence numbers. In addition, a survey of newly-promoted captains with DORs which predate and postdate Jodl's DOR confirms that, regardless of the exceptions already noted, promotion to captain was also based on the principle of seniority.

Because seniority was the norm, favoritism or personal influence could play little or no role in the promotion system at the junior officer level. Consequently, it would serve no purpose to analyze the type of junior officer promoted in terms of unit, noble pedigree, geographic area, or branch of service. In this regard, it is significant that Jodl and other officers who had completed

General Staff candidate training by 1930 were given no special pre-
ference for promotion to captain. If completion of General Staff
training was the most important step on the road to an outstanding
career, it did not serve as a special advantage for promotion in
the junior officer ranks.

The promotion experiences of Zorn and Jodl show that their
time-in-grade as lieutenants differed considerably. Yet, as the
following analysis will demonstrate, it does not follow that Zorn,
who spent a shorter period of time as a lieutenant, was offered
better prospects for career advancement. Appendix 6, table 4 is a
numberical listing of the authorized and assigned strength of the
officer corps for the period 1924-1932. In general, there is a
close correlation between authorized and assigned figures, which
indicated that, in terms of the number of officers promoted each
year, a reasonably stable balance was maintained. Nevertheless,
the lieutenants and first lieutenants present a glaring exception
to the general picture, and this is also apparent in appendix 6,
table 5, which shows the yearly totals of newly-promoted officers
for each of the grades. Not surprisingly promotion opportunities
in the Reichswehr, as in all professional armies, became progressively limited during the officer's career. Even in the lower
ranks relatively few officers were promoted each year, and, as in
Jodl's case, the time-in-grade for lieutenants could reach nearly
ten years.

The figures in appendix 6, table 6, which are provided by two
officers who worked in the Personnel Office after Seeckt left office, show comparative figures for age and time-in-grade at the
time of promotion for the years 1931, 1928, and 1913.[8] As of 1931,
most officers were being promoted at an age which would enable the
"best" to reach the rank of brigadier general by the time they entered their fifty-first year. On closer examination, the situation, particularly for junior officers, was less optimistic. In
Jodl's case, he served nearly ten years as a liutenant and six as a
first lieutenant before his promotion to captain. Although he
reached captain by age thirty-four, the age considered appropriate
by Reichswehr planners, his future prospects were not particulary
promising. Assuming that Jodl served the full time-in-grade for
each rank, he would reach the grade of major at age 47, lieutenant
colonel at 52, colonel at 55, and general at 58. Only if the arti-
ficially adjusted the promotion system could Jodl become a general
by age fifty-one.

The reasons for Jodl's unfavorable promotion future are due
not only to the structural problems of the professional army.
Rather, the very size of Jodl's lieutenant and first lieutenant
promotion groups created severe problems for a promotion system
that required smooth, steady, rapid advancement in order to function effectively. It was Jodl's group, for example, that was responsible for the instability apparent in the force structure figures described above. In effect, Jodl's group was creating a bottleneck for junior grade officers like themselves and those like
Zorn, who were following in their wake.

The problem originated in the immediate postwar years of reconstruction when an extraordinarily large group of lieutenants was

accepted into the officer corps. Like Jodl, these lieutenants had
DORs dating from the war years. Why such a large number of wartime
lieutenants was admitted is not entirely clear. A frequent explanation for the imbalance is provided by officers, like Hossbach,
who blame the situation on the stipulations of the Versailles Treaty. To be sure, the number of staff officers and the strength of
division-size units were fixed by the terms of the Treaty. The
Treaty also limited the number of "superior" or field grade and
general officers to 20 percent of the 4,000-man officer corps.
Nevertheless, if the total figure of officers assigned to the junior ranks was fixed by law, the Treaty was silent on precisely how
this figure was to be distributed among the grades of lieutenant,
first lieutenant and captain. In this case, at least, the Versailles Treaty was not responsible for the initial imbalance in the
junior officer ranks.

As Hossbach also admits, this problem developed partly as a
result of policy decisions and partly because of unavoidable circumstances.[9] It is well-known that the Reichswehr planners consciously desired to include a sizeable number of vererans in an
Army that needed experienced officers for reconstruction purposes.
Although one might conclude that they over-estimated the requirement for lieutenants considerably, it is more likely that the real
dilemma they faced was not entirely of their own making.

As noted earlier, the initial postwar unpopularity of the Army
resulted in a severe shortage of officer candidate recruits. The
officer candidate system, furthermore, could not be expected to
produce the first class of lieutenants until the winter of 1924-
1925. When one considers that first lieutenants were in short supply in any case, it is clear that the planners felt that the bleak
outlook for the future left them no choice but to overload the
lieutenant grade. To do this, they were forced to accept lieutenants whose DORs were concentrated in the narrow 1915-1917 year
groups.

In the first few years of the Reichswehr's existence, the situation presented no serious problem. The small number of officers
promoted to lieutenant during the first four years could easily be
absorbed into the lieutenant ranks without de-stabilizing the force
structure. Only a few isolated voices, like that of First Lieutenant Paul Mahlmann, were raised in public criticism of the problem.
In 1922, Mahlmann published an article in the Militär-Wochenblatt
in which he predicted that eventually the Army would have forty-
year-old lieutenants and forty-five-year-old captains. Although he
was officially reprimanded for his pessimism, his career did not
suffer as a result.[10]

By 1925, on the other hand, the officer recruitment situation
appeared very different. With Weimar's internal revolutionary period over, recruitment for the officer training program was rising,
and the first substantial number of new lieutenants trained under
the four year program were entering the Army. It was obvious that
the situation had been stabilized, and the Reichswehr could look
forward to a steady supply of new lieutenants every year. This, in
turn, put pressure on the Personnel Office to take action on Jodl's
enormous group senior lieutenants. At the same time, these wartime

lieutenants were approaching ten years in grade, an extremely long period of time to serve as an officer at the bottom of the military and financial ladder.

As the figures in appendix 6, table 4 indicate, the decision was made in 1925 to reverse the ratio of lieutenants to first lieutenants, which meant that now the first lieutenant grade would be overloaded with a hugh block of officers with the same DOR. At the same time the time-in-grade was shortened to approximately four years for lieutenants who had entered the officer corps under the four-year training program. As a result, the problem of imbalance was perpetuated in the first lieutenant grade, and lieutenants like Zorn, who were promoted after Jodl on the basis of seniority, found their careers obstructed until the large group ahead of them had been promoted. The long-range consequences of the initial imbalance of lieutenants and the 1925 inflation of first lieutenants is difficult to determine, but certainly the bottleneck that was produced in thos ranks make career prospects unfavorable for most officers in Jodl's group and those who followed them -- and that fact was a continuous source of discontent in the junior officer ranks.[11]

*   *   *

For most senior officers, promotion opportunities were hardly more promising that those for their subordinates. In both cases, a relatively large number of officers was competing for a limited number of available promotions. Unlike the situation facing junior officers, however, the selection process for field grade officers was far more rigorous and competitive. For one thing, the Reichswehr, like all armies, devoted more attention to the promotion of senior officers because the command responsibilities associated with them were greater. Moreover, because of the extremely close association of rank and assignment in the senior grades, promotion was determined by the availability of the particular assignment as well as the officer's qualifications forthe post. In the Reichswehr, the limited number of assignments for senior officers resulted in an extremely competitive environment. Finally, the very fact that a smaller number of candidates were competing in the higher grades enabled the Personnel Office to scrutinize field grade officers more carefully. The Reichswehr's greater interest in senior officer promotions is reflected in the more elaborate procedures and criteria required in the preparation of their OERs. Nevertheless, a survey of newly-promoted majors, lieutenant colonels, and colonels shows that for field grade officer promotions, as for those of junior officers, the Reichswehr seldom deviated from the rule of seniority (see appendix 6, table 7). Clearly, because seniority was the key to promotion, most officers advanced through the regular promotion system in normal fashion, and positions appear to have been made available by means of attrition rather than by violation of the seniority system.

A profile of the officer who survived the selection process in the three field grades indicated that, first of all, aristocrats fared very well in each of the three grades (see appendix 6, table 8). The average figures of 20 percent for majors, 38 percent for lieutenant colonels, and 31 percent for colonels compare more than favorably with the Army-wide average of 21 percent. A significant number were assigned to key staff and field positions, which demonstrates that the criterion of leadership potential for the next higher grade -- in addition to current performance -- was an important factor in the selection process.

The most revealing statistics are found in the area of branch representation. While it is understandable that the infantry and artillery branches are well-represented, it is interesting to find the cavalry, despite its enduring prestige, with the lowest numbers of newly-promoted officers in the senior grades. In fact, often the number of officers in the various technical or auxiliary arms was higher. Indeed, the latter officers are highly visible throughout the period. There is little evidence available to indicate that these officers were particularly outstanding or especially favored, and most were promoted in normal sequence. Their high representation, in comparison to their total strength in the officer corps, probably lies in the fact that they constituted a small, yet vital element in the modern Reichswehr. Any loss, for whatever reason, would severely cut into the strength of the technical branches. When one recalls that Army policy, especially during the Heye period, emphasized technically-trained officers, it is evident why such officers, despite the well-known absence of glamour surrounding the auxiliary arms, were prominent on the lists of newly-promoted field grade officers.

Available information provides no definitive picture of the typical officer promoted in the senior ranks. The most that can be said with certainty is that the officer is more likely to represent either the infantry or artillery than the cavalry, and that he could easily be an aristocrat. Perhaps most important, the Reichswehr's promotion system appears to have been remarkable successful in its quest to reward qualified officers. By means of a promotion system based on seniority, the Army seems to have recognized especially competent field grade officers whose responsibilities lay primarily in key staff and command positions.

*   *   *

Given the fact that most senior officers were promoted on the basis of seniority, what were the prospects for favorable career progression in the field grades? Certainly for officers in a professional army, the main hurdle on the road to general officer rank is the promotion from captain to major -- from junior grade to senior grade officer. The Army required a proportionately larger number of junior officers to handle training responsibilities, but fewer senior senior officers to fill command and staff positions. The Reichswehr was authorized 1,098 captains but only 372 majors, or a reduction of 66 percent. With only between 75 and 100 new majors promoted each year, promotion prospects, irrespective of policy decisions, were extremely limited (see appendix 6, tables 4 and 5). Organizational requirements alone made the promotion to major especially difficult.

Moreover, the fact that traditionally in the German Army the promotion from captain to major had been the most critical in an officer's career would serve to highlight its importance in the Reichswehr. In the Imperial Army, the so-called "major's corner" had been the greatest hurdle for most officers, and personal influence and social origins were considered by critics of the process to have been more important than merit. Although there is little evidence to indicate that politics unduly continued to influence the "major's corner" in the Reichswehr, this promotion nevertheless remained the most crucial one.[12]

For major, accessible evidence suggests that the number of officers eligible and number selected were very close. In this way the Reichswehr avoided the discontent which could have resulted from only a few being selected from a large number of eligibles. Those selected, furthermore, were normally awarded their DORs with a delay of no more than a few months. Here again, potential criticism was forestalled by promoting selected captains promptly. The fact that only a very few captains were promoted in any given year was just one aspect of the unfavorble career prospects for senior captains. Closely related to this and most discouraging for the Reichswehr captain was the negative trend regarding time-in-grade prior to eligibility. In 1924, captains with just under nine years in grade were being promoted to major, but by 1932, the time-in-grade had increased progressively until the newly-promoted major had spent over thirteen years as a captain (see appendix 6, table 7). In fact, the 1932 Rangliste still listed four captains whose DORs predated the official formation of the Reichswehr. If these four captains represent an extreme case, the fact remains that promotion from captain to major was slow and could lead to morale problems in the professional army.

Promotion prospects improved for majors and lieutenant colonels who survived the demanding selection process. In 1923, new lieutenant colonels had served just under seven years as majors; a decade later, time-in-grade had decreased to approximately four years. Moreover, the number of new lieutenant colonels rose steadily until, by the late Weimar years, the annual turnover of lieutenant colonels was nearly one-third of the total authorized. Promotion to the rank of colonel likewise shows a decreasing figure for time-in-grade prior to eligibility, and after Heye assumed command, colonels experienced a yearly turnover rate of nearly 50 percent. Clearly, the limited number of authorized positions for lieutenant colonels and colonels, as well as the leaders' emphasis on the youth, account for the increasingly rapid turnover in these ranks during the late Weimar period. Heye's Chief of Personnel, Joachim von Stülpnagel, in particular, was determined to move the outstanding senior officers through the higher ranks as rapidly as possible.[13]

The Army's general officers, of course, represent the most select group in the officer corps. One might expect that favoritism or special application of the procedures would, if they were to play a significant role in the promotion system, be evident in general officer promotions. But evidence suggests that the promotion picture remains very similar to that of the field grade officers

(see appendix 6, table 9). The general officer normally represented either the infantry or artillery (see appendix 6, table 10).
Cavalry officers were as underrepresented in the general ranks as
they were in the field grades. Interestingly enough, officers of
the auxiliary arms were nearly nonexistent among general officers.
Even several weapons inspector commanders, who dealt with the individual technical branches, like Brigadier General von Bonin (the
Signals branch in Bonin's case), were officers from the infantry or
artillery. Evidently, the Reichswehr felt that the increased command responsibilities associated with general rank could not be met
by most officers who had been trained in the auxiliary arms. Officers were also moved through the general ranks rapidly, and the
turnover rate was high. On the whole, the promotion opportunities
for generals, like those for lieutenant colonels and colonels, improved during the Heye era.

It is clear that for field and general grade officers, the
Reichswehr favored a policy of progressively rapid adancement
through the senior ranks. As indicated by the strict application
of the seniority rule, the rapid progression in the upper ranks was
achieved primarily by means of officer attrition. On the other
hand, this was not the only method used to advance the "best" officers. A more positive method, and one common to all armies, was
the use of the preferential promotion (merit promotion) or the
backdating of rank.

*   *   *

From the sample listings of new majors, it is apparent that
several were awarded preferential advancement before their contemporaries. In 1927, for instance, Captains Erich Fromm and Hans
Reinhardt were promoted two years earlier than fellow officers with
the same DORs, and thereby gained a significant advantage over them
(see appendix 6, table 7). These two examples raise key questions
about the procedures, policies, and effects of the preferential
promotion system. Reichswehr personnel planners continually spoke
of the need to create "air" in the promotion system.[14] Their solution was the use of preferential promotion, or "promotion by selection." This enabled the Army to provide incentives to outstanding
officers and to ensure that future leaders would be recognized and
assigned responsible, challenging posts at an early age. Because
promotion by seniority alone could not guarantee that the "best"
officers would advance as rapidly as necessry, the preferential
promotion system served as a corrective to the regular program.

The 1926 OER regulation is very clear on the purpose of the
preferential promotion system: "In order to bring leaders to the
head of the Army who have energy and the vigor of youth, there is
need for the promotion of specially-fitted officers by selection."[15] The procedures for awarding preferential promotions were
similar to those for the regular system. In March of each year,
the Personnel Office published the list of officers eligible according to their DORs and distributed it to the units. There the
individual commanders nominated their deserving officers and entered them on Recommendation List 1. This list was attched to their

OER, which was prepared in the fall, and submitted up the chain-of-command to the Personnel Office. Officers chosen from the lists received a DOR advantage of from one to two years for major and one year for lieutenant colonel. Those officers not selected could be renominated until the DOR advantage had expired.

In theory, every outstanding officer with the required DOR qualification was eligible for a preferential promotion. The essential question, of course, is precisely what criteria did the officer have to satisfy in order to be considered outstanding. From the Reichswehr's inception, preferential promotions created problems for the high command because invariably too many candidates were nominated. Seeckt, in November 1921, declared that the number of officers proposed exceeded the total number of promotions available for officers under both the preferential and regular systems. Because of this, Seeckt defined the eligibility criteria more narrowly and specifically.

Basically, preferential promotions would be restricted to General Staff officers eligible for promotion to major and lieutenant colonel. Non-General Staff or line officers would be considered in "exceptional cases" only. To be nominated, captains had to have demonstrated the potential for the post of General Staff operations officer (Ia), a major's assignment. For majors, the criterion was the ability to assume the duties of chief of staff at division level, a lieutenant colonel's assignment. Furthermore, no General Staff officer, no matter how competent, could be proposed before he had completed a tour of duty with a field unit. Seeckt was very sensitive to criticism, which dated from the postwar years, that General Staff offices were not "Front," or combat-qualified officers. He repeatedly pointed out that General Staff officers were every bit as qualified to hold field command assignments as their line officer counterparts. To justify his contention, he required General Staff officers to serve up to three years in field units prior to their nomination for a preferential promotion.[16]

Seeckt's problem diminished little during the following years. In March 1923, he returned to the topic and admitted that his earlier attempt to limit the number of nominations had proven ineffective. In addition, from the last group of OERs it was impossible to determine the most deserving officers. Seeckt's solution was to set a numerical limit of 15 percent of the total number of captains and majors eligible for promotion in any given year. In effect, each division could nominate two majors and three captains for preferential promotions each year.[17]

Although the problem of too many nominees was never entirely solved, by 1923 the Reichswehr had firmly established its criteria for preferential promotion: General Staff qualification, field experience, and command potential for the grade in question. Because of these demanding requirements and the introduction of quotas, preferential promotions were reservd for a very select group of officers. But what type of officer was selected and what was the impact of the preferential promotion system on the officer corps?

Here an analysis of Bavarian majors is very instructive.[18] The records indicate that during the period 1924-1932 a total of 125 majors served in Divisioin VII. Only seven of these officers were assigned to the division from outside Bavaria. Of the 125, 26 received a preferential promotion (see appendix 6, table 11). Although in percentage terms this figure is rather large, it must be remembered that because it is the total for an eight-year period, it is not as significant as it first appears.

As a result of a policy change in 1927, the preferential promotion to lieutenant colonel was eliminated entirely and captains awarded the special promotion to major were selected three rather than two years before their normal eligibility date.[19] Beginning with Major Wilhelm Wimmer, the future Luftwaffe general, this change is reflected in the Bavarian ranks. The number of these promotions, however, continued to be very limited. If 26 Bavarian majors received the coveted promotions, there remained 29 with General Staff credentials, in addition to the large number of regular line officers, who did not.

What type of officer received the preferential promotion? Was he, in fact, more likely to be a General Staff officer? In Bavaria's case the answer is yes because fully 19 of the 26 officers were General Staff officers, and the status of Majors Dietl and Konrad is unclear. All nineteen had served the required tour of duty in the field at some point prior to their promotion. Most of the officers represented the infantry, with the artillery bringing up a distant second. As for social background, it was not an objective factor in the selection process. Only 3 of the officers were nobles, and 2 of these were non-Bavarian.

There is no reason to doubt that the officers chosen met the high standards established for selection. Most were General Staff officers who had proven themselves in the field. Moreover, if the Reichswehr was promoting them on the basis of their future potential, it was also assigning many to important, prestigious posts during the Reichswehr period. Albert Kesselring, for one, served mostly in the Truppenamt's Organization Branch (T2) as its management rationalization expert. Erwin Janecke and Erich Brandenberger attended the prestigious "Reinhardt Course," and the majority of the remaining twenty-three served as division General Staff operations officers. Sixteen reached the rank of general in the later Wehrmacht, and this figure could well be higher.[20]

If preferential promotions were restricted to the chosen few, they were indeed highly coveted promotions. Selectees -- like Halder and Ritter von Speck, for example -- received an advantage over their fellow captains of 200 places in the Rangliste. Officers promoted after the 1927 policy revision might be jumped as many as 275 places, which meant that they would move through the senior ranks rapidly and reach the general grade at the youthful age considered essential. Significantly enough, none of the fifteen majors on the list who were promoted before Wimmer received early advancement to lieutenant colonel. Therefore, the preferential promotion to major, at least in the Bavarian case, was the most crucial in the career of officers likely to qualify for such promotions. This becomes more important when it is remembered that the preferential promotion to lieutenant colonel was eliminated after Heye assumed command of the Reichswehr. In essence, for the extremely able, ambitious General Staff captain, the "major's corner" was doubly important in his career.

This analysis of the Bavarian majors demonstrates that the Reichswehr's preferential promotion criteria of field duty, General Staff training, and outstanding ability and performance were met in the selection of the twenty-six officers. There is no reason to assume that the Bavarian situation, here as in other facets of the promotion picture, is unique and not applicable to other areas and to the Army as a whole. Indeed a comparison of regular and preferential promotion figures for Bavaria and her sister divisions makes it clear that the Bavarian record is not exceptional.[21] The analysis also shows that preferential promotions were limited to a very few, exceptionally-qualified future leaders. This is to be expected because a large number of special promotions would adversely affect the authorization tables and, more importantly, increase discontent within the officer corps. Indeed, with a fixed authorization figure, every preferential promotion meant that one less regular promotion was available.

Even though such promotions were few in number and difficult to receive, they altered for some the generally dismal view of career prospects characteristic of the regular promotion system. They also provided the Army with a method of ensuring that a youthful group of outstanding leaders would become generals, and served as an incentive for the highly-motivated officer to do so. Especially for a junior officer like Jodl, who was jammed in among so many other first lieutenants with the same DOR, it must have been comforting to know that his successful General Staff experience meant that his chances for an early promotion and subsequent career progression were very promising. The preferential promotion system was one method by which the Reichswehr could eliminate the type of obstruction that was noted earlier in the junior officer grades.

Nevertheless, whether the preferential promotion system was, as its defenders maintain, the most effective method of creating "air" in the career pattern is debatable.[22] Because the yearly number of officers dismissed from the Army normally exceeded the number of those who received early promotions, it can be argued that the officer elimination program was the key to a smoothly functioning system. In any event, at least the preferential promotion system was a more positive method and, despite its competitive nature, less likely to produce dangerous discontent in the officer corps.

*   *   *

That a general feeling of dissatisfaction about promotions existed in the officer corps is not open to question. One need only peruse the Militär-Wochenblatt to discover the widespread sense of frustration especially in the junior officer grades. The authors, who deplored the "increased insecurity" in their careers, referred to a "wretched promotion system" in an officer corps that had "grown too old." Captains, in particular, faced an "extraordinarily hard test of patience" because many had to serve more than twelve years time-in-grade.[23] Almost to a man, the former

Reichswehr officers interviewed by Harold Gordon agreed that promotion opportunities were discouraging and the subject of considerable criticism. Nevertheless, they also agreed that such discontent never reached the point of threatening the unity of the officer corps and the Army's combat effectiveness.[24] Then why did the friction present in the promotion system remain within manageable proportions.

One reason, paradoxically, is certainly the factor of conformity that was discussed in other portions of this study. Most officers would hesitate to become too vociferous because of the impact such outspokenness could have on their careers. But if the tendency to conform served in a negative way to lessen the discontent over disagreeable promotion opportunities, it was a factor that did not please the authorities. They preferred to keep the friction under control by defending the promotion system. For one thing, it was convenient and effective to blame outside forces for whatever problems might be at hand. After all, the restrictive organizational structure of the professional army which made career progression difficult and slow was not of Germany's making. Not only had such a system been forced on Germany, but all efforts to have it modified were opposed by the authors of the Versailles Treaty. Supporters of the Reichswehr's promotion policies, like later general Curt Liebmann, also reminded their critics that prospects in the Reichswehr compared favorably with those in other postwar professional armies and were better than they had been in the Imperial Army.[25] To the many officers who had served in the prewar army and were willing to listen to reason, these arguments were effective.

Equally convincing was the line of argument that stressed financial benefits and the security provided by the military profession. To be sure, the economic factor is double-edged. On the one hand, the threat of forced dismissal from the Army did not foster job security, and the low pay of the Reichswehr officer was a continual subject of concern. A reasonably competent officer could expect to survive elimination, however, and he had to realize that the economic situation for military officers improved during the course of the 1920s. During Heye's tenure, in particular, pay for junior grade officers improved, which was especially beneficial to Jodl's group of first lieutenants. Significantly enough, most criticism of the poor financial state of military officers occurred during the late Seeckt and early Heye periods, when Germany's internal political and economic situation was relatively stable. After 1929 such criticism was undermined by the effects of the Depression. While many Germans joined the ranks of the unemployed, the competent Reichswehr officer, no matter how desperate he might consider his situation to be, could not forget that at least he had a secure job and a regular income. At such a time, criticism of the promotion system was seldom voiced. Indeed, malcontents were far more likely to vent their criticism on the policy of forced dismissal -- in fact, it is not inconceivable that Army leaders deliberately channeded potential discontent into the officer elimination program.

Above all, the authorities were able to defend the promotion system effectively because it was administered fairly and career opportunities were equal for the vast majority of officers. To be sure, favoritism or internal politics was not entirely absent from promotion or career decisions. Take the case of Kurt von Schleicher, for example. His preferential promotion to lieutenant colonel ensured that his advancement would be rapid, but during the entire Reichswehr period he did not serve outside the Defense Ministry. Futhermore, Schleicher's loyal subordinates, Eugen Ott, Erich Marcks, and Kurt von Bredow, received preferential promotions to major while they worked for Schleicher. Although these officers were undoubtedly very able men, their accelerated advancement through various staff rather than line assignments did not endear them or Schleicher to their fellow officers. It is not surprising to find that National Socialist criticism of the "Schleicher clique" touched a responsive chord in the officer corps or that Schleicher failed to receive much needed support from the officer corps during the twilight years of the Weimar Republic.[26]

Despite these and other exceptions that have been discussed, most officers realized that the promotion system was equitable. In theory, every officer was provided the same opportunities for promotion, and in practice, this ideal approached reality. The preceding analysis of the promotion system confirms that the principle of seniority was followed for promotion in all grades in the officer corps. Furthermore, the use of preferential promotions to advance outstanding officers was unlikely to a very small number of officers each year. Although most selectees were General Staff officers, the majority of General Staff officers were denied selection. Moreover, because every junior grade officer was required to take the District Examination, he was forcibly offered the chance to compete for General Staff candidate selection. In general, if promotion opportunities in the Reichswehr were less than outstanding, this situation was inherent in the professional army and everyone suffered accordingly.

Much of the credit for the success of the promotion system was due to the leader's ceaseless efforts to improve the quality of OERs from the field and the means by which officers could be evaluated effectively. Every year the commander-in-chief published his evaluation of the current OERs and, during Heye's tenure, local commanders were made more responsible for the reports they submitted. Under Heye, rating officers who lacked the desire or ability to meet the reporting standards required were criticized by superiors in their own OERs.

More important were the efforts within the Personnel Office to improve the decision-making process. To overcome the difficulty of evaluating officers from different geographic areas and branches of the service, officers were assigned to the Personnel Section 1 for a lengthy tour who could be expected to become experts in specific areas of responsibility. For example, Lieutenant Colonel von Perfall, who spent four years in the P1, was responsible for Bavaria, his native state, and the cavalry, his branch of service. As former General Rudolf Hofmann has pointed out in his study of the OER system,

> Because of his broad perspective and his personal knowledge, the examiner could decide whether and to what degree

> the evaluations...were justified in the light of overall
> requirements. In normal times the specialist in the Per-
> sonnel Office knew the spirit of the officer corps of each
> specific unit, and he could thus judge the appropriateness
> of the ratings awarded. The differences between the stan-
> dards applied in various units were adjusted in the Per-
> sonal Office...[27]

Headquarters personnel officers also broadened their perspective
through frequent visits to the field and by participating in the
Reichswehr's tactical ride evaluation program. In this way, they
could keep the field formations informed of headquarters policies
and expand their own knowledge of individual units and officers.

Nevertheless, it must be remembered that, if the Reichswehr's
system for identifying and promoting the "best" officers was generally effective, it was, in a sense, a very personal system. In the
small, professional army it was possible for Reichswehr authorities
to staff the Personnel Office with officers who could become experts in their areas and devote personal attention to individual
branches, areas, units, and officers. In a larger army, the additional officers and units would make any such personal system like
the Reichswehr's much less effective. This, in fact, is precisely
what happened when the professional Reichswehr was replaced by the
conscription-oriented Wehrmacht. It is ironic that in the case of
the Reichwehr's personnel policy, as in so many other areas, this
so-called Army of the future was, in truth, operating very much
within the constraints and realities of the present.

On balance, it is difficult to evaluate precisely the results
of the promotion system in terms of the quality of the officers
promoted. Despite the Heye regime's emphasis on character, it is
unlikely that it was successful in its effort to eliminate conformism and weed out the flagrant careerist. The highly competitive
nature of the promotion system and the concern for personal security made the success of such an effort almost impossible. In the
less subjective area of identifying and promoting the "best" officer, the Army leaders appear to have been more successful. Objective criteria called for technical efficiency in current assignments and the ability to perform effectively the duties associated
with the next higher grade. For the most part, these criteria were
met in awarding junior, senior, and general officer promotions.
Indeed, Army leaders may well have been correct to claim that the
Reichswehr could look to the future with a solid core of professional, technically-proficient officers.[28]

7.
Officer Dismissals

The single most divisive issue within the Army, and a major factor in all personnel planning, was the officer elimination (Verabschiedung) program. Unlike the situation in the conscript army, the small professional Reichswehr's restricted personnel authorizations and twenty-five year service commitment meant that officers whose ability otherwise may well have warranted their retention faced the prospect of separation well before their normal retirement dates.[1] Discontent surrounding the elimination program was a dangerous undercurrent throughout the Reichswehr's history. No officer could be expected to accept his separation without at least a certain amount of bitterness. Not only would he feel personal rejection; he could not look forward to living comfortably in Germany on a military pension alone. His fellow officers, too, would share his bitterness, and his unit would have to find a replacement and minimize the disruption in unit an individual training. Finally, Reichswehr leaders disliked administering a negative program that threatened their authority and the officer corps' homogeneity. These constraints made the elimination program an integral part of every Reichswehr personnel policy decision. Officer replacements and the availability of promotions and assignments depended largely on the number of vacancies created by dismissing serving officers. Because these programs were interrelated, personnel planners were forced to pursue several competing objectives. When it is considered that personnel goals included providing high quality officers, securing youth in the corps, and placing the best officers in the key posts -- without creating excessive unrest in the ranks -- the challenge facing the planners in their efforts to maintain stability was monumental. Despite the subject's importance, no thorough study of the program has so far been undertaken. For information, one must refer to general works on the Reichswehr, memoirs of retired officers, or to indirectly related works. What is needed is an analysis of the program's procedures and problems and impact on the Reichswehr.[2]

$$*\qquad\qquad *\qquad\qquad *$$

Appendix 7, table 1 shows the career profiles of thirty-five Bavarian officers who were dismissed during the period 1926-1929. The experience of one representative member of the group, Captain Friedrich Walther, who was discharged in March 1928, is a useful illustration of the procedures and criteria for involuntary retirement of Reichswehr officers. Walther had a history of substandard performance that was well-documented in his OERs. By 1925, at the latest, it was clear that Walther was in trouble because in that year he received a special, non-periodic OER from his regiment commander. Under normal circumstances Walther would receive an OER only in even-numbered years. Furthermore, when it came before Division Commander Major General Frhr. Kress von Kressenstein, it was apparent that Walther's performance was weak. Kress, consequently, formally admonished him that he needed to develop "a more decisive and confident bearing" and "greater vigor and skill" as a squadron leader.[3]

Before Walther's OER was sent to the Personnel Office, his regimental commander was required to inform him verbally of the unfavorable OER comments -- a procedure called "disclosure" (Eröffnung) -- the ostensible purpose of which was to make the officer aware of his shortcomings so that he would have the opportunity to improve. But looking ahead to possible separation, the Reichswehr was absolutely determined, too, that such a step not come as a total surprise to the individual. Disclosure was thus important also as a means of keeping discontent to a minimum. Nevertheless, officers often were shocked, and the leaders had considerable difficulty ensuring that rating officers performed the unpleasant duty of notifying colleagues of their shortcomings.[4]

Although Walther's OERs for 1926 and 1927 are not available, it is apparent that his performance as squadron commander did not improve because in 1927 he was listed among the Division VII's weakest captains. Furthermore, he received another non-periodic OER and was included on Recommendation List VIII, the list for "officers no longer performing [their] duties capably."[5] Once an officer found himself on this list, he could not expect to remain in the Army much longer.

On December 8, 1927, Brigadier General Joachim von Stulpnagel, Chief of the Personnel Office, issued the preliminary notification of discharge (Vorbescheid). It stated that the commander-in-chief agreed with the division commander's evaluation that "Captain Walther does not possess the ability for his current assignment as squadron commander." Furthermore, his dismissal "is desired for official reasons because it would permit the promtion of an officer in a lower service grade." Walther's regimental commander was instructed to notify him immediately that under these circumstances the commander-in-chief sincerely regretted that, "despite his full appreciation for Captain Walther's service in war and peace," he could not allow him to remain in the Reichswehr beyond March 31, 1928.[6]

In the preliminary notification Walther was also reminded that, under the terms of Article 26 of the defense law, he had the right to appeal the decision to the Defense Minister within one month. He chose not to appeal, however, but to go through the formal procedures to obtain his financial entitlements. Although he was scheduled to serve on active duty only until January 31, he would continue to receive his full salary through April. He was reminded that, according to the Defense Minister's decree of August 15, 1927, he was authorized a separation allowance to ease the transition to civilian life. Finally, he was granted a full pension and the privilege of wearing his uniform at military functions. As of March 31, 1928, Walther was no longer a member of the Reichswehr.

Following his retirement Walther seems to have been active in border defense work in the Nurnberg area. Division VII records indicated that the division was able to secure military-related work in Bavaria for officers who were separated. Most were employed by the Army itself in positions like pensions officer, psychological testing officer, and other civil-service type occupations characteristic of most military organizations. Others were used as so-called "L'Angestellte" officials, who supervised the state defensive recruitment training measures which were, at best, semi-legal.[7]

On balance, the Reichswehr's objectives in the case of Captain Walther appear to have been satisfied. A weak officer was correctly identified, given adequate opportunity to improve, and then discharged in the interest of upward mobility in the officer corps. In the process, local input was important at every stage of evaluation, and Walther seems to have been treated as fairly as possible under the circumstances.

                    *   *   *

For the Army as a whole, Rangliste statistics make it possible to develop a portrait of the dismissed Reichswehr officer and to examine the rate of losses and their impact on the different grades and units. Appendix 7, table 2 specifies the numerical and percentage figures of officers separated during the period 1924-1932. In terms of yearly losses, it is evident that Reichswehr and Bavarian figures fluctuated in relation to the periods associated with the three commanders of the Army. During the Seeckt period, Rangliste years 1924-1927, the yearly totals stabilized at approximately 160 after the first two years. From 1928 to 1931, the years in which Heye determined policy, the high figures reflect the increased quotas, with those for 1928 and 1930 the highest in Reichswehr's history. In 1931 the numbers decline once again, and it is known that the unpublished 1933 Rangliste figures were close to the 1932 totals.

This same pattern of fluctuation was noted for the promotion statistics for the Weimar period. Not surprisingly, the highest figures for newly-promoted officers occurred during the Heye period, which also experienced the highest elimination rates. In this regard, the restrictive nature of the professional force and the close relationship between promotion and elimination are clearly demonstrated. Because the number of promotions depended largely on the number of vacancies that resulted from dismissals, the latter was the most important method of increasing mobility in the officer career structure.

Among the different ranks, the Stabsoffiziere received the highest priority for dismissal throughout the period. Their total was high in 1924, remained so throughout the Seeckt period, and then rose during the Heye years until in 1931 it amounted to 50 percent of the total number of officers dismissed. In every year their percentage of losses was higher than the percentage of Stabsoffiziere in the Reichswehr as a whole. The latter comprised 18 percent of the total authorized officer strength.

The figures for junior officers were also consistently high. The most stable rank was captain, which contributed nearly fifty officers per year until 1931. More fluctuation was visible in the lieutenant and first lieutenant ranks, although here too the numbers were high. Clearly the lower totals for Seeckt's last two years are accounted for in these grades. It was noted earlier in Jodl's case that his first lieutenant promotion group first appeared in the 1926 Rangliste. It was this group that, as lieutenants, was responsible for the high lieutenant losses in 1924 and 1925 and, as first lieutenants, the high rate in 1928. If Stabsoffiziere received the highest priority, junior officers were far from ignored. Generally, officers in all grades were eliminated, and no one was particular grade seems to have predominated.

Another facet in the general composite of the elimination picture that must be discussed is social background. It was suggested that the Bavarian program seemed to place no particular emphasis on social origins. For the entire Reichswehr, the statistics show a much more striking picture (see appendix 7, table 2). Indeed, the number of officers drawn from the aristocracy dismissed each year never fell below 20 percent of the total, and was usually higher. It is important to note, however, that critics of the Reichswehr's high percentage have failed to examine the same question in the context of officer elimination. Dismissed noble officers likewise represented a consistently high percentage of yearly losses and also showed an increase during the late Weimar years. There is no evidence to suggest that the Reichswehr, whether the program was officer selection or elimination, followed a specific policy concerning the social background of its officers or potential officers. In any event, scholars who stress the social origins of the Reichswehr officers should be aware that, if the Army attracted more than its share of nobles, it also did not hesitate to eliminate noble officers in proportionately large numbers. In this regard, an officer's performance rather than his social background seems to have been the decisive criterion.

In terms of branch representation, it is not surprising to

find the infantry with more than twice the total for the other two main branches combined (see appendix 7, table 3). In spite of the small size of the technical arms, however, they too suffered substantial losses. In general, the yearly branch statistics conform to the pattern for the three periods described above. During the Heye years, for example, all branches were affected by the requirement to raise the number of eliminations. Most interesting are the yearly figures that do not fit the pattern. Why, for instance, are the cavalry numbers especially high for 1925 and low for 1931? Or, why were the artillery and technical branches so low in 1932? The cavalry especially is a constant surprise, and it may be that the Reichswehr's increasingly technical orientation during the late Weimar years is the answer.

Because of the potentially disruptive effects of officer eliminations, it is useful to evaluate the impact of the losses in the different areas of the Reichswehr. This can be done by examining the Rangliste, which lists the officers dismissed each year for the period 1924-1932. As expected, most of the officers separated from Defense Ministry and other higher headquarters assignments were Stabsoffiziere and generals. Likewise, the high rate among Stabsoffiziere assigned to garrisons and training areas is not surprising. In both cases, the Seventh Division conforms to the general pattern.

It is also evident that the line regiments bore the brunt of the dismissals. If the yearly losses for the twenty-one infantry regiments are examined, it is apparent that they were hardest hit, contributing at least one-third of the yearly total (see appendix 7, table 4). Yet how much of a problem the losses created for specific regiments is more difficult to determine. Rangliste statistics provide no conclusive evidence in this area. In fact, the yearly losses seem to be rather evenly distributed among the regiments. On the other hand, the statistics also cannot explain why the 13th and 21st Infantry Regiments had relatively low total figures for the Weimar period. At least in the Bavarian case, there is no evidence to indicate that the 21st Regiment either had difficulty recruiting officer replacements or included better officers than the other regiments.

Significantly, favoritism appears to have played no major role in the elimination picture. This is perhaps best illustrated by the fact that neither the 9th Infantry Regiment, the most prestigious Prussian infantry regiment, not the 19th, its Munich-based counterpart, were exceptions to the general pattern. Both experienced relatively high officer loss rates. The remaining artillery and cavalry regiments and the technical branches show few exceptions in terms of their yearly losses. On the whole, their losses conform to the pattern noted for the Seeckt, Heye, and Hammerstein-Equord periods.

Several tentative conclusions can be drawn from this statistical survey of the Reichswehr's elimination program. For one thing, the Heye period, with substantially higher loss rates, stands out as the exception and the major factor in the fluctuating pattern. Throughout the Army's history, furthermore, the dismissal of Stabsoffiziere in all branches received the highest priority.

To be sure, branch and district quotas provided working parameters for the elimination program. But within these guidelines, branch representation, assignment, and social background appear less significant than the objective of removing the weakest officers. The fact that the actual losses in the different grades often varied from the precise quota figures tends to support this conclusion. Although the statistics alone cannot show the effects of the losses for specific units, they suggest that the losses were apportioned fairly evenly and that favoritism was not prevalent. Here, too, the main emphasis seems to have been on identifying the weak officer.

                *   *   *

From the preceding analysis it is evident that the elimination program confronted the Reichswehr with two basic problems. The first concerned the most effective method of recognizing and removing weaker officers. The second involved the establishment of a systematic way of eliminating a sufficient number of officers each year to provide mobility without producing instability and discontent.

Seeckt's answer to the problem of selecting the right officers for dismissal was improved OER quality and better compliance with the Recommendation Lists VII and VIII requirements.[8] Because divisions were always reluctant to put their officers on lists for what amounted to certain elimination, the Reichswehr planners had to turn to the OERs to select the additional officers. As Seeckt always observed, however, the poor quality of the reports made it very difficult to distinguish between the competent and incompetent officer. Too often reports tended to be verbose, colorless, and plagued by what the leaders called Wohlwollen, the rater's practice of describing and emphasizing only the positive side of the officer's performance, ability, and character. Reichswehr OER critiques repeatedly condemned the prevalence of Wohlwollen, and the threat this posed to the quality of the officer corps was highlighted in the OER regulation itself:

> The best interest of the service is the decisive factor in judging an officer...Complete good will [Wohlwollen] must be maintained during the forming of the estimate. This good will must not, however, lead to silence concerning actual faults; important interests of the service are menaced thereby.[9]

The regulation further specified that should officers be assigned to posts for which they were unqualified, the harm done to the officer corps, the general public, and the individual would far outweigh the extent of personal injury that a more objective report might have caused the officer.

However, despite the many directives calling for an end to excessive Wohlwollen and more objectivity in reporting, the problem persisted. The leaders attributed this to the poor state of the German economy.[10] Even after the Dawes Plan of 1924 brought a mea-

sure of stability to the economy, Seeckt believd that reporting officials were reluctant to contribute to a fellow officer's dismissal because of the meager benefits that awaited him.

And, indeed, such benefits seem to have been exiguous.
Reichswehr veterans almost invariably consider salary and pension
benefits the most negative part of their experience, and Lieutenant
General Reinhardt, one of the most objective and astute senior officers, found the situation particularly shocking. In November
1925 he told the Seventh Division commander that the personnel not-
ices

> present a sad picture of the economic situation and the
> average family's position in the officer corps. Nearly all
> officers are propertyless. Larger families are the rarest,
> and even most of the older married couples have only one or
> two children. In the struggle to improve our economic con-
> dition, especially regarding transfer and housing allow-
> ances, these facts must not be passed over in silence.[11]

Although a certain amount of progress had been achieved by the time
of Seeckt's resignation in late 1926, the quality of the OERs was
still of major concern to the leaders, who continued to pursue an
economic solution to the problem.

The task of identifying the right officers for elimination was
closely related to the question of how many officers in what grades
to dismiss each year. Because the elimination program had to be
planned in conjunction with the other personnel programs and the
uncontrollable variable of voluntary separation, systematic, long-
range planning was extremely difficult if not impossible. Furthermore, organizational confusion and political turmoil, especially in
the early years, added to the uncertainty of the situation. Only
by late 1924, when it was clear that the Republic would continue to
survive, could the elimination program, as well as the other officer programs discussed earlier, be stabilized. Now Seeckt could
introduce quotas and be reasonably certain that the divisions would
comply with them. The elimination figures for his last two years
reflect his burden on the junior officers.

Partly because the number of first lieutenants dismissed in
1926 and 1927 declined, the priority continued to be on Stabsoffiziere. In fact, in September 1925, Seeckt not only reaffirmed
this objective but stated that the number of Stabsoffiziere proposed for dismissal must be increased. If the figure for 1926
Stabsoffiziere eliminations shows only a slight percentage increase, the higher 1927 figure seems to reflect the regime's intention to raise the Stabsoffiziere dismissal rate (see appendix 7,
table 2).

Nevertheless, despite the appearance of stability and the emphasis on Stabsoffiziere eliminations during Seeckt's last years,
it is evident that certain influential officers believed that the
elimination program was not meeting its objectives of increased mobility and better promotion and assignment opportunities. To these
officers, Seeckt had become complacent and unwilling to uphold a
program that personally he found very disagreeable. His protection

of senior officers, in particular, convinced his detractors that he was no longer interested in maintaining a youthful officer corps.[12]

One of Seeckt's severest critics was Joachim von Stülpnagel, whose appointment as Chief of the Personnel Office in early 1927 signaled a new era in the officer elimination program. Although Seeckt left behind a system that was operating fairly smoothly, his successor, Wilhelm Heye, was determined to improve the means of identifying weak officers and to raise the annual dismissal rate. The battle was led by his two key subordinates, Stülpnagel and Werner von Blomberg, the new Chief of the Truppenamt. They intended to revitalize what they considered to be a flabby, aging, unmodern Army that was unprepared for future challenges. Stülpnagel, in particular, was the driving force behind the changes in personnel policies and programs that occurred during Heye's tenure as commander-in-chief.

For most of his career, Stülpnagel had been a Seeckt protege and intimately involved in many important decisions of the early Reichswehr years. But after openly criticizing Seeckt's training and personnel policies, he was quietly banished in 1925 to the "Front," where he served as commander of the 17th Infantry Regiment.[13] When he returned to the Defense Ministry in early February 1927, he found that decision-making had become more decentralized following Seeckt's departure. Heye, who had neither the temperament nor inclination to fill the authoritative shoes of Seeckt, has been generally portrayed by most scholars as a kindly grandfather figure whose weak, vacillating policies reflected his inability to replace Seeckt.[14] In the personnel area, however, a completely different picture emerges -- one of dynamic, forceful leadership bent on making substantive changes. Although Stülpnagel, who apparently was allowed a free hand in personnel matters, was certainly the key man behind the changes, he later admitted that Heye had forced him to fight hard for his decisions and had been far more than a mere rubber stamp.[15]

The changes began in March 1927, when Heye issued a scathing critique of the 1926 OERs and the general state of Reichswehr personnel policies. OERs, he said, were of such poor quality that it was almost impossible to identify weak officers for elimination. He considered it wholly improper to use the economic situation as an excuse for the excessive Wohlwollen producing inflationary reporting and a leveling effect on the standards of the officer corps. Because it was so difficult for the Personnel Office to identify weak officers from the OERs, Heye now required submission of divisional merit lists for Stabsoffiziere and captains eligible for promotion. He further instructed the divisions to include their weaker captains, regardless of promotion eligibility. With the merit lists, Heye went beyond the OERs and the Recommendation Lists to force the divisions to discriminate more carefully among their officers.[16]

In addition to the improved evaluation procedures, Heye took a step toward clarifying the thorny problem of determining how many officers should be eliminated from the different ranks each year. It was at this time that the increased quotas were issued. Renewed emphasis was placed on Stabsoffiziere who now, in contrast to the

Seeckt period, were to be scrutinized to ensure that they were still "fresh" and vigorous in their current assignments. All commanders were to receive an annual rather than a biannual OER. Captains approaching the "major's corner," moreover, were to be evaluated more carefully, and first lieutenants, too, were to feel the sharp edge of the elimination knife. As Heye pointed out, it would be better for the Army and the individual if the careers of weak junior officers were terminated early.[17]

This communique is significant for its tone as well as its substance. Along with the changes in policy, it shows a new seriousness and intensity in the leaders' approach to personnel objectives. Heye's intention to promote vigor and youth in the officer corps clearly meant that the peacetime Reichswehr was becoming much less secure for the marginal officer.

In his major address to the Reichswehr in September of that year, Heye defended his goals and discussed what they signified for the officer corps:

> The requirement for the dismissal of officers can exclude no officer of any grade who is contributing to the danger of an overaged officer corps. This question is very serious today. It is correct that younger officers want to advance. This can only be achieved if approximately 200 officers are separated each year.[18]

Furthermore, it was not sufficient for an officer to perform satisfactorily in his present assignment. He also had to "qualify for the next higher." After all, Heye warned, "insecurity was inherent in the nature of the officer profession."[19]

It was in this address, which emphasized the dangerous problem of conformity, that Heye implied that the weak officers that must be identified for dismissal were not to be confused with mavericks and nonconformists who performed capably. The results of the 1927 changes can be seen in the 1928 Rangliste, which shows that Stabsoffiziere and junior officer losses rose considerably, while the total figure for the Army far exceed the goal of 200 (see appendix 7, table 2).

In March 1928, Heye again evaluated the previous year's OERs, concentrating on a defense of his policies. Reflecting on the opposition that had surfaced during the past year, he stated that too many of the officers recently separated took their dismissal as a personal injustice rather than a necessary consequence of the enemy's imposed treaty (Feindesdiktat) and their own lack of ability. Many had initiated the formal protest procedure. Heye was disturbed as much by the nature of the complaints as he was by their high number. It seems that the protestors had accused their superiors, particularly their rating officers, of disloyalty. Heye's response was that such complaints showed that their authors had charcter flaws and should have been eliminated long ago. He was also alarmed that the elimination notifiction seemed to come as a complete surprise to many officers, whose superiors avoided responsibility by blaming higher headquarters personnel officers for the decision.[20]

It is clear from Heye's comments that discontent surrounding the elimination program had risen substantially and was becoming a major threat to the discipline and homogeneity of the officer corps. Whether such opposition compelled Heye to reduce the number of dismissed officers the next year is uncertain. Nevertheless, the figures in the 1929 Rangliste show a decrease in eliminations and, significantly enough, after only one year the submission of divisional merit lists for all captains was discontinued.

The decline in eliminations certainly did not reflect the leaders' satisfaction with the program. Indeed, Heye saw little improvement in the quality of the 1928 OERs, and his criticisms echoed earlier comments on such problems as Wohlwollen and the failure of the divisions to nominate enough officers for Lists VII and VIII. As was Heye's custom, he stressed character as the single most important criterion in the officer's evaluation. No mention was made of the previous year's unrest, but he did imply that the leaders should not be considered insensitive to the plight of the involuntarily retired officer. After all, it was very successful in finding military-related work for the officers recently dismissed. But at the same time, he warned that because of the insufficient number of nominations, more captains and first lieutenants would be separated the next year.[21]

This project increase is reflected in the 1930 Rangliste, which shows that first lieutenants provided the major share of the increase (see appendix 7, table 2). The 1931 Rangliste totals, which are reasonably high, represent the work of Heye's last year in office. In the fall of 1930 he retired to make way for a more youthful successor.

There is no question that Heye had a significant impact on the Reichswehr in the personnel area. Changes certainly were warranted. The method of identifying weak officers needed improvement, and Heye's reforms undoubtedly introduced more discrimination into the evaluation process. Heye could also argue that promotion and assignment opportunities increased as a result of the large yearly losses in all grades. Stulpnagel, furthermore, has contended that he did everything possible to minimize the impact of separation on the individual officer and to ensure that the divisions were involved in the decision-making process. From his point of view, the Heye period was one of great progress. Its personnel policies cleared the Army of much dead wood and provided the necessary mobility for outstanding officers to move rapidly through key assignments. Most significantly, he attributed the swift rise of the Wehrmacht to the high quality of the officer corps that was achieved by the personnel reforms of the Heye years.[22]

Nevertheless, it is also quite clear that in the ranks the so-called reforms in the elimination program produced much disgruntlement, which was expressed in the high number of individual protests and divisional complaints. Such discontent was easily fanned by the political extremists who monitored the state of the Reichswehr's morale. If, to his admirers, Stulpnagel was known as "Joachim of the Future," to severe critics like the National Socialists he was the "hangman" (Henker).[23] Even after one makes all due allowances for National Socialist exaggeration, it must be assumed that their criticism reflected a significant degree of discontent concerning the elimination program.

Heye's successor in October 1930 was General Kurt von Hammerstein-Equord. It was apparent to him that, at a time when political and economic conditions were already aggravated, the high loss rates of the Heye years had to be reduced to ease the pressure on the units and lessen the discontent. At the same time, he wanted to retain the most positive aspects of Heye's reforms. The thrust of Hammerstein's approach to the elimination program is seen best in the review of procedures and policies that occurred during an adjutant's meeting held in Berlin from March 19-21, 1931.

The significance of Heye's work was acknowledged by the fact that the participants condensed Heye's OER critiques of 1926, 1927, and 1928, and used the abbreviated version as the basis for future policy. Consequently, the meeting's comments on OER policy and procedures show little change in the prevailing standards. The meeting minutes indicate, however, that the planners were still haunted by the problem of too few divisional nominees for dismissal. In light of the worsening Depression, they tried to reassure the raters that dismissed officers, would, in most cases, continue to find employment in the Defense Ministry. Perhaps Heye's efforts to improve the quality of the officer corps were already becoming apparent because Hammerstein believed the low number of officers proposed for elimination reflected the higher quality of the officer corps in the early 1930s.[24]

In all likelihood this explains his additional steps to improve officer evaluation techniques. Not only were the merit lists retained and the captains' lists reinstated, but new lists, referred to as Scala, were introduced. Now all Stabsoffiziere and captains eligible for promotion were ranked in one of four categories based on performance and future potential. Colonels were not included. Although it is not clear whether each division was assigned specific quotas for each category, the new lists promised far more discrimination in officer evaluation that previous methods.[25]

In addition to improving the method of identifying weak officers, Hammerstein reduced the yearly elimination figure to 170, which he considered a realistic goal for subsequent years. Even more significantly, after ten years Reichswehr personnel planners now devised a plan to guarantee mobility and stability in the officer's career. Elimination would occur only in the ranks of first lieutenants, senior captains (the "major's corner"), and colonels. Officers in the other grades would not be affected, and, ideally, the competent officer should be able to end his career as a colonel. Furthermore, to improve upward mobility, field assignments in divisions, regiments, battalions, and companies would be stabilized, while certain staff assignments would be intentionally destabilized and experience a high turnover rate. Because stability could not be achieved in all assignments, the leaders were emphasizing those assignments that most directly affected the training status and combat performance capability of the Army.[26]

Unfortunately, the planners admitted that this plan could not be implemented immediately. Rather, it was a solution for the fu-

ture.   In the meantime officer dismissals would occur in all
grades, and stability in officer assignments would continue to be a
major concern.   From all indications, the plan was still in the
theoretical stage on the eve of the Third Reich.

*   *   *

On balance, the Reichswehr personnel planners handled the
elimination program as well as could be expected.   Of the two major
problems they faced, they were more succesful with the identification of weak officers.   To be sure, criticism of OER quality was
steady throughout the period, and it seemed that the planners'
criticism always fell on deaf ears.   Despite their attempts to improve financial entitlements, it is unlikely that the solution to
the problem of officer reporting could be found entirely in the
area of economic benefits.   At bottom, the culprit, which the
Reichswehr preferred not to recognize, was human nature.   Every
military report by one officer on another was inherently subjective
and affected by the idiosyncrasies of the rater.   Furthermore, in
such a personal rating system, the rater tends to minimize his
critical remarks.   Not only is criticism of fellow officers distasteful in itself, raters hesitate to chastise their subordinates
if they cannot be certain other raters are doing likewise.   The result is inflation in the rating system and a leveling tendency in
the officer corps.   If all officers are rated high, then it is difficult to distinguish the outstanding from the mediocre.
In a small professional service like the Reichswehr, with limited personnel authorizations and a forced selection-out policy,
the problem was especially acute.   During the Seeckt period, the
Army was well aware of the danger and relied on official demands
for more objectivity in reporting and the Recommendation List,
which were to provide more discrimination in officer evaluations.
Yet, because the Recommendation Lists, as the name implies, recommended more than they evaluated, the reporting system remained unsatisfactory in the Seeckt era.   Although Heye made the first significant improvement by requiring the divisions to rank their officers on merit lists, his solution was only partially successful.
Hammerstein went a step further with the Scala lists, which, in effect, put the officers ranked on the merit lists into evaluative
categories.
This was about as far as the Army could progress without issuing the divisions quotas, by which only a certain number of officers could be entered in each of the Scala list categories.   Even
this measure would be little more than marginally effective without
an assignment corrective.   It would do little good, for example, to
differentiate officers by category if the different assignment responsibilities were not taken into account.   But, can this be done
effectively?   Indeed, it is doubtful whether quotas or any other
alternative could do more than limit the subjective aspects of the
evaluation system.   The Reichswehr, it must be admitted, handled
this problem reasonably well.   Through use of the lists, as well as
the communications channel between Berlin and the districts, the
Army was able to identify weak officers much more effectively than

its criticism of the problem would imply.

The personnel planners were less successful in their attempts to find some way of determining the "correct" number from the "correct" grade to eliminate each year. Certainly the contradictory objectives made a long-term, systematic policy very elusive. At bottom, only two alternatives were available. Relatively speaking, one could have either a low loss rate with a low level of discontent or a high loss rate with a high level of discontent. Neither was completely satisfactory. During Seeckt's last two years, the high command followed the first alternative. However, in doing so, it compromised the objectives of mobility in the officer's corps. Heye, on the other hand, chose the second alternative. Although his improvements were substantial, they also produced instability and unrest in the field units. If their long-term impact was a higher level of quality in the officer corps, their immediate result was a clear threat to the leaders' authority and the officer corps' sacred homogeneity.

With Hammerstein we see a return to the strategy of low loss rates with less friction. Despite his statements concerning the higher quality of the officer corps, it is unlikely that by itself the lower number of yearly dismissals could produce significant mobility in the officer structure. In this regard, his proposed plan of furthering mobility and stability in certain grades and assignments is very intriguing because it confined dismissals to certain ranks. At the same time, however, it seemed to offer no solution to the thorny problem of deciding which ranks should receive the highest priority. Here, too, the task was nearly insoluble. Hammerstein's plan proposed avoiding Stabsoffiziere elimination until the grade of colonel. But by forcing the junior officers to bear the burden, the profession would appear less attractive to potential officer replacements.

Given enough time, his plan may have been the best possible way to satisfy the various objectives. He, at least, had a plan. Meanwhile, he consciously chose to reduce the discontent and instability in the field. Was he successful? Although it is difficult to correlate the internal operation of the Reichswehr with particular contemporary political conditions, it is nevertheless suggestive that in the fall of 1932 the leaders believed that the discipline and homogeneity of the Army had weakened to the point where its reliability in the internal crisis could not be assured. This was the conclusion of the Ott Plan, or war game prepared by Lieutenant Colonel Eugen Ott for the government. If the Army were faced with an emergency created by extremists of the political left or right, he concluded that it could not suppress the uprising.[27]

Despite the various approaches to the problem, the elimination program remained all but unmanageable for the planners throughout the period. Balancing the objectives of elimination, assignment, promotion, and officer recruitment programs seemed beyond the organizational abilities of the leaders. All the personnel officers could do was try to apply the criteria as objectively as possible. In the elimination program, this seems to have been done because neither individual officers nor units were subjected to favoritism. Generally, the close cooperation that existed between

Berlin and the divisions in this area ensured that standards would
be upheld and weak officers identified.

Nevertheless, the fact remains that the elimination program
was a negative, unpopular program that had the potential to do serious damage to the officer corps. Unlike the promotion system, the
elimination system could not be compared favorably with a similar
program in the old Imperial Army. It is not at all unusual to find
that discontent was always present. Indeed, it would be surprising
were this not so. Stülpnagel, for one, has remarked that most of
the officers lived with the fear that they would be separated at an
early date. Heye's comment, that insecurity was a necessary part
of the profession, was hardly reassuring. If, as seems the case,
the system affected primarily the weak or marginally competent officer, most officers realized that they could not take their positions for granted. They also knew that such a problem would not
exist in a national, conscription-based army.

The leaders viewed the elimination program's problems in the
general context of the professional army. Because it could not
hope to alter its status militarily, it attempted to have it modified politicially. The first step was removal of the Inter-Allied
Military Control Commission established by the Versailles Treaty.
Although the commission was dissolved in early 1927, it led to no
major changes in the Reichswehr's legal status. German compliance
continued to be monitored by the League of Nations and especially
by the French.[28]

The second and major objective was to gain for Germany equality of status (Gleichberechtigung). Although this goal was pursued
continuously at the various disarmament conferences held during the
later Weimar years, it was not until December 1932 that Chancellor
Schleicher's government was granted its request. By that time it
was much too late for it to be effective.

There was, of course, another solution of sorts. The Reichswehr could violate the legal 5 percent limit on replacements and
dismissals and list as separated various officers who were still
involved in military activities. It is well-known that this was
done in some cases. The Russian connection, for example, was handled by officers who, like Bavarian Major Ludwig Ritter von Radlmaier, were listed as dismissed in the Rangliste but, after their
return from Russia, resumed their active duty commitments.[29]

This phenomenon was discussed earlier when, in the promotion
program, it was discovered that several Bavarian officers in Jodl's
promotion group were discharged and later reactivated. In this regard, the top secret November 1930 roster of Reichswehr flying officers is very interesting (see appendix 7, table 5). Fully 53 of
the 167 officers do not appear in the 1930 Rangliste, while many
are not found in the 1931 Rangliste. Although this curious situation shows that the Rangliste must be used with care and that the
elimination program was used for other than its stated objective,
the important question concerns the extent of the Army's violation
of the 5 percent clause. While a complete answer to this question
is elusive, it would appear that the Army's clandestine activities
requiring personnel document manipulations and falsifications did
not involve most officers. The vast majority of dismissed officers

were not separated with the intention of readmitting them to the Reichswehr.

On balance, such use of the elimination program ws not extensive, and the high command was resolved to make the program at hand work as well as possible. Certainly many officers, beginning with Seeckt, saw the conscript army as the only solution to the Reichswehr's difficulties. But some of these same officers would later bemoan the decline in quality produced by the rapid expansion of the Wehrmacht. Above all, the Reichswehr could pride itself on the high quality of its officer corps in the technical-military sense of the word. In view of the widespread criticism of the elimination program, it is ironic that this program was perhaps more responsible than any other for the high quality of the force. Every Reichswehr officer was forced to excel or face the prospect of elimination.

However, if the elimination program contributed to the high standard of the officer corps, it did so at a great price because its means were fear, compulsion, and insecurity. The result was an unhealthy spread of conformity and careerism. These were tendencies that endangered the success of the very objective most prized by the leaders -- the high quality of the officer corps. Heye was one of the few officers who recognized and confronted the ambivalent nature of the elimination program. He demanded higher standards of quality and performance from his officers, and those who did not perform did not remain in the Reichswehr. For the problem of conformity he offered character education (Charaktererziehung), which he promoted incessantly throughout his four years in office.

It is sadly ironic that Heye's reform measures may have aggravated the very problems he sought to eliminate. While higher standards and higher losss rates certainly contributed to better individual advancement opportunities and a more competent officer corps, they also bred insecurity and discontent. Excessive competition can prove counterproductive if officers became overly concerned with personal security and career advancement. Such officers possess little imagination and what Stülpnagel has referred to as civil courage.[30] Heye's emphasis on character education was not misplaced. It is unfortunate that it was so ineffective because if, as many believe, a lack of civil courage explains much of the German officer corps' tragedy during the Third Reich, the seeds of that tragedy were present and recognized in the Reichswehr. Clearly the elimination program was a major contributor to this problem.

8.
Operational Training

Operational training is the most important function of the peacetime army because the state of the army's training efficiency is the best test of its striking power in time of war. Historically, the Prussian-German Army emphasized training at all organizational levels, and made it the particular responsiblity of General Staff officers. This additional interest and concern was continued by the Reichswehr. Indeed, training efficiency was considered by Reichswehr officers to be a matter of national survival. Only by means of a superbly-trained corps of officers could the Treaty-shackled Army hope to overcome the burden which insufficient personnel and equipment imposed on its ability to defend the Fatherland. For the vast majority of officers, life in the 100,000-man Army was the regular daily performance of training responsibilities, the Alltagsarbeit of the officer's existence. Even those assigned to higher headquarters staff posts, which normally involved no direct command of troops in the field, were not excluded from training requirements. Although the importance of operational training is not a matter of dispute, it has seldom been the subject of intensive research. Most scholars have been satisfied to describe the training system that Seeckt established and allow it to stand unaltered for the entire Weimar period.[1] More recently, other scholars equally interested in the Reichswehr's political problems have plunged into the labyrinth of the Army's illegal mobilization and the rearmament efforts of the late 1920s.[2] The result has been to neglect the officer corps' major activity of military training in the world of the Weimar Republic. Indeed, operational training is of fundamental importance for an understanding of the Reichswehr. The Army faced the dilemma of achiev-

ing contradictory aims by attempting to train the best possible officer corps while maintaining stability of command at the "Front."
Seeckt and Heye responded differently to this problem, and their
approaches illustrate a fundamental disagreement regarding the role
of the professional army. Operational training best reflects the
way in which the Reichswehr viewed its role in the Republic as well
as its mission as an integral part of the future national revival.

*   *   *

When Lieutenant Eduard Zorn was accepted into the officer
corps in December 1924, he was no stranger to the Reichswehr's
training program. His four-year officer candidate training program
was designed to prepare him to assume his role as a junior infantry
officer without major adjustment problems. His training as an NCO
provided him with first-hand knowledge of the troops he would command, while his tours at the Infantry School and in the field units
exposed him to theoretical and practical instruction in the tactics
of combined arms operations. The transition was made easier by the
fact that from the late fall of 1924 he had been taking part in the
First Battalion's training program at Munich as a Senior Ensign.

In mid-December, Zorn reported to the Third Battalion's Ninth
Company in Lindau, on the shores of Lake Constance. His commander
was a First Lieutenant Kaiser, a General Staff officer and the
third commander of the company in the previous three years. Kaiser's company was one of two stationed at the Lindau garrison administered by the 19th Infantry Regiment from Munich through battalion headquarters in Kempten. The 19th's decentralized organizational structure was characteristic of the Reichswehr, which maintained approximnately 127 garrisons spread throughout the country.[3]

It had been Seeckt's policy to favor decentralization and close
contact with the population in order to prevent the Army from becoming a mercenary force. Therefor, although individual initiative
was encouraged by the leaders, it was also a consequence of the
dispersed nature of the Army. For example, even though Kaiser was
required to follow established training guidelines, he possessed a
good deal of freedom in the actual operation of his company. In
this way, it was expected that Kaiser would develop initiative and
maintain a high level of motivation among his officers and enlisted
men. Under these conditions, the Reichswehr planners understandably placed a great deal of emphasis on uniformity of training and
the responsibilities of the regiment commanders.

When Zorn arrived, the Ninth Company was in the midst of its
winter training program. Winter training occurred during the six-
month period that commenced on November 1. During this period, the
same type of theoretical and practical training was administered in
all branches at every level of the Reichswehr. The general objective was to improve individual and small unit efficiency and prepare officers for summer exercises and maneuvers. Within the six-
month period, Zorn participated in three different, yet closely related categories of training.[4]

The first category, which was called theoretical studies, included several tactical exercises and problems designed to develop

the individual qualities of leadership. Most important were the map exercise (Planubung), the war game (Kriegsspiel) which was normally performed using the sand table, and the terrain evaluation without troops (Gelandebesprechung) conducted in the vicinity of the garrison. It will be remembered that these were the same kinds of theoretical, tactical exercises that Jodl performed during his General Staff candidate training. They stressed the same common framework for solving problems, and all emphasized the tactics of combined arms under conditions of mobile warfare. As a new lieutenant, Zorn participated only as a team member and was excluded from the more advanced instruction provided selected junior officers at regimental headquarters in Munich.

In addition to the tactical exercises, Zorn's theoretical training included lectures and problems of a tactical and contemporary military-political nature. Lectures consisted of military-technical or political-historical topics. Usually, new weapons technology and the experiences of the First World War were the main subjects. Following normal practice, Zorn was required to conduct an extemporaneous discussion of the subject rather than deliver a formal lecture. The tactical assignments dealt with a variety of combat situations that could be expected to confront a small Army forced to rely on combined arms tactics and rapid movement to neutralize an attacking force. Zorn's contemporary military-political question, interestingly enough, required an analysis of the impact of the Dawes Plan on Germany and Europe. Lessons of this nature appear to have been the only means of providing political instruction for junior officers assigned to the field units during the Seeckt period.

The second category of winter training was called field service (Felddienst), a general term which referred to small unit combat training. It was through field service that Zorn first developed platoon leadership techniques and trained his unit as a cohesive force. Specific types of training included marching, various combat maneuvers, supply support exercises, security measures, intelligence reporting, and engineering work. The guidelines for field service were outlined in the Reichswehr's standard, comprehensive tactical manual on use of the combined arms. Like other categories of winter training, Field Service prepared officers and their units for participation in the larger terrain exercises and maneuvers that began in the spring.

The third category was called "practical" instruction and included such individual outdoor activities as horsemanship, athletics, fencing, and target practice. The latter was given special priority because Army leaders believed firing proficiency offered one of the few ways in which the small Army could counteract the weakness in arms and equipment. Because the Third Battalion was assigned the special mission of training for mountain warfare, Zorn's practical training included skiing and practice with the unique euipment required for operations in the Alps.

In addition to the three major categories of winter training, Zorn spent his normal share of time supervising the care and maintenance of the Lindau garrison as well as dealing with the problems of his platoon members. When not involved with formal winter duties, he was expected to study both the latest technical and tactical studies distributed by the Defense Ministry and the tactical problems that frequently appeared in publications like the Militär-Wochenblatt. Winter training officially ended in late March following the regimental commander's inspection of the garrison. There is little doubt that winter training, with it variety of challenging mental and physical tasks, was a strenuous experience for Zorn.

The Reichswehr's summer training period began with small field exercises in April, and officers were now expected to apply what they had learned during the winter months. In May Zorn took the part in the small border reconnaissance patrols his battalion sent into the high Alps from April through June. During the spring he also participated in the weekly garrison terrain exercise (Standortgelandebesprechung) and the troop terrain exercise (Truppengelandesbesprechung). The former stressed combined arms tactics and included officers from the different branches, while the latter emphasized the tactics of the infantry service only. The framework of the exercises was normally the company or battalion, although officers and senior NCOs wer the main participants.

In the summer, Zorn's company was ordered to join the other elements of his battalion at Grafenwohr, the division training site near the Czech border, for several weeks of firing practice and tactical training in preparation for the fall maneuver. Like the terrain exercises performed without troops in the Lindau area, the Grafenwohr exercises were characterized by thorough planning beforehand and critiques of the different phases of the operations afterward.[5]

The climax of the summer training period and the yearly training cycle occurred in September with large-scale formation maneuvers. For Zorn and his fellow officers in 1925, this amounted to field operations at the level of the reinforced infantry regiment, consisting of an infantry regiment, an artillery battery, an infantry trench mortar company, and a cavalry regiment. Normally only one infantry regiment per division took part in the so-called division maneuvers. The others were either conducting smaller-scale exercises, participating in divisional artillery and engineering skeleton, i.e., understrength, exercises, or performing as a supplemental force in a division maneuver outside Bavaria. A crucial part in the fall maneuvers was played by the umpires, the officers responsible for directing the course of events and ensuring that all phases of the operation were handled as realistically as possible. Emphasis was placed on communications and resupply efforts as well as the tactical employment of the combat forces. The Reichswehr also made every attempt to ensure that the local population was inconvenienced as little as possible.

Although the Reichswehr scheduled division maneuvers every fall, these did not involve large, division-size formations until 1926, Seeckt's last year in office. Only in the 1926 maneuver did the Second Group Command pit division-level forces against each other. In the earlier years, the "division" maneuvers involved only elements of the particular division combined in a reinforced regiment. Although the division maneuver of 1925 was the largest that Zorn had experienced, it was still only a reinforced regiment formation maneuver.[6]

The Army, furthermore, faced a difficult task in its efforts to provide realistic training. Enemy forces had to be represented by flag troops while the friendly forces had to resort to canvas-covered "tanks" and defend against "assumed" aircraft attacks. To be sure, the Reichswehr was progressive in its tactical operations and well aware of contemporary developments in weapons technology. Yet the scale of operations remained small throughout the early years, and the absence of the equipment prohibited by law gave an air of artificiality to the field training program.

After the 1925 maneuver, Zorn, like most officers and troops of the Reichswehr, took his annual holiday which lasted approximately two weeks. When the new winter training cycle began in November, priority was again the mistakes and lessons of the summer exercises and maneuvers. For specific guidance, all units in the Army consulted the yearly critique of the training program published by Seeckt in December.

In addition to the elements of the winter and summer training programs, two other major types of training were available to officers more senior in rank than Zorn. Although both have been described briefly in conjunction with Jodl's General Staff work, they must also be examined in the context of operational training. The first consisted of instructional courses (Lehrgänge) that were held at various locations throughout the training year (see appendix 8, table 1). The Seventh Division, like most divisions, supplemented these courses with several of its own which were held in Munich. The courses were largely theoretical and technical in nature and ran the gamut from refresher to advanced training courses. It was primarily by means of the instructional courses that the Army disseminated new technical-tactical information in the officer corps. Because the courses drew officers from all branches and geographic areas, however, they also served to promote uniformity and reduce parochialism.

Since the Army considered it essential that junior officers spend sufficient time familiarizing themselves with all facets of life in the small field unit, officers were not permitted to attend instructional courses until they had completed three years of service as an officer. In Zorn's case, a partial exception was made because, as a member of the Alpine unit, he was required to attend two ski instructor courses in the late winter of 1925.[7]

The other type of training from which Zorn was excluded in 1925 was the tactical instructional ride. Appendix 8, table 2 shows the Defense Ministry and division staff rides, which were normally scheduled in the spring of every year.[8] Although the tactical rides were not an innovation in the Reichswehr, Seeckt developed the system to a fine art. They were designed to familiarize officers with larger tactical situations in different types of terrain, promote tacticl uniformity, and screen officers for more responsible positions of leadership. They also prepared officers for specific leadership posts in the summer and fall exercises and maneuvers. Perhaps reflecting a realistic evaluation of the Army's combat capability and the need for small unit training, the tacti-

cal situations in different types of terrain, promote tactical uniformity, and screen officers for more reponsible positions of leadership. They also prepared officers for specific leadership posts
in the summer and fall exercises and maneuvers. Perhaps reflecting
a realistic evaluation of the Army's combat capability and the need
for small unit training, the tactical ride problems did not deal
with situations calling for large military formations. Even in the
commanders' ride (Führerreise), which was led by the commander-in-
chief, seldom did instruction involve forces of strength greater
than the reinforced infantry division. Zorn could not expect to
participate in the staff ride program until he, like Jodl, had been
accepted into the General Staff training program.

There is no need to describe Ferdinand Jodl's experience during a typical training cycle. Despite the fact that he was an artillery officer and more senior in rank than Zorn, training for him
was conducted along similar lines. From Zorn's experience in the
late Seeckt period, the Reichswehr's training program presents the
appearance of a well-organized system in which winter and summer
training were closely dovetailed. Within a common organizational
framework, instruction began with individual and small unit theoretical and practical work in the winter period and then expanded
progressively to larger field exercises and maneuvers in the summer
and fall months. One year's mistakes were made the subject of the
next year's instruction. Throughout the year's cycle, emphasis remained on the concepts of combined arms tactics in mobile combat
situations. Individual initiative was stressed to encourage freedom of decision within a common framework as well as to maintain a
high degree of motivation (Dienstfreudigkeit).

*   *   *

Although Zorn's experience shows how the system functioned and
what the officers were expected to learn, it does not indicate how
well the officers performed their duties or how effective the program was for the Army as a whole. Like all armies, the Reichswehr
emphasized both individual and unit training. Not only does Zorn's
experience bear this out, it also shows that the Reichswehr training program was pursuing the two fundamental objectives established
by Seeckt at the Army's inception. The new German Army was to be
both an army of leaders (Führerarmee) and a highly mobile shock
force capable of defending the country.[9] Other armies have pursued
similar goals but have not received the acclaim accorded the
Reichswehr. What made its training program particularly outstanding and the subject of widespread admiration?

Certainly one must turn first to Seeckt, who set high standards for individual behavior and unit training efficiency. As a
result, officers were trained in the "mould of Seeckt" that Liddell
Hart describes so eloquently.[10] At the heart of his effort was
what he continually called the "education" (Erziehung) of the officer corps. To Seeckt this included individual technical and tactical proficiency, but character building was its fundamental ingred-
ient. Not surprisingly, character education was as important in
the operational training program as it was in the other programs

analyzed in this study. As he noted in one of his training critiques.

> The most important foundations of an army are its morale
> and its character...The war has shown us what demands are
> to be made on the strength of mind and on the independence
> of single men...The appreciation of technology must not
> make us forget that it is the man who decides and will al-
> ways decide the battle...[11]

The end product was to be the leader capable of assuming responsibility and motivating the men under his command.

The yearly training program critiques that were published
every winter during Seeckt's tenure provide interesting insights
into the Reichswehr's ability to perform its basic mission of national defense. His critiques were based on his own observations
and the branch efficiency reports compiled by the weapons inspectorates. The format, which never varied, consisted of two sections. The first dealt with such topics as education and training,
compliance with regulations, exercise and maneuver experiences,
combat tactical problems, and the role of umpires and critiques in
the training program. The second section contained detailed comments pertinent to each branch of the Army. Although much of this
information clearly came from the reports of the branch inspectors,
Seeckt noted that he incorporated only those observations with
which he agreed. Like most commanders, he used praise sparingly
and directed his attention to the areas requiring improvement.

Three subjects dominated every critique. The first was World
War One. From the critiques it is clear that the First World War,
and especially trench warfare, had a profoundly negative impact on
the German military mind. In Seeckt's view, the four years of war
on the western front were devoid of any type of leadership and had
closed men's minds to individual initiative. Consequently, he felt
compelled to overcome an entire mind-set, and his comments reflect
his emphasis on independent, individual decisions within the broad
framework of the regulations.

In his 1921 report, for example, he flatly condemned what he
called schema, or stereotyped reactions to tactical situations. He
had observed this tendency even in small units. The key to over-
coming this pattern of thinking was concentration on mobile warfare
and "mental elasticity."[12] Regulations were to guide, not to
rule. In every critique he stressed the need for officers to use
their imaginations and to free their minds from set-piece responses. In 1924 he declared typically that "it is of fundamental
importance that our subordinate leaders be trained to think and to
act independently."[13] Only after the 1925 training year had ended,
however, could he conclude that "the field maneuver proved that we
are succeeding in freeing the Army from the chains of position
warfare under which it is still laboring."[14] Seeckt's unflinching
battle against mental formalism must be considered one of his
greatest contributions to the military education of the officer
corps.

In an even more positive sense, Seeckt was also determined to

apply the war's relevant technical and tactical lessons to the
Reichswehr and to his conception of future warfare. Indeed, his
critiques are infused with the concepts that later became hallmarks
of the German Army. Mobile or movement warfare was made the characteristic form of combat training. Reflecting on the Reichswehr's
handicaps, Seeckt repeatedly stated that mobility was the "prime
requirement" of the Army.[15] If mobile warfare was the Army's characteristic form of training, combined arms operations was its chief
expression. This was particularly evident in the emphasis placed
on liaison between infantry and artillery elements and the appreciation of the increased role of firepower in all combat situations.
As Seeckt stated in 1921 and repeated many times thereafter, "the
key purpose of maneuvers is training in the combined arms."[16] The
concepts of mobile warfare and combined arms operations, of course,
were important not only for the Reichswehr, but the future Wehrmacht as well.

Seeckt's second major concern in the critiques was realism in
the training program. Generally speaking, all military training in
peacetime is artificial because leaders can only assume how the
next war will be fought, and must make concessions to the civilian
world in which the army trains. The Reichswehr's situation was
made more difficult by the Treaty provisions. Live ammunition often could not be used because it was in short supply, while enemy
forces normally had to be "represented" by flag troops and modern
equipment by "mock-ups." The danger here was that Seeckt's emphasis on free minds and mental elasticity would produce training conditions that bore no relation to what could be expected in wartime. For instance, although problems involving the use of tanks
and aircraft were always included in combat situations, they were
too often worked without proper appreciation of the capabilities of
the weapons. Because the Reichswehr had neither weapon, their "represented" deployments were often judged to be erroneous. Too much
imagination clearly could be harmful. Seeckt was well aware of
this danger and continually criticized tactical problems that assumed too much and were patently unrealistic.

Closely related to the problem of artificial training conditions was the ever-present concern for morale and motivation. Re-
petitious, artifical training tends to be boring and a threat to
morale and motivation. Seeckt's priority on mental elasticity and
individual initiative was one means of attacking the weakness.
Another was his stress on realism in the program and his constant
appeal to the patriotism of the individual officer and enlisted
man. In terms of specific measures, he also encouraged fewer drill
periods and inspections and a reduction in the physical requirements during exercises and maneuvers.

The third theme that emerged from the Seeckt critiques was the
state of training in the separate branches and his approach to modern warfare. It is in the realm of modern weapons and technical
developments that Seeckt, particularly during his later years as
commander-in-chief, has been criticized -- by Heinz Guderian, among
others -- for unprogressive thought. It must be said, however,
that his remarks in the critiques do not completely justify this
criticism. His comments regarding the technical branches reveal a

realistic sense of their importance for the Army. In his view, the officers and their units had to be trained thoroughly in the technical requirements of their work before tactical proficiency could be developed. Above all he demanded that they be trained by the infantry as combat troops and made a part of all exercises and maneuvers. Seeckt was never satisfied with the progress of the technical arms and, not surprisingly, he paid more attention to them in the critiques than he did the main branches.

Seeckt's evaluation of the role of the tank and airplane shows that his mind was open, yet skeptical about the future of these weapons. It should be remembered that in the decade following the war there was no universally accepted doctrine governing their use. Seeckt's Army, perhaps reflecting contemporary fear of the airplane's effectiveness and mindful of its own lack of an air arm, only trained against "supposed" enemy air attacks. All exercises included air defense (Luftschutz) measures, and each division was responsible for conducting a yearly air defense study.

Although dummy tanks were also included in all exercises and defensive tactics against tanks were considered very important, the slow speed and vulnerability of the tank could hardly be expected to convince Seeckt that this weapon would ever be anything but an adjunct to the infantry. Nevertheless, the Army during Seeckt's tenure always published the latest foreign studies on the development and employment of tanks, and officers like Oswald Lutz and Guderian were permitted to pursue their own ideas on the role of the tank, although it is true that the Reichswehr's faith in combined arms tactics would mean that later Guderian's conception of an independent armored force would encounter strong opposition.

Regarding the cavalry, a branch oriented to the past rather than the future, Seeckt was ambiguous. Even though he admitted that "the bullet is faster than the horse" and in open ranks formation attacks against any force other than opposing cavalry were a thing of the past, he could still contend that the mounted attack was here to stay. He seemed convinced that the cavalry's traditional advantages of mobility, surprise, and the ability to alter operations rapidly could still be useful because of its increased firepower. He even went so far as to state that "I do not demand as much from any other arm as from the cavalry."[17]

Seeckt, for a commander of his time and of an Army with the Reichswehr's limitations, appears to have been progressive and well aware of the impact of modern technology on warfare. His emphasis on morale and character revealed a concern for the timeless virtues promoted by all military leaders, while his concepts of mobile warfare and combined arms tactics demonstrated an appreciation of the Reichswehr's operational situation in the postwar world. Because of their importance in the future Wehrmacht, Seeckt must also be credited with farsightedness.

On the other hand, a focus on strategic concepts was largely absent from the training program. As he said flatly in 1926, "operations with mixed troops on the terrain must not be concerned with large tactical or strategical considerations."[18] More than likely, his disdain for strategic problems in training scenarios is explained by the need to ground the units thoroughly in tactics as well as the Reichswehr's inability to mount successful strategic offensive operations.

Although Seeckt's Reichswehr appears to have applied the lessons of the war in a realistic manner, it is significant that many of his most important criticisms reoccur throughout the critiques. Despite his occasional words of praise and the favorable comments of foreign observers, there is good reason to believe that Seeckt's disappointment reflected major and continuing weaknesses in the state of the Army's individual and unit training programs. The problems centered on the Reichswehr's inability to set its yearly training sights higher than the individual and the small unit.

In 1921, for example, the goal was to establish organized formations in the divisions, and this objective was achieved. In that year's review, Seeckt stated that until late 1922 emphasis should be on individual instruction to overcome difficulties in unit training. Yet, in the 1922 critique it was clear that the situation remained unsatisfactory because Seeckt declared that training should continue to stress individual proficiency and proficiency in the units "from the bottom up." The following year he was forced to admit that, despite some progress, the goals still had not been entirely achieved. In particular, junior officers continued to require much improvement in combined arms training, a deficiency he attributed to the political turmoil that had interrupted routine troop training. For 1924, emphasis again was to be on individual training and combined arms instruction in the smallest units. In the 1925 critique, Seeckt's last, he declared that the responsibilities of the individual, especially in the area of independence of action, must be increased.

It is apparent that throughout the Seeckt period the Army's most important training objectives were individual and small unit proficiency. Although exercises and maneuvers were held as a matter of course, priority remained on the individual and the small unit. Evidently Seeckt was never satisfied that the individual Reichswehr soldier had mastered the basic training associated with his own arm and the concept of combined arms in small unit formations. His overriding concern with fundamental instruction suggests that the general state of the Reichswehr as a combat-ready force was not encouraging.

*   *   *

By the time that Eduard Zorn entered the officer corps, the contradictory nature of the Reichswehr's mission could no longer be overlooked. Officer leadership training posed a threat to unit effectiveness and, by extension, to the combat efficiency of the Army. Field units complained that they had too few officers available to accomplish the many tasks required of them. The seriousness of the problem precipitated a major debate within the Reichswehr hierarchy which resulted in a reorganization of the training program and a reevaluation of the Reichswehr as a professional force.

At the heart of the issue was the problem of detached duty (Abkommandierung). There is no question that this problem was genuine and a major source of friction throughout the Army. Seeckt's response to the dilemma in the summer of 1924 showed that by this time it had reached crisis proportions and demanded a radical solution:

> Frequent complaints from various officers within the Defense Ministry attest to the fact that the officer corps in the field units [Truppenteile] is no longer in a position to accomplish the varied tasks presently required of it. The number of officers serving at the Front is so limited that the officers available either forego important work altogether or devote insufficient time to their duties.[19]

Seeckt's solution was to have senior NCOs do the work previously done by officers. Because the number of NCOs was not considered sufficient, however, junior enlisted men would have to assume the duties of NCOs.

Seeckt's comments are significant because they further understanding of the Reichswehr's conception of leadership training. Rabenau was correct, in part, when he stated that the Reichswehr initiated training in higher levels of responsibility in order to combat boredom and produce an army of leaders. Such training, the high command believed, would provide the cadre force for a future expanded army. But if this type of leadership training was Army policy, it is also apparent that the Reichswehr had no choice but to follow this course of action. In other words, the impetus for the training was not as positive as Rabenau has asserted. The Abkommandierung problem dictated that all personnel must be trained for higher leadership positions if the Army expected to field an effective combat force. If Seeckt was determined to train an army of leaders for the future, he was also motivated by the realities surrounding the small professional army.

The comment in September 1924 by Major General Kress on the significance of the Abkommandierung problem for the Bavarian division provides a sound assessment of the difficulties experienced in the Reichswehr's training program:

> The deficiences evident in the unit strength reports are known to the District Command. They are a natural consequence of a small army and the fact that the training of junior officers has been neglected for so long...Furthermore, they are a consequence of a leader army which requires officers to be trained in as many different areas as possible.[20]

Kress affirmed that the most severe problem was the large number of required training courses that drew so many officers from their assigned duties in the field units.

It is difficult to determine how frequently and for what length of time officers were absent from their units. The Rangliste seldom shows detached duty assignments, and the unit training records are incomplete. But from the list of courses presented in appendix 8, table 1, it must be recognized that the number of officers affected was substantial. Reichswehr policy at this time, of course, was to send all officers to as many courses as possible. Significantly, not every course was designed for advanced or specialist training. Ferdinand Jodl, for example, attended a basic artillery course in 1924. His experience was similar to that of many junior officers who, because of wartime necessity, had never attended the basic weapons course for their branch. Before they could take advantage of the advanced courses, they had to be schooled in the fundamentals of their branch. Not until the middle of 1927 were the basic courses finally discontinued.

In effect, throughout most of the Seeckt years the units labored under the burden of an Abkommandierung problem that severely limited the effectiveness of combat training in large formations. By 1925 Seeckt could no longer ignore the situation, and in August of that year he announced that henceforth the frequency of courses and the number of officers attending them would be reduced:

> From now on a whole series of courses will be held every other year. In order to keep the highest number of officers in the field units, only such classes will be required which are essential for the education and advanced training of suitably qualified instructor personnel.[21]

Units were instructed to contact the Defense Ministry if the absence of officers became unbearable and replacements could not be found within the battalions. Considering the fact that each district conducted its own series of training courses and that even normal duty absences could hamper unit training, the Abkommandierung problem assumes added significance. It is difficult, therefore, to agree with the judgment that the problem of officer absences was only a temporary phenomenon.[22]

The Abkommandierung situation illustrates the contradictions in the Reichswehr's training program. Training was designed to provide both an effective combat force in time of war and corps of leaders whose comprehensive, individual training would enable them to assume greater responsibilities in a future army. But in attempting to achieve the latter goal, the Reichswehr threatened to destroy its credibility as a combat-ready army. Under the Seeckt training program, there seemed to be no way that both objectives could be achieved satisfactorily. Seeckt's August 1925 message concerning training courses was an indication that the Reichswehr was increasingly required to reassess its competing training objectives. At the same time, Germany's domestic situation and its role in the international arena were changing and influential senior officers were arguing that the training program should be adjusted to reflect these new conditions. Their proposal, which involved a comprehensive reorganization of officer and enlisted men training, affected the very nature of a professional army in Weimar Germany.

*   *   *

The crucial 1926 debate on training has not received the attention it deserves. Few scholars have discussed it, and those that have fail to emphasize the significance of the decisions taken. The problem was first described in Rabenau's biography of Seeckt, and authors writing later have followed his lead. Rabenau has noted that Seeckt was always concerned about the monotony and artificial nature of training which, he believed, threatened to destroy the motivation of the troops and limit the Army's combat capability. Apparently, in the early years an attempt was made to divide the training period for enlisted men into stages. This was considered preferable at a time the Reichswehr was admitting recruits of widely varied competence. By 1925-1926, however, the Army was beyond its initial organizational problems, many enlisted troops were halfway through their service career, and Seeckt and others believed that changes were necessary to make training more meaningful for both the officer and the long-serving enlisted man. Although mention was made of a type of two-year program established at this time, it is not clear precisely what, if any, program was discussed or implemented.

Throughout late 1925 and much of 1926 discussion of the training program continued. Although the eventual decision was made after Seeckt left office, his biographer contends that it was due to Seeckt's initiative. If this is correct, the outcome of the review would hardly have pleased its initiator. Indeed, the changes resulted in a new view of the Reichswehr's mission and its role in the Weimar Republic.[23]

The key document in this controversy is the memorandum of November 6, 1926, which was prepared by the Truppenamt's Organization Branch (T2). At issue was the type of training program most suitable for a professional army serving a republican, democratic government.[24] The document and the circumstances surrounding it are worth examining in detail. The authors viewed the Reichswehr's history from the end of the war to 1926 as a transitional period. They concluded that the Army, faced with difficult foreign and domestic problems, had developed in a very brief time into a capable force which based its field training program on experiences of the First World War. Because of the constant need for combat readiness during these years, the difficulties associated with the professional force, particularly the "true character of the twelve-year service obligation," were relegated to the background.[25]

But in recent months circumstances had altered the situation in a fundamental sense. Cited were international developments, including the Locarno treaties, Germany's entry into the League of Nations, and the country's improved economic position. As a result, they said, the German public no longer considered desirable a military solution to national problems, and the earlier reliance on force of arms had disappeared:

> In its place stands the reality of the inexorable constraint of the twelve-year service obligation, which is having a growing impact in all areas of the German Army. Obviously, we stand at a turning point. The time of transition is over, the time of the new army, the professional army with the twelve-year obligation, has begun...[26]

The authors believed that more could be done to improve peacetime training for the individual without sacrificing the Reichswehr's combat effectiveness, although they admitted that, even if the proposed changes satisfied present conditions, the Reichswehr still had to overcome the "impossible constitution through a reduction of the service commitment, an increase in the size of the officer corps, and a military system better suited to the national character."[27]

This memorandum was much more than an obscure position paper produced by a few junior officers in the Defense Ministry. It was the subject of a major conference held in Berlin on November 8 and attended by the division commanders and other senior officers. The significance of the Army's review of training lies not only in the fact that an important segment of the high command considered the program ineffective. It was also a result of the Reichswehr's belief that changes were required because of the new domestic and foreign political conditions. It would be a mistake to view this review only from the narrow military perspective of an attempt to improve training. Rather, it was closely related to the Reichswehr's military-political policies undergoing review at precisely the same time. Training, in fact, was an important element in what has been termed Heye's "New Course," or the "Move to the Left." Heye and his key subordinates were prepared to end the Reichswehr's isolation and work more closely with the government of the Republic. If they meant to do this on their own terms, as the Reichswehr's critics suggest, they were also ready to change the Army to conform to these new conditions.[28]

In December 1926, for example, Schleicher, who was the driving force behind this new political course in the Army, circulated among key departments within the Defense Ministry a memorandum proposing that the Army work closely with a Republic which, he argued, was here to stay. By doing so, the military could better achieve the objectives it set for itself. A few weeks later, furthermore, the Reichswehr leaders agreed to cooperate with the government on the financing of illegal rearmament and mobilization activities that it had pursued independently since 1925. From these developments, it is clear that Seeckt's departure had opened the way to "reform" from within the Army.[29]

As noted earlier, in late 1926 the Army also faced a dangerous attack from its political opponents in the Reichstag, one that ironically came at exactly the time that Reichswehr leaders were inclined to cooperate with the Republic. Never again during the Weimar period would the Army be so inclined. But if the New Course never fulfilled its promise, the changes it brought were significant. This study has shown that Heye's policies were more than refinements implemented by a caretaker for Seeckt or a stopgap regime on the road to the Wehrmacht. His regime was a watershed in the history of the Reichswehr and the Republic because it marked the end of the Army's isolation from the Republic it had heretofore never condoned. Especially in the military sphere, Heye's New Course resulted in a military training program that more realistically reflected the problems facing a small professional army in Weimar Germany, while at the same time it provided the framework necessary for planning the army of the future.

During these years military observers of the Reichswehr's maneuvers were impressed by the spirit, morale, tactial efficiency,
and the ability of the Army to accept new ideas and employ them in-
telligently in its training.   Nonetheless, if the Reichswehr was
prepared to fight a modern war mentally, it remained woefully weak
in men and equipment. Heye, like Seeckt before him, could do little to change this situation. On the other hand, it is doubtful
that a combat-ready force was his major objective at this time because his program argued against this. Heye's purpose was to raise
the level of proficiency by extending the yearly program to three
years and conducting training in progressively more difficult stages. Such a program was well-suited to a professional army with a
long service commitment.   The depth of training knowledge and experience was to be complemented by a new cohesiveness in the units
which would suffer less from frequent absences of their leaders.
Along with this, the Heye Reichswehr would be come a skeleton army
in a double meaning. Leaders would continue to be trained as cadre
for the future national army, while, at the same time, the three-
year program would provide an organizational framework for the experimentation and adoption of new equipment and tactical formations.   The new organizational framework also was ideally suited
for an illegal mobilization and rearmament program that required
time as well as money. Because of the improved domestic and international conditions, Heye, unlike Seeckt, could afford to gamble on
a lengthy developmental training program.

*   *   *

It is not known when the final decision to restructure the
Reichswehr's training program was made. Following the Berlin meeting, Heye's political difficulties, his efforts to assemble his own
team in the Defense Ministry, and the need for careful study of the
probable effects of the proposed changes all argued against hasty
action.   A lengthy review of operational training, furthermore,
would tend to reduce internal opposition and better prepare the Army for the new system. By the late summer of 1927 the review was
completed, and on September 1 the new program was published in regulation form as "Instructions for Training in the Forthcoming
Years" (Richtlinien fur die Ausbildung der Nächsten Jahre).   The
"Instructions," which described all facets of individual and unit
training, represented a major break with past training and deserve
to be discussed in some detail.[30]
The new regulation was a comprehensive, thirteen-page document, which was supplemented by several lengthy appendixes dealing
with specific categories of training. Heye's plan established a
three-year intensive training program, which was scheduled to begin
on April 1, 1928 and terminate on March 31, 1931. As he noted, the
new plan was required because individual and unit responsibilities
required several years of intensive training. Heye first described
the principles that governed the new plan. Above all, the focus
would be on the "education of the personality" (Erziehung zur Per-
sönlichkeit), the general character-building effort that Seeckt had
initiated and now Heye was determined to continue. Individual com-

manders were responsible for developing their own training plans within the general guidelines, and higher headquarters would inter- fere only in cases of financial stringency or when the uniformity of training was endangered.

The training of the field troops was of the utmost importance, and stability had to be the guiding objective. The main effort would be to keep the highest number of officers in the field units at all times. Because at present junior officers did not have enough uninterrupted time at the "Front," instructional courses and exercises would not be conducted at the expense of troop training. Each individual had to be challenged to reach the highest limit of his personal potential as a leader. In this regard, the goal would be the thoroughness rather than the extent of knowledge. Challeng- ing training could not be limited to the officer corps. Indeed, because of the continuing shortage of field officers in the small army, NCOs would still be required to assume officer responsibil- ites. Regimental commanders would continue to play a central role in training and were responsible for balancing the competing inter- ests in the program.

The thrust of Heye's plan was organizational, and it is in the organizational structure of the new program that his changes are best seen. Three levels of training were discussed. First was in- dividual training. Enlisted men and NCOs were to be assigned to classes and would progress through various leader and instructor- oriented schools. Officers would serve as instructors. The second level of training was "outline" (Rahmen) or skeleton organizational training in which the imagination of the leaders was to be develop- ed by training in understrength units. This level would serve as a transitional stage from individual to formation training in various types of combined arms units. Heye distinguished between annual and biannual training goals for each of the three levels.

The most intriguing part of the new plan was the section on general education. Heye declared that general education and in- struction were to be emphasized much more than had been the case previously. "In a professional army," he said, "education, espec- ially in the area of personality development, must replace drill as the primary method of character building." As he further noted, "general education is not only beneficial preparation for civilian life, it is valuable in itself and necessary if military training is to be meaningful." Heye's emphasis on significant training was also evident in the sections on the separate arms, where he stressed the importance of realism in combat training, combined arms tactics, and motivational instruction.

But at this point it is fair to question the Reichswehr's ability to field a combat-effective force while simultaneously en- gaged in an intensive, incremental three-year developmental pro- gram. Although Heye repeatedly stated that combat capability would not be impaired, it must be assumed that the success of Strese- mann's foreign policy and favorable domestic conditions encouraged the Reichswehr to risk the three-year training program.

*   *   *

How did Heye's plan work in practice? Here it is best to focus on the major categories of training, beginning with winter
training. The training cycle was adjusted to conform to the government's budget year (April 1 to March 31), but the existing division into winter and summer training was left unchanged. Zorn, for
example, would have experienced the same type of winter training
during 1928-1929 that he did the first winter of his career in the
officer corps. On the other hand, he would have noted that technology was receiving more emphasis and training was far more intensive. Although the objectives were fewer in number, sufficient
time was not available to achieve them.

Within the Defense Ministry, winter training centered more on
strategic problems under Blomberg's supervision than had been the
case during the Seeckt years. These problems were of two kinds,
war games performed by officers assigned to the Defense Ministry
and strategic or operational lessons (operative Aufgaben) required
of General Staff officers stationed in the field units. The Defense Ministry problems reflected not only the growing importance
of technology in the Reichswehr, but Blomberg's demand for imaginative tactical and strategic thinking from his officers.[31] With a
man of Blomberg's inclination commanding the Truppenamt, it is not
surprising to find more flexibility and realism in the operational
planning for a small army with limited means. This trend continued
throughout the Heye period. As Gaines Post has indicated, the Heye
years showed increased cooperation between Reichswehr officers and
foreign office officials in the military-political area of strategic planning. This, too, was a part of Heye's New Course.[32]

The three-year plan also included the three major categories
of training that were a part of the Seeckt training program: instructional courses, tactical rides, and exercises and maneuvers.
Heye's directives on instructional courses were designed not only
to maximize individual training but to solve the old Abkommandierung problem. Already in May 1927 he had issued an order limiting
the number of officers subject to detached duty to one-eighth of
the total number of officers in the unit.[33] In the "Instructions"
he cautioned that, despite increasing technical specialization,
theory was not to replace the practical application of knowledge in
the field units. Only those courses would be held which offered
something new, especially in the field of technology and weapons
prohibited to the Army, and which could not be administered in the
units themselves. The idea was to continue the change made during
Seeckt's final year of training instructors for the units rather
than training every unit officer. Junior officers, in particular,
were to be sent to the courses dealing with technical subjects. In
order to ease the burden on the units, most courses were to be compressed into a three-month period during winter training.

Whether Heye's plan dealt effectively with the Abkommandierung
problem must remain unanswered. To be sure, the number of officers
attending courses yearly was certainly less and the burden on the
units more bearable. Yet, as appendix 8, table 3 shows, the number
of courses and officers affected for 1928-1929 was still substantial, and this listing includes neither the sixteen optional courses that were offered the same year nor those conducted in each of

the divisions. Furthermore, despite Heye's intention, the courses were not confined to a single three-month period. Although a number of courses were shortened or cancelled during the three years, others were added because of the technical and organizational changes that occurred after 1927. On balance, Heye appears to have achieved only limited success in his attempt to solve the Abkommandierung dilemma.

This problem was also a factor in the second major area of training, the tactical ride program. Heye stated the detached duty for this program must not interrupt field training. Specifically, no company, battery, or squadron commander was to participate during the first year of his assignment. In general, the three-year staff ride program followed the same pattern evident in the Seeckt years. Most rides took place during the spring months, and tactics was the main focus of instruction (see appendix 8, table 4). In this area of training, Heye's changes are best seen in the addition of several supply and technical rides and in the reduction of the number of rides required yearly. If the program showed no major changes, it was nevertheless more flexible and better organized and administered than the Seeckt programs.

The third category of training consisted of exercises and maneuvers, and this was the most elaborately organized section of the plan. The exercises and maneuvers were designed for five types of units, and every unit at each level underwent training according to specific objectives that were made progressively more difficult every year. For the fall maneuvers, the two Group Comands alternated responsibilities. The three-year exercise and maneuver program culminated in the 1930 grand maneuver (Grosse Rahmen Übung), in which every type of unit in the Reichswehr took part. Heye led this maneuver, which was the largest field maneuver held in the Reichswehr's history. Although the leaders called the maneuver a great success, the correspondent for the Militär-Wochenblatt was less enthusiastic. He observed that, despite the fact that valuable training in directing large tactical formations was achieved, a skeleton exercise, no matter how large, could not take the place of full-strength field formations.[34] However, he neglected to concede that the Reichswehr could not hope to field full-strength maneuver forces on such a scale as long as the Treaty provisions were in effect. At least Heye experimented with larger organizational units and challenged the leadership cadre that might one day expect to direct large, full-strength formations.

Not only did the three-year plan call for training in larger tactical formations, it also provided for a greater technical orientation under Blomberg. Several technical branches underwent major organizational changes, and the horse-drawn supply corps was even disbanded entirely. Test units appeared to allow the experimentation with new artillery equipment and the use of tanks, and Heye specifically stated that a technical branch assignment should in no way damage an officer's career. Although the lack of modern equipment remained a severe training handicap, the Army's technical studies and experiments kept it mentally fresh and in the forefront of contemporary military thought. This was an important professional and motivational facet of the Reichswehr's training program, as well as a vital development for the future.

If Heye's regime must be recognized for its tactical and technical progress, it must also be cited for its awareness that too much emphasis on tactics and technology could prove harmful. The danger of an exclusively tactical orientation was discussed earlier in this study. Despite Heye's determination to encourage general education and expand the mental horizons of the officer corps, the danger was great that a small army that realistically could only perform tactical field training would produce an officer corps with a narrow military outlook. This certainly explains Blomberg's concern with strategic problems during winter training.

Moreover, in one area an attempt was made to provide outstanding junior officers with a better appreciation of the military's relationship with the wider world. This intriguing experiment was the so-called "Reinhardt Course," the brainchild of General Walther Reinhardt (ret.), who was strongly supported by Heye and Defense Minister Otto Gessler. From 1928-1931, twelve of the best young minds in the Reichswehr assembled each year at the University of Berlin for instruction that centered on liberal arts subjects and their importance for the military. Among the professors was Theodor Heuss, the prominent educator and politician, whose later recollections reveal a strong commitment to this type of training for military leaders.[35]

Despite the promise that this kind of broad, general educational training offered, its impact on the Army was slight. Obviously, the small number of junior officers could hardly be expected to make a significant impact on the force at this stage in their careers. The program, in addition, was under constant attack from Defense Minister Groener and others who opposed it because of personal animosity toward Reinhardt or skepticism regarding the value of such training at a time of growing economic hardship. Reinhardt himself died shortly after initiating the course, and when the Heye team departed opponents gained the upper hand and soon eliminated the program.

The other means by which the Army might have broadened the general perspective of its officer corps was university education leading to advanced degrees. Even though a number of officers, including future Wehrmacht general Hans Speidel, earned Ph.D.'s during the Weimar period, the Reichswehr apparently had no organized program to send selected officers for advanced degree training.[36]

Although the Reinhardt Course was a commendable attempt to provide much needed liberal educational training, neither it nor an unsupported higher degree program could prevail against the current belief in the overriding importance of tactical training. Indeed, despite Heye's interest in the non-technical area of education and training, he offered generalizations but did not specify how liberal education was to be implemented in the officer training program. Certainly the non-technical officer courses of these years show little if any change in number and content. In practice, his changes to the training program consisted of organizational modifications, which help explain the increasingly important role of tactics and technology in officer training during the Heye years. The exercises and maneuvers held during the three years of Heye's

plan were designed to test the tactical and technical readiness of
the Army for combat. All of the concepts that were noted during
the Seeckt period -- mobility, combined arms tactics, speed, and
rapid decision-making --were practiced under Heye's leadership.
Especially in the areas of artillery and motorization, the new developments were absorbed into the training program and made a part
of the Reichswehr's approach to war.

On balance, there is no doubt that the Heye training program
was a significant phase in the Reichswehr's development. Of the
various attempts to create a realistic training program, it came
closest to balancing the competing objectives pursued by the small,
professional army. When Heye retired in October 1930, six months
before the three-year plan was completed, he left behind a better
trained Reichswehr, which his successors were determined to point
in the direction of military expansion and political intrigue.

                *   *   *

On the surface, the Reichswehr's training program appears to
have changed very little during the two years preceding Hitler's
appointment. Hammerstein, the new commander-in-chief, retained the
same yearly cycle of winter and summer training. The instructional
courses, tactical rides, and exercises and maneuvers for this period show that, on the whole, the subject matter remained unchanged.[37] On closer inspection, however, training in the Reichswehr
had altered significatntly. Training messages for 1931 and 1932
described the need for "war strength" units in exercises and for
more night operations and forced marches. Intensive training in
the fundamentals of individual and small unit combat had to be
stressed, and leadership training stepped up in all units. Furthermore, the problem of dealing with Communist unrest was made the
focal point of training throughout the Army.

In effect, the entire training program seems to have been adjusted to provide rapid and effective response in the event of an
imminent crisis. Less attention was directed to intensive, long-
term training and more to immediate readiness training. Gone were
the days of relative peace and security of the Heye years. Once
again, as in the Seeckt period, the Reichswehr seemed to be functioning as an emergency force faced with impending conflict. Under
these circumstances Hammerstein reverted to the all-inclusive one-
year training program with its objective of maximum effectiveness.

Details on the transition from Heye's three-year program to
the yearly plans of 1931 and 1932 are very sketchy. Nevertheless,
by analyzing certain key events and personalities, it is possible
to construct a reasonable explanation not only for the change but
also for the state of the training program and the condition of
the Reichswehr itself during these years.

Part of the explanation must lie in the realm of personalities. The change of command in 1930-1931 brought to prominence the
so-called Schleicher clique, which included the new commander-in-
chief. These men had never admired or trusted Heye, and it was unlikely that they had as much faith in the three-year program. Although his efforts to cooperate with the Republic were not entirely

unwelcome to them, he wanted to work with the existing government, not change it to meet the demands of certain influential military officers and politicians. Heye's critics also could not but be alarmed by the growing dissension in the officer corps. His well-known penchant for cavorting with enlisted men, as well as the changes he introduced in many areas, seemed to threaten the discipline and homogeneity so carefully nurtured by Seeckt.

Although Heye's authority declined almost from the beginning of his term in office, clearly it resulted more from organizational and personnel changes within the Defense Ministry than internal dissension in the field units. For example, Schleicher's control of the newly-created Ministeramt in early 1929 meant that a type of undersecretary stood between the Defense Minister and Heye, which the latter deeply resented. Moreover, from 1928, when Groener replaced Gessler as Defense Minister, Heye was subjected to steady inroads into his tradtional areas of responsibility. Groener, for one, was in the habit of conducting inspections of field unit facilities and demanding responses from Heye when conditions appeared substandard. As Gordon Craig has pointed out, Groener was also accorded the unique privilege of criticizing the fall field maneuvers. Such measures did nothing to enhance Heye's prestige and authority in the officer corps.[38]

By the end of 1929, Heye's two chief subordinates had been transferred. In October Stülpnagel left the Personnel Office and, thoroughly disillusioned, retired prematurely.[39] In the same month, Blomberg was exiled to East Prussia after receiving shoddy treatment that left him permanently embittered.[40] Heye followed them a year later. As a military officer in the more traditional mold, he had little taste for political intrigue and could hardly be expected to participate in the creation of Schleicher's presidential disctatorship supported by a praetorian guard Reichswehr. Neither Heye nor his three-year training program was considered appropriate for an Army facing an alarming internal political and economic crisis.

The clash of personalities during a period of internal strife was certainly one reason for the change to a yearly training program emphasizing constant readiness. Equally important was the mobilization and rearmament factor. The three-year program, among other things, was designed to prepare the Reichswehr for future expansion. By all accounts, Heye's plan had done much to fulfill this purpose, and the new leaders believed that immediate expansion could and must be achieved.[41]

Although Germany's efforts to gain an international equality of forces agreement were finally rewarded in December 1932, a unilateral decision to expand the Army had been made long before. In April 1930, the mobilization plan calling for a peacetime establishment of twenty-one infantry divisions was adopted, and in January 1932 Hammerstein set April 1, 1933 as the target date.[42] Clearly Army leaders were convinced that the seriousness of the situation facing the Reichswehr from within and without justified the risks associated with expansion. Indeed, such a violation of the Versailles Treaty would either expose Germany to foreign intervention or, at the very least, produce a governmental crisis.

Internally, the crisis was already at hand as the growing political radicalization and economic misery threatened to shatter the weak fabric of Weimar society. Now the Reichswehr could no longer enjoy the luxury of a long-term developmental training program suited to a professional army looking to a nebulous future threat. The Army had to be ready for immediate action, and the training program amended accordingly. Consequently, Hammerstein felt compelled to introduce a training program designed for immediate combat readiness.

The effectiveness of the new yearly plans cannot be determined because the Army was never used in a military capacity. Rather, it served as a political instrument in the internal struggle for power. Even the Ott Plan was politically motivated and used to buttress Schleicher's claim to the chancellorship. It was hardly a reliable indication of the Reichswehr's ability to perform in combat. Although by late 1932 the Army was clearly suffering from disunity, this seems to have been more the result of the political-military machinations than the friction created by Heye's attempt to make the professional Reichswehr a professional army in fact as well as in theory.

*   *   *

During the Weimar years, the Reichswehr's training programs reflected the policies pursued by its three commanders. Under Seeckt, training emphasized combat readiness and established the groundwork for a superbly trained cadre of officers capable of serving an expanded army. Hammerstein also stressed immediate readiness while moving rapidly toward expansion. Heye's Reichswehr served as a bridge between the two. Given the good fortune of more stable internal and foreign conditions, he adopted a developmental program that realistically pursued the objectives of challenging individual leadership training and progressive tactical and technical proficiency.

Because the Heye program conformed more to contemporary needs, yet prepared the Army for the future, it was uniquely suited to the limitations and advantages of the professional army in the Weimar Republic. If favorable conditions account for much of Heye's success, he nevertheless took advantage of the opportunities and maintained his program in the face of significant opposition. The importance of his three-year program cannot be overestimated. When one searches for the keys to the future Wehrmacht's outstanding corps of officers, one cannot merely refer to the period of growth under Seeckt. Indeed, the Heye era served as the real bridge between the past and the future.

9.
Conclusion

From the outset, the Versailles Treaty's provisions affecting the Reichswehr's size, organization, and composition created an artificial situation. Not only was the small professional force an alien institution in the eyes of many Germans, it was also an Army that did not reflect a realistic assessment of Weimar Germany's requirements for national defense. Moreover, it was given little or no prospect of legally altering the situation in the future.

Nevertheless, if external forces were primarily responsible for limiting the Reichswehr's freedom of action, its own leaders' response to these conditions compounded the Army's inability to perform as an effective military force. By attempting to achieve two fundamental missions simultaneously, it severely weakened the chances of fulfilling either one satisfactorily. The objectives of the elite, mobile shock force were different from those of the cadre army. The former had to contend with the existing military threat and emphasize stability in unit training for officers and "other ranks." A cadre force of leaders, on the other hand, set its sights more on the education and training of the individual and weapons, equipment, and doctrine applicable to future conditions. In an army like the Reichswehr, which was forced to operate within an artificial framework, these objectives were not only competing but contradictory. For ten long years the Reichswehr attempted to balance its contradictory goals before admitting defeat, and its accomplishments, despite ultimate failure, were remarkable.

Herbert Rosinski, who produced the first major study of the German Army, argued that "the Reichswehr lived in the past and the future and not in present. It was rooted in the cult of the Old Army, living for the new nation which was to be."[1] His view of the Reichswehr has received widespread support ever since the publication of his book in 1940. Admittedly, if the Reichswehr's political relationship with the Republic is the focus of attention, Rosinski's charge has merit. The officer corps was composed largely of former Imperial Army officers who felt little love for Weimar and looked forward to the day when Germany would once again field a national conscript army to replace the small professional force that had been imposed from without.

On the other hand, this study of the Reichswehr officer's career structure has shown that Weimar's professional army lived very much in the present. However much the leaders found the Republic and the Reichswehr's constraints distasteful, it operated largely within the framework established by the Versailles Treaty. To be sure, the Army engaged in clandestine operations that technically violated certain provisions of the Treaty. Developmental programs abroad, most notably the Russian connection, as well as various border defense measures were pursued throughout the Reichswehr's existence. These activities are well-known and have been discussed in this study and elsewhere. Yet, most scholars have overstated the importance of such violations to the Reichswehr. Most officers had very little, if any, direct connection with these activities, and it is doubtful if many in the higher echelons took them seriously. Throughout the period illegal operations remained peripheral to the Army's basic work of education and training in the performance of its missions. Indeed, the striking fact is that, for the most part, the Reichswehr functioned within rather than outside the Versailles system.

In the selection of officer candidates, for example, the number of recruits was determined primarily by the number of projected vacancies in the officer corps. Selection criteria were demanding and the leaders did not compromise its objective of quality by admitting candidates who could not meet the high educational, performance, and character standards. Even during the early years when qualified recruits were in short supply, Seeckt preferred to accept fewer than the desired number rather than endanger the quality of the officer corps. Furthermore, never did the Reichswehr seek to admit an excessive number of candidates in order to create a clandestine reserve force. On the contrary, the high command chose to implement a lengthly officer candidate training program that would provide the officer corps a relatively small, yet extremely well-trained, number of replacements. Army leaders realized that rapid turnover of officer personnel would not only invite foreign reprisal but would also de-stabilize the force structure and produce continual friction within the officer corps.

Likewise, the selection of General Staff candidates was managed within the framework of the limitations imposed on the Army. Although one can look back from the perspective of the Wehrmacht period and note that the expanded army was able to draw on officers who had some General Staff training during the Weimar period, the Reichswehr at no time attempted to create a reserve of General Staff officers for the future. Rather, the number of candidates, as in the prewar army, was determined by the size of the force. Although the Seeckt years witnessed an overabundance of candidates, as the "Year of Practice" demonstrated, this problem was corrected by Heye, and thereafter the number of candidates rigidly conformed to the needs of the small professional army. A five and one-half year General Staff training program does not suggest that the priority was to produce a large number of General Staff officers for the future. It was always a problem to find enough General Staff assignments for those officers on hand.

Training in the Reichswehr was conducted realistically and also within the Versailles framework. For all line and staff officers, as well as officer candidates, training was administered from the standpoint of the Reichswehr's ability to meet the current threat. Technical study, the tactics of the combined arms, and mobility -- basic priorities for the small professional army -- were the cornerstones at all levels of training. If the Reichswehr's progressive theoretical studies were important for future developments, its field training program was designed to make it an effective combat-ready army.

The three major personnel programs -- assignments, promotions, and dismissals -- also showed that the Reichswehr largely conformed to the restrictive conditions it faced. Quality rather than quantity was the key objective in all three programs. In the assignment area, authorities adhered to the table of organization very closely, and the number of unauthorized assignments was very low. Promotion in the Reichswehr was slow because of the small number of positions available, the absence of excessive favoritism, and because Army leaders rigidly followed the principles of seniority and professional merit. Likewise, in the elimination program planners pursued a policy of recognizing and discharging weaker officers despite the friction that resulted and the fact that they would have remained in a larger army. No effort was made to establish a reserve of officers who had been prematurely discharged from the Reichswehr.

The limited career advancement opportunities for the Reichswehr officer reflected the realities surrounding a small professional army that conformed to established procedures. The evidence indicates that in administering the three interrelated programs the personnel planners operated within rather than outside the restrictive framework. Because the Army conformed to Treaty provisions, this conclusion, and not the Reichswehr's illegal activities, deserves to be emphasized.

*   *   *

It is also evident that Reichswehr leaders faced a herculean task in their efforts to make the officer's career structure function effectively. Seeckt, for one, found the problem all but insolvable. Only by the end of 1924 had the Reichswehr achieved any appreciable degree of stability, and many in key positions recognized that the situation was tenuous at best. If the officer candidate system was now producing the first in a steady stream of new officers trained under the four-year program, their future impact on the force structure was uncertain. The number of General Staff candidates far exceeded the Army's ability to absorb them, and only a drastic cutback could alleviate this problem. In the personnel area, promotion opportunities were a continual source of concern

rather than satisfaction. Severe promotion group imbalances, especially among junior officers, seriously endangered the prospects
for steady advancement through the higher grades. Although the
elimination program had finally achieved some degree of stability
after years of tension between Berlin authorities and local leaders, the yearly figures were set at lower levels which threatened
the Reichswehr's vaunted policy of youth. Perhaps most seriously
affected of all was the training program, in which the Abkommandierung problem continued unabated. Here, the conflict between the
two missions was most evident, and it appeared that Seeckt might
produce an elite army or a cadre army but not both.

By 1925 the new political stability compelled colleagues of
Seeckt to advocate internal changes in order to adjust the Reichswehr to new political realities. But Seeckt temporized and could
not bring himself to alter what he had begun. Consequently, his
last two years in office were years of drift and uncertainty in
which the Reichswehr continued to maintain the fiction that it
could perform both missions. In reality, it was performing neither
mission satisfactorily. The opposition surfaced most forcefully in
the 1925-1926 debate over training and the function of the elite
army. Even though more study of the crucial decisions of these
months is warranted, it is clear that the Army leaders were motivated as much by problems within the professional army as they were
by their political attitudes. The "Young Turks" who led this
Fronde against Seeckt found in Wilhelm Heye the man they needed to
reorient the professional army along more practical lines.

Heye has been the forgotten man in the history of the postwar
German army, and the reasons are not difficult to understand.
There is no question that the Reichswehr was largely the creation
of its founder, Hans von Seeckt, and most scholars have concentrated on his work of constructing the Army out of wartime defeat
and Versailles restrictions. An accompanying tendency has been to
move ahead to the final three years of Weimar when Schleicher and
others were involving the "non-political" Army more directly in the
political affairs of the day. John Wheeler-Bennett, for example,
has included in his book three successive chapters entitled "The
Seeckt Period (1920-1926)," "Courtship, Honeymoon, and Separation
(1920-1926)," and "The Schleicher Period (1926-1933)."[2] This is
another case of looking at history backwards. Historians, in other
words, have been viewing the Reichswehr from the vantage point of
the National Socialist takeover. Not only has this perspective focused attention on the Army's political history, it has largely excluded crucial military developments that occurred during the period from Seeckt's departure in 1926 to the appearance of Hammerstein
in 1930.

The few scholars who have described the Heye years have treated them either as a continuation of the Seeckt era or the fertile
breeding ground for Schleicher's machinations.[3] The developments
that took place within the Army during Heye's tenure, however, are
important for understanding the role of the Reichswehr as a professional army in the Weimar Republic. The evidence shows that the
traditional view of the Heye years is incorrect. This period cannot be considered superficially as a mere transition between the

beginning and end of the Republic's army. Neither can Heye be
viewed as nothing more than a stopgap for a stronger Reichswehr and
Hammerstein over its death, Heye must be credited with developing
an efficient military instrument that achieved a large measure of
success in the performance of both its missions. In doing so, he
left behind an important legacy for the future Wehrmacht.

Heye, in fact, served as the bridge to the future, and the results of his New Course were evident in every Reichswehr program.
Stability within the Army was his overriding priority. In the officer candidate system, he achieved a stable selection and training
program and introduced psychological testing procedures into the
selection process. More evident was his work in the General Staff
program, in which he implemented a stable two-year program at division level, reflecting the increasingly technical orientation of
the age.

Youth was the central theme of his work in the personnel
area. Assignments and promotions, especially for the exceptionally
competent officer, were never better than under Heye, while the
higher elimination figures reveal his determination to weed out
those who failed to meet the demanding standards. Never were the
criteria observed so closely as under Heye; never was the emphasis
on quality more apparent. As a result, the goal of a youthful officer corps of superior quality was realized, and this was an essential objective for an army whose mission was to develop a cadre
of leaders.

Heye's impact was also felt in the field of operational training. Under his three-year plan, new technical equipment was developed and ineffective units eliminated or reorganized. For the
first time Reichswehr leaders implemented comprehensive, graduated
training for the individual and enlisted man as well as for units
at every organizational level. Finally, the plan provided the
framework within which mobilization and rearmament studies could be
pursued more effectively. Scholars who have supported Rosinski's
view that Heye's reforms were only refinements of the Seecktian
system have been very short-sighted. During his tenure, the
Reichswehr, for the one and only time, approached the goal of
achieving a workable balance between the two contradictory objectives.

Ultimately, even the Heye Reichswehr could not perform both
missions successfully. Of the two tasks, Heye was more effective
in dealing with the cadre mission than with maintaining a combat-
ready mobile shock force. In effect, taking advantage of improved
political conditions, he tacitly reduced emphasis on preparedness
and concentrated on developing a cadre force designed to anchor a
future expanded army. Even so, combat readiness did not suffer ap-
preciably. In fact, it can be argued that the purpose of the elite
force was accomplished better under Heye than Seeckt or Hammerstein
because the Heye Reichswehr continued to perform the field exercises and maneuvers that were essential for combat readiness. Indeed, the Heye Reichswehr was a better professional long-serving
army because its training was more progressive and its officer
corps of higher quality. The Heye Reichswehr came closest to balancing both missions within the artifical framework, and it did

this with fewer evasions of the Versailles provisions and with more cooperation from the Republic's political officials.

                    *   *   *

In view of the Reichswehr's serious liabilities, it is some-what surprising that the officer corps attained a high level of efficiency and gained an outstanding reputation in military circles. Captain Truman Smith, one of the most astute analysts of Reichswehr and Wehrmacht conditions, observed in 1936, during his second tour of duty as American Military Attache in Berlin, that the Reichswehr officers corps "was, in the opinion of all competent foreign observers, the most highly trained, efficient and forward looking officer corps in the world."[4]   Since the time of Smith's comment, scholars have cited various reasons to explain the secret of German military success. Most recently, T.N. Dupuy has discussed "genius" that supposedly was institutionalized in the German General Staff corps, although the little evidence he presents is far from convincing.[5]   The Reichswehr possessed no special genius or formula for achievement.   Rather, it accepted the liabilities of a small professional army that attempted to perform contradictory missions and turned them to its own advantage.

Among the many factors that contributed to the Reichswehr's achievement, four were particularly prominent. For one thing, good organizational procedures were an important element in the Reichswehr's success. The leaders maintained an unusally effective balance between central direction and local initiative and responsibility. Certainly tradition played a role here because decentralized operations were characteristic of the old army.   In the Reichswehr, much of the responsibility for officer selection, training, and personnel management continued to be centered at the regimental commander level. This was especially remarkable in view of the disruptive conditions of the early Weimar period when, despite the strong hand of Seeckt, achieving uniform standards was a serious problem. Even though the decentralized nature of Reichswehr operations was a subject of controversy among officers throughout the 1920s, Army authorities were never prepared to abandon the emphasis on local control in matters of training and personnel. It was perhaps the tension that developed between central and local direction that contributed to the Reichswehr's creative responses to its problems.

A second factor that distinguished the Reichswehr was its management of programs affecting the officer's career structure. Given the unpredictability of personnel management in any bureaucratic institution, effective long-term planning presents a special challenge. On the whole, Reichswehr personnel planners met this challenge successfully. They seriously attempted to match individual officers with assignments for which they were most suited and to recognize the "best" officers at an early point in their careers. Likewise in the promotion system, favoritism was minimized, and those who advanced did so on the basis of seniority and professional ability. A youthful high quality officer corps required involuntary separation, but the planners never compromised the standards established at the outset. Above all, the personnel programs were effective because they were administered fairly and objectively. Ironically, in the personnel field, as in so many others, the Reichswehr's liabilities forced it to stress quality and performance among its officers.

Thirdly, the Reichswehr established uniform standards at every level of its training program. Whether the area examined is officer candidate training, General Staff training, or regular staff and line officer training, the problem-solving method and subject matter for all theoretical and practical training seldom varied. In fact, the only major variable was the organizational level of instruction. Consequently, when an individual advanced from officer candidate through progressively higher ranks, he experienced a training program that was familiar to him. In this way, the Reichswehr was able to implement a uniform doctrine and common approach to tactical situations.

The fourth factor, although less tangible than the other three, was no less important. The Reichswehr successfully attracted men to whom the appeal of elitism, tradition, and the idealism of the military profession were important. Harold Gordon has observed that the burden of the twenty-five year commitment served to make a career in the Reichswehr attractive primarily to men who thought of the army as an ideal. Furthermore, such officers would hardly become less "army-minded" during the course of their careers.6 Although this sense of idealism was common to the officer corps as a whole, it was particularly evident among General Staff officers. For an army like the Reichswehr, which relied on a decentralized structure, the role of General Staff officers was especially vital. Because they held line and staff assignments at all levels in the Reichswehr, their motivation was a critical factor in enhancing the level of professionalism throughout the Army.

*   *   *

What type of individual was the Reichswehr officer? What was he expected to learn, and how well did he learn it? Despite the conclusions of Carsten and Sauer, among others, the evident suggests that social origin was not the test of an individual's ability or status in the Reichswehr. This was as true for officer candidates as it was for officers selected for General Staff training. Mastery of technical knowledge and tactics rather than social background was the key to success. It is significant to note that the Reichswehr, because of the Abitur requirement, recruited officer candidates with a good general educational background. Training, however, encouraged technical expertise and not the attributes of the generalist. Even in the General Staff program general education was not emphasized. The Reichswehr recruited and trained men like Eduard Zorn and Ferdinand Jodl. If they represented the "best" type of officer, their experiences were not uncommon. The Reichswehr wanted motivated officers who were technically and tactically competent because these were the kind of officers best suited to the needs of the small professional army.

There is no question that the Army was successful in its quest

for this type of officer. And yet, this achievement was made only
at great cost. Scholars who have studied the Reichswehr's attitude
toward the Republic see in the lack of political and general education and the Army's abstract concepts of loyalty the major contri-
butors to the German officer's failure to demonstrate civil courage
and moral fortitude during the period of National Socialist domina-
tion.[7] Seeckt had established the policy of "überparteilichkeit"
for the "non-political" Reichswehr, by which the officer corps
washed its hands of politics and merely did its military duty.
Carried to an extreme, an officer corps imbued with this attitude
would obey and political government that promised the army freedom
to pursue its objectives undisturbed. This happened during the
Third Reich. Nevertheless, the Reichswehr's political attitude is
an insufficient explanation for the officer corps' inability to
demonstrate political initiative and the courage of its convictions.

In fact, it is the Reichswehr officer's career structure that
is primarily responsible for producing officers who would seldom
question higher authority, whether it be military or political.
Education and training in the Reichswehr fostered the narrow viewpoint of the tactical-technical specialist and not the broad outlook of the generalist. From the military standpoint, such training, as contemporary observers of Reichswehr operations pointed
out, would become a serious handicap when problems involving modern
strategy had to be confronted. Moreover, the deficiencies that resulted from the narrow outlook of the tactical specialist were not
confined to the military sphere. As Liddell Hart has noted,

> The Seeckt-pattern professional became a modern Pontius Pi-
> late, washing his hands of all responsibility for the or-
> ders he executed. Pure military theory deals in extremes
> that are hard to combine with wise policy. When soldiers
> concentrate on the absolute military air, and do not learn
> to think of grand strategy, they are more apt to accept po-
> litical arguments that, while seeming right in pure strat-
> egy, commit policy beyond the point where it can halt. Ex-
> treme military ends are difficult to reconcile with modera-
> tion of policy.[8]

If the Reichswehr officer's narrow outlook was largely a result of the type of training he underwent, it was reinforced by the
nature of the personnel programs in the professional army. Because
favoritism was not widespread, all officers had to work within the
career structure and advance solely by means of professional
merit. With promotions and assignments in the small army severely
limited, competition was very intense, and the Army's emphasis on
quality and performance served to heighten the competitive nature
of the system. Moreover, the forced selection-out program created
an atmosphere of insecurity in which the officer lived in constant
fear of dismissal if his performance fell below standards.

It is this unhealthy competition inherent in the small professional army that explains the careerism and conformity that were
such prominent characteristics of the Reichswehr officer's career--

and that flourished later in the Wehrmacht. To be sure, all armies experience these problems to some degree. At times criticism of military policies and nonconformist thinking are equated with disloyalty, and officers so identified can easily find their careers severely damaged or even terminated. In a small professional army, like the Reichswehr, the problem was particularly prevalent. Few Reichswehr officers were willing to voice controversial opinions, when the consequence could be permanent identification as troublemakers. Officers were more inclined to follow the high command's lead and master the tactical and technical elements of their profession. Indeed, it is the professional nature of the Reichswehr, not its political outlook, that explains the absence of civil courage among Reichswehr officers.

At this point it should be pointed out that it was the Reichswehr's professional nature that both Rosinski and Dupuy overlooked in their search for the secret of this unique armed force. If the Reichswehr looked to the past and the future, as Rosinski claimed, it was fashioned largely by its present-mindedness -- and the challenge of mastering the postwar technological world. Dupuy's "genius" was, in fact, the Reichswehr's superior command of tactics and technology -- expressed most visibly in General Staff training but present at all levels of Reichswehr education and training. It is ironic that this "non-political" officer corps of technocrats and tacticians was made so by the very enemy-imposed Treaty it despised. Indeed, the Versailles Treaty, more than any other single factor, was responsible for making the officer corps into the perfect tool for use by Adolf Hitler.

The Reichswehr officer's tendency to conform also was encouraged by the leaders' emphasis on character. The terms character, personality, and character education appear over and over again throughout the Weimar period. At bottom, character was a major element in the evaluation of every officer and served as a vital component in measuring ability and performance. The problem with such a concept lay in its subjectiveness. At no time did any Reichswehr commander give it precise definition. As Seeckt used the concept, it became a catch-all for everything wrong with the officer corps. Deficiencies were viewed as character failings and consisted of everything from curfew violations to substandard performance in the field. But when Seeckt's comments are analyzed, his meaning becomes quite clear. It included the elements of discipline, obedience, and loyalty. These, of course, were the traditional virtues of the Prussian officer and gentleman, and these were the attitudes that Seeckt wanted to instill in his officer corps. Perhpas it is understandable that Seeckt stressed these qualities in view of the postwar decline of values and the political confusion of the early Weimar years. His interpretation of character, nevertheless, came to haunt the officer corps because the overriding emphasis on obedience and duty did not encourage individual initiative and independent thinking. As Blomberg and Stulpnagel have testified, Seeckt did not easily tolerate the independent officer.

Heye took a somewhat different approach to the problem. To be sure, he, too, stressed discipline, obedience, and loyalty, as any

military commander must do. As his comments about officers who
protested their dismissals indicated, he could assess opposition to
his policies in terms of character deficiencies. On the other
hand, he went beyond Seeckt's negative use of the concept by encouraging individual initiative and non-conformist thinking in the
officer corps. Heye wanted the type of officer who, within the
regulations, would think for himself and demonstrate the courage of
his convictions, even if the action taken was not always popular.
He specifically directed that such officers should not find their
careers jeopardized on this account. But was he successful?

Unquestionably, it is difficult for an army or any other conservative institution, for that matter, to promote independent
thinking among its members. Yet, the promise is worth the effort
because officers schooled to think for themselves could also be expected to demonstrate this same quality outside the military
sphere. It is to Heye's credit that he recognized the need for
this type of Reichswehr officer and made a serious effort in this
direction. Unfortunately, he was only able to achieve a limited
degree of success. Not only had Seeckt done his work too well, the
very nature of the professional army argued against him. What Heye
needed was time and authority; but time was not on the side of the
Reichswehr, and Heye could never achieve the dominance over the Army that Seeckt enjoyed. Ironically, Heye himself largely destroyed
what little chance he had for success because his reforms, which
admittedly improved the quality of the officer corps, not only contributed to a greater emphasis on tactics and technology but also
increased the competitive nature of the programs and produced widespread discontent within the officer corps. Scholars who take note
of the internal criticism that resulted from Heye's cooperation
with the Republic's politicians fail to point out that his attempt
to improve the quality of the officer corps generated equally dangerous internal opposition.

Ultimately, there was no satisfactory solution to the problems
facing the small professional Reichswehr. If Heye achieved the
most success in balancing the missions of the elite army and cadre
army, he too failed in the end. Heye, in fact, made the last serious attempt to operate within the framework of the Versailles Treaty. Those who came after him had decided that the professional army could not be made to work. The remarkable thing is that only
after ten long years was this decision finally taken. It is well-
known that Schleicher and his group were motivated by their political ideas for the state. Although more research into the crucial
events of the final years of Weimar is still needed, the conclusion
nevertheless seems inescapable that the tensions within the Army
resulting from the officer's career structure were a prime factor
in the decision to abandon the professional army. Political historians who evaluate the Reichswehr from the vantage point of the
National Socialist takeover must also examine the Army from within. Independently of Hitler, Reichswehr leaders had concluded that
the professional army had failed and expansion could not be post-
poned.

The fate of the Reichswehr, Germany's professional army, offers important lessons for any interested observer seeking to un-

derstand contemporary military institutions. The problems that the Reichswehr experienced attempting to create and maintain an effective career structure for its officer corps serve to remind us that quality is often achieved only at great sacrifice. The competition and friction that affect all military institutions are particularly dangerous in the professional armed force which necessarily operated under restrictive conditions. Education and training in the professional force can produce officers of outstanding ability within the narrow confines of military expertise. But military and civilian authorities must be aware that the structure of the officer's career does not necessarily promote initiative and broad-mindedness but rather the reverse. The professional army, which finds itself more isolated from its social base than the national conscript army, requires special attention from within and without if the promise of military professionalism is to be realized.

End Notes

PREFACE

[1] On professionalism, see Lieutenant General Sir John W. Hackett, The Profession of Arms (London: The Times Publishing Company Limited, 1962; reprint ed., United States Air Force Academy, Colorado: USAF Academy, 1974); Samuel P. Huntington, The Soldier and the State: The Theory and Politics of Civil-Military Relations (New York: Vantage Books, 1957), pp. 7-18; Brian Bond, The Victorian Army and the Staff College, 1854-1914 (London: Eyre Methuen Ltd., 1972), pp. 7-45.

[2] Harold J. Gordon, Jr., The Reichswehr and the German Republic, 1919-1926 (Princeton: Princeton University Press, 1957), p. 169.

[3] U.S., Department of State. The Treaty of Versailles and After: Annotations of the Text of the Treaty. Conference Series Pubn. No. 92 (1947); reprint ed., (New York: Greenwood Press, Publishers, 1968), pp. 318-337.

[4] Herbert Rosinski, The German Army (Washington, D.C.: The Infantry Journal, 1944), pp. 129-130; Friedrich von Rabenau, Seeckt: Aus seinem Leben, 1918-1936 (Leipzig: von Hase and Koehler Verlag, 1940), pp. 474-475.

[5] John W. Wheeler-Bennett, The Nemesis of Power: The German Army in Politics, 1918-1945 (New York: St. Martin's Press, 1967); Wolfgang Sauer, "Die Reichswehr," in Die Auflösung der Weimarer

Republik, ed. Karl Dietrich Bracher (Stuttgart: Ruig Verlag, 1955); Gordon A. Craig, The Politics of the Prussian Army, 1640-1945 (New York: Oxford University Press, 1964).

6 F. L. Carsten, The Reichswehr and Politics, 1918-1933 (Berkeley: University of California Press, 1966); Michael Geyer, "Das zweite Rustungsprogramm (1930-1934)," Militärgeschichtliche Mitteilungen, no. 1 (1975), pp. 125-172; Martin Kitchen, A Military History of Germany: From the Eighteenth Century to the Present Day (Bloomington: Indiana University Press, 1975).

7 On Reichswehr rearmament activities, see especially Berenice A. Carroll, Design for Total War: Arms and Economics in the Third Reich (The Hague and Paris: Mouton, 1968). Among notable studies of particular weapons are: Karl-Heinz Völker, Die Entwicklung der militarischen Luftfahrt in Deutschland, 1920-1933: Planung und Massnahmen zur Schaffung einer Fliegertruppe in der Reichswehr (Stuttgart: Deutsch Verlags-Anstalt, 1962); Walther Nehring, Die Geschichte der deutschen Panzerwaffe, 1916 bis 1945 (Berlin: Propylaen Verlag, 1969).

8 Michael Geyer, Aufrüstung oder Sicherheit, Die Reichswehr in der krise der Machtpolitik, 1924-1936 (Wiesbaden: Franz Steiner Verlag GMBH, 1980).

9 Harold J. Gordon, Jr. Hitler and the Beer Hall Putsch (Princeton: Princeton University Press, 1972), pp. 140-164, 507-523.

10 Warren L. Young, Minorities and the Military: A Cross-National Study in World Perspective (Westport, CT.:   Greenwood Press, 1982).

11 NA, 79, 73, p. 721, passim.

12 Gen. A. D. Joachim V. Stülpnagel to Harold J. Gordon, Jr., 23 March 1960, Gordon Papers, Stülpnagel: Reichswehr MSS. and Testimony Folder.

CHAPTER 1

1 See, for example, studies by Gordon, Reichswehr and German Republic; Hans Meier-Welcker and Wolfgang von Groote, gen. eds., Handbuch zur deutschen Militargeschichte, 1648-1939, 7 vols. (Frankfort am Main; Bernard and Graefe Verlag für Wehrwesen, 1970), vol. 6:   Reichswehr and Republik (1918-1933), by Ranier Wohlfeil and Edgar Graf von Matuschka; To be referred to subsequently as Wohlfeil, Handbuch; Telford Taylor, Sword and Swastika: Generals and Nazis in the Third Reich (Chicago: Quadrangle Paperpacks, 1952).

2 Wohlfeil, Handbuch, pp. 177-178; Hans Meier-Welcker, "Der Weg zum „Offizier im Reichswehr der Weimarer Republik," Militärgeschichtliche Mitteilungen, no. 1 (1976), pp. 147-149; Karl Demeter, Das Deutsch Offizierkorps in Gesellschaft und Staat, 1650-1945 (Frankfurt am Main: Bernard & Graefe Verlag fur Wehrwesen, 1964), pp. 47-56.

3 Manfred Messerschmidt and Ursula von Gersdorff, Offiziere im Bild von Dokumenten aus drei Jahrhunderten (Stuttgart: Deutsche Verlags-Anstalt, 1964), p. 224.

4 Waldemar Erfurth, Die Geschichte des deutsche Generalstabes von 1918 bis 1945 (Berlin and Frankfurt: Musterschmidt-Verlag, 1957), p. 82.

5 NA, T-79, 56, p. 212.

6 Quoted in Christian Müller, Oberst i.G. Stauffenberg: Eine Biographie (Dusseldorf: Droste Verlag, 1970), p. 65.

7 This study will use the terms Abitur and non-Abitur to designate candidates with and without the Abitur qualificaion, respectively.

8 Commissioned Reichswehr grades and their United States equivalents are:

Reichswehr grade	Equivalent U.S. grade
Leutnant	(Second) Lieutenant
Oberleutnant	First Lieutenant
Hauptmann or Rittmeister	Captain
Major	Major
Oberstleutnant	Lieutenant Colonel
Oberst	Colonel
Generalmajor	Brigadier General
Generalleutnant	Major General
General der Inf.,Kav.,Art.,usw.	Lieutenant General
Generaloberst	General

Gordon, Reichswehr and German Republic, p. 191.

9 Messerschmidt and Gersdorff, Offiziere im Bild, p. 225.

10 Ibid.

11 Demeter, Deutsche Offizier-Korps, pp. 63-108; Craig, Politics of the Prussian Army, pp. 217-251; Peter Paret, Clausewitz and the State (London: Oxford University Press, 1976), Chapter 12; Manfred Messerschmidt, "Militär und Schule in der wilhelminischen Zeit," Militärgeschichtliche Mitteilungen, no. 1 (1978), pp. 51-77.

12 Geyer, Aufrüstung oder Sicherheit, pp. 1-15, 76-97.

13 Klaus Epstein, The Genesis of German Conservatism (Princeton: Princeton University Press, 1966), pp. 3-25.

14 Gordon, Reichswehr and German Republic, p. 193.

15 Wohlfeil, Handbuch, p. 177.

16 NA, 79, 56, p. 296, passim; NA, 79, 64, p. 1046; BA-MA, Pers 6/2091 (Eduard Zorn).

17 Richard Scheringer, the key defendent in the celebrated Leipzig trial of 1930, quoted his regimental commander on this subject. See Richard Scheringer, Das grosse Los unter Soldaten, Bauern und Rebellen (Hamburg: Rowohlt Verlag, 1959), p. 143.

18 NA, 79, 56, p. 261.

19 Ibid.; Wohlfeil, Handbuch, p. 177.

20 NA, 79, 56, p. 193, 198.

21 National Archives Microcopy No. 137 (Groener Papers), Roll 25, Stuck 225.

22 NA, 79, 56, p. 198.

23 Ibid., p. 211.

24 Ibid., p. 179.

25 Ibid., p. 679.

26 Friedrich Doepner, "Zur Auswahl der Offizieranwärter in 100000-Mann Heer," Wehrkunde 22 (1973): 201.

27 NA, 79, 56, pp. 631-632.

28 Carsten, Reichswehr and Politics, pp. 255-256.

29 Demeter, Deutsche Offizier-Korps, pp. 53-54; Sauer, "Die Reichswehr," p. 258.

30 Carsten, Reichswehr and Politics, pp. 214-215.

31 Nicholas v. Preradovich, "Die soziale Herkunft der Reichswehr-Generalität 1930," Vierteljahrschrift für Sozial-und Wirtschaftsgeschichte 54 (December 1967): 481-486; Harold J. Gordon, Jr., personal letter.

32 Demeter, Deutsche Offizier-Korps, pp. 54-55.

33 Doepner, "Zur Auswahl der Offizieranwärter," pp. 200-201; Gordon Papers, Müller-Hillebrand: Reichswehr Testimony Folder,

1919-1926.

34 Hermann Teske, "Analyse eines Reichswehr-Regiment,"
   Wehrwissenschaftliche Rundschau 12 (May 1962): 252-269.

35 NA, 79, 53, p. 986, passim; Capt. Hugh W. Rowan, "Psychological
   Tests for Candidates for Commission in the German Army," M.A.
   Rpt. No. 2016-1151, August 29, 1932.

36 Rabenau, Seeckt, p. 490.

37 See especially the following issue: Militär-Wochenblatt, March
   11, 1932, p. 1213.

38 Kurt Hesse, "Praktische Psychologie in der Wehrmacht,"
   Militär-Wochenblatt, September 18, 1930, pp. 401-404.

39 Carsten, Reichswehr and Politics, Chapter VI.

40 NA, 79, 78, pp. 1230-1233; Joachim von Stülpnagel, 75 Jahre
   meines Lebens (Dusseldorf: By the Author, 1960), p. 251.

41 NA, 79, 78, p. 1190, passim.

                              CHAPTER 2

1 These attributes of leadership are discussed in "Instructions
  for the Training and Examination of Officer Candidates" (March
  14, 1923), in NA, 79, 56, pp. 727-731.

2 Hauptmann [Gerhard] Kauffmann, "Offizierkorps und
  Offiziernachwuchs," Wissen und Wehr 12 (1931): 24-31.

3 Messerschmidt and Gersdorff, Offiziere im Bild, p. 230.

4 NA, 79, 56, p. 177.

5 Ibid., pp. 84-85, 72, 182, 279. Weapons included the rifle,
  light machine-gun, cannon and howitzer. The group, which
  consisted of approximately ten men, was the equivalent of the
  squad in the U.S. Army.

6 Ibid., pp. 284, 682, 730, 211-213.

7 Ibid., pp. 222-225, 642, passim.

8 Instructions for the Training and Examination of Officer
  Candidates, M.A. Rpt. No. 2277-B-18, January 28, 1924.

9 Ibid. The following analysis of the weapons schools is based

primarily on this regulation, which includes brief descriptions
of each subject's content as well as instructional objectives.

10 Ibid.

11 Zorn was number two among eighty-four cadets in his promotion
group of 1.12.24 His performance on the Officer Examination was
most important in determining the ranking. NA, 79, 64, p. 67;
Rangliste 1925; Col. Wolfgang Bujard (ret.) to Harold J. Gordon,
Jr., February 1978, Gordon Papers, File Bujard: Reichswehr
Personnel Data Folder.

12 NA, 79, 56, p. 729.

13 Ibid., p. 211.

14 Ibid., p. 730.

15 NA, 79, 53, pp. 1008-1009.

16 NA, 79, 56, pp. 679-682, 236-237.

17 Ibid., pp. 727-730. The changes were reflected in the 1927
revised regulation.

18 Messerschmidt and Gersdorff, Offiziere im Bild, p. 230.

19 NA, 79, 56, pp. 728-729.

20 Ibid.

21 Ibid. The Fähnrichsvater played a key role in this area.

22 For the most comprehensive account, see Harold J. Gordon, Jr.,
Hitler and the Beer Hall Putsch (Princeton: Princeton
University Press, 1972).

23 Wheeler-Bennett, Nemesis of Power, pp. 157-164.

24 F. Schraml, "Aus unserer Infanterieschulzeit 1923," Gordon
Papers, Schraml: Infantry School Folder.

25 Messerschmidt and Gersdorff, Offiziere im Bild, p. 233; NA, 79,
56, p. 655; NA, 79, 65, pp. 460-461.

26 NA, 79, 56, pp. 554-555; Zorn was cited for helping to suppress
the putsch. See Ibid., p. 401.

27 NA, 79, 62, pp. 830-831.

28 NA, 79, 78, pp. 1236-1240.

29 NA, 78, 279, pp. 6226662-6226672.

30 NA, 79, 78, p. 1150, passim.

31 Wheeler-Bennett, Nemesis of Power, p. 96.

CHAPTER 3

1 U.S., Department of State, The Treaty of Versailles and After, p. 320.

2 Col. T. N. Dupuy, A Genius for War: The German Army and General Staff, 1807-1945 (Englewood Cliffs, N.J.: Prentice-Hall, Inc., 1977). The best of the major works are: Erfurth, Geschichte des deutschen Generalstabes; Walter Goerlitz, Der Deutsche Generalstab: Geschichte und Gestalt, 1657-1945 (Frankfurt: Verlag der Frankfurter Hefte, 1951); Hansgeorg Model, Der deutsche Generalstabsoffizier: Seine Auswahl und Ausbildung in Reichswehr, Wehrmacht und Bundeswehr (Frankfurt am Main: Bernard & Graefe Verlag für Wehrwesen, 1968); Wiegand Schmidt-Richberg, Die Generalstabe in Deutschland 1871-1945 (Stuttgart: Deutsche-Verlags-Anstalt, 1962).

3 See Jodl, Ferdinand, Personnel Folder. This document is found in what I have titled [General Staff Officer Personnel File] which is housed at U.S., Department of the Army, Office of the Chief of Military History, Washington, D.C.; BA-MA, Pers 6/203 (Ferdinand Jodl).

4 NA, 79, 56, pp. 347-349; The 1921 District Examination, M.A. Rpt. No. 2016-960(2), December 11, 1924.

5 NA, 78, 370, pp. 6332533-6332535.

6 Ibid., pp. 6332552-6332554, 6332265-6332532.

7 Ibid., p. 6332537; Col. Creed F. Cox, "Notes on Education of Officers of the Reichswehr," M.A. Rpt. No. 2016-960(2), December 11, 1924; NA, 79, 56, p. 348.

8 Friedrich von Cochenhausen, Die Truppenführung: Ein Handbuch für den Truppenführer und seine Gehilfen (Berlin: E.S. Mittler & Sohn, 1927).

9 See Hermann Teske, Die silbernen Spiegel: Generalstabdienst unter der Lupe (Heidelberg: K. Vowinckel, 1952); Friedrich Hossbach, Die Entwicklung des Oberbefehls über das Heer in Brandenburg, Preussen und im Deutschen Reich von 1655-1945 (Würzburg: Holzner-Verlag, 1957), pp. 142-145.

10 NA, 79, 56, p. 760; Hossbach, Die Entwicklung des Oberbefehls, p. 143.

11 Rangliste 1926; NA, 79, 64, p. 1376; NA, 79, 73, pp. 607-609.

12 NA, 79, 64, pp. 1061-1065.

13 Ibid., p. 1124.

14 This composite is drawn primarily from the works of Teske, Erfurth, and Model.

15 NA, 78, 370, pp. 6332265-6332532.

16 Ibid., p. 6332302.

17 District Examination 1924, M.A. Rpt. No. 2016-961(8), February 9, 1925.

18 NA, 78, 370, pp. 6332574-6332595.

19 Model, Deutsche Generalstabsoffizier, p. 27.

20 Teske, Silbernen Spiegel, p. 37.

21 Kurt Weckmann, "Fuhrergehilfenausbildung," Wissenschaftliche Rundschau 6 (1954): 268.

22 NA, 78, 370, p. 6332554.

23 Harold J. Gordon, Jr., personal letter; Rangliste, 1923-1932.

24 Erfurth, Geschichte des deutschen Generalstabes, p. 140.

CHAPTER 4

1 See, for example, Schmidt-Richberg, Die Generalstäbe in Deutschland 1871-1945, pp. 55-72.

2 NA, 79, 56, p. 435, 915.

3 The remaining selectees were assigned to Divisions I and VI. The following description of Jodl's three years of training is based primarily on his training file, which is found in NA, 78, 370, and NA, 78, 371.

4 Normally the group consisted of ten to twenty officers. Although motorized vehicles were used for some rides late in the Weimar period, horses remained the main mode of transportation. See Karl Wilhelm Thilo, "Generalstabsreisen," Wehrkunde 13 (1964): 516-520.

5 NA, 79, 77, pp. 125-126.

[6] NA, 78, 368, pp. 6330585-6330587.

[7] Rabenau, Seeckt, p. 501.

[8] "Brother combinations" is used as a category to denote names of officers which appear more than once in the Rangliste as of May 1, 1932.

[9] Model, Deutsche Generalstabsoffizier, p. 36; Gunther Gillessen, "Wie Man Generalstabler heranbildet," Frankfurter Allgemeine Zeitung, May 6, 1967, sec. Bilder und Zeiten.

[10] Heinz Guderian, Panzer Leader, trans. C. Fitzgibbon (London: Michael Joseph, 1952), p. 460. On the historical precedent, see Cyril Falls, A Hundred Years of War (London: Gerald Duckworth & Co. LTD 1953), pp. 62-63.

[11] Model, Deutsche Generalstabsoffizier, pp. 51-53; NA, 78, 375, pp. 6339194-6339203.

[12] Hans Speidel, for example, had completed the first two years by the summer of 1924 but was not allowed to continue with the third year because he was considered too young. Hans Speidel, Aus unserer Zeit (Berlin: Propylaen Verlag, 1977), p. 40.

[13] NA, 79, 81, pp. 933-936; NA, 79, 65, pp. 184-185; Col. Creed Cox, "Notes," M.A. Rpt. No. 2016-960(2), December 11, 1924.

[14] See Appendix 4, table 7 for a list of these officers.

[15] NA, 79, 56, pp. 782-785.

[16] Ibid.

[17] NA, 79, 81, pp. 923, 933-936.

[18] NA, 78, 370, 371; Rangliste 1923-1932.

[19] Rabenau, Seeckt, p. 517, NA, 79, 77, p. 929.

[20] Carsten, Reichswehr and Politics, Chapter VI.

[21] Ibid., p. 516; NA, 79, 65, p. 184.

[22] NA, 79, 65, p. 184.

[23] Col. Cox, "Notes," M.A. Rpt. No. 2016-960(2), December 11, 1924.

[24] Walter Goerlitz, The German General Staff, 1657-1945, trans. Brian Battershaw (New York: Frederich A. Praeger Publishers, 1953), p. 227.

[25] U.S., War Department, Military Intelligence Division, eds., The

German General Staff Corps: A Study of the Organization of the German General Staff (Washington, D.C.: Government Printing Office, 1946), p. 5.

26 Col. A. L. Conger, "Third Division Officer Schools," M.A. Rpt. No. 2016-1004(25), n.d. 1926.

27 Gen. Günther Blumentritt (ret.), "Instruction at the Military Schools," MS#B-322, 1947, Foreign Military Studies Series, Modern Military Records Division, Record Group 338, National Archives, Washington, D.C.; Weckmann, "Führergehilfenausbildung," pp. 271-274.

28 Rabenau, Seeckt, p. 516.

29 Carsten, Reichswehr and German Republic, pp. 219-220; Wheeler-Bennett, Nemesis of Power, pp. 95-102.

CHAPTER 5

1 Hermann Ramcke, Vom Schiffsjungen zum Fallschirmjaeger-General (Preussisch, Oldendorf: Verlag K.W. Schutz, KG, 1972), p. 155.

2 The basic sources for assignments are : D.V.P1 No. 291, Bestimmungen über Aufstellung und Vorlage der Offizierbeurteilungen (Beurteilungsbestimmungen B.B.), July 30, 1921: To be referred to subsequently as the OER regulation; Hans Black, et al., Untersuchungen zur Geschichte des Offizier-korps: Anciennität und Beförderung nach Leistung (Stuttgart: Deutsche Verlags-Anstalt, 1962), pp. 140-141: To be referred to subsequently as Black, Anciennität und Beförderung.

3 For caraeer profiles of Wehrmacht generals, see Wolf Keilig, Das Deutsche Heer 1939-1945, Part II: Die Generalität des Heeres im 2. Weltkrieg 1939-1945 (Bad Nauheim: Podzun-Verlag, 1956), pp. 210-219: To be referred to subsequently as Keilig, Generalität des Heeres im 2. Weltkrieg.

4 NA, 79, 73, pp. 744-747, 781-784, 971-975, 982.

5 OER regulation, sec. 5, 6, 7, 14.

6 NA, 79, 77, pp. 74-80.

8 NA, 79, 65, p. 358.

9 NA, 79, 56, p. 859; NA, 79, 83, p. 125.

10 NA, 79, 65, p. 560; NA, 79, 73, pp. 602-603.

11 NA, 79, 56, pp. 70-71, 374, 376, 425, 978.

12 Hossbach, Die Entwicklung des Oberbefehls, pp. 142-147.

CHAPTER 6

1 Gordon   Papers,   Guderian: Reichswehr   Testimony   Folder,
1919-1926.

2 Black, Anciennität und Beförderung, pp. 140-149.

3 Rangliste (1925-1929); Bujard to Gordon, Gordon Papers.

4 Frequently the Militär-Wochenblatt published Patent eligibility
figures.   In Zorn's case, see "Die neue Rangliste 1927,"
Militar-Wochenblatt, June 4, 1927, p. 1664; M.A. Rpt. No.
2016-1113(3), n.d. 1926.

5 There are no published guidelines on Patent adjustments for
"reactivated" officers. Gordon to the Author, 8 January 1978.

6 Analysis of Jodl's promotion group history is based primarily on
Rangliste information and his personal file, BA-MA, Pers 6/203
(Ferdinand Jodl).

7 The nine officers in question are Lts. Plaschke, Gaze,
Veith, Meister, Weber, Wieband, von Richthofen, Holle, and
Notz.   "Liste der Fliegeroffiziere des Reichsheeres nach dem
Stand vom 1.11.30," in Volker, Entwicklung der militärischen
Luftfahrt in Deutschland, pp. 255-259; Appendix 7, table 5.

8 Kauffmann, "Offizierkorps und Offiziernachwuchs," p.   31;
Hossbach, Die Entwicklung des Oberbefehls, p. 149.

9 Hossbach, Die Entwicklung des Oberbefehls, pp. 136-141; U.S.
Department of State, The Treaty of Versailles and After, pp.
318-323.

10 Paul Mahlmann, "Beitrag zur Psychologie des Frontoffiziers,"
Militär-Wochenblatt, September 23, 1922, pp. 248-250; Gordon
Papers, Mahlmann: Reichswehr Personnel Data Folder.

11 See the following articles in the Militär-Wochenblatt:
"Offiziersatz-und Beförderungsverhältnisse in Reichsheer," July
11, 1927, pp. 59-62; "Gendanken zu den Beförderungsverhältnissen
in Reichsheer," November 11, 1928, pp. 708-709.

12 Alfred Vagts, A History of Militarism (New York: The Free
Press, 1959), p. 298.

13 Stulpnagel, 75 Jahre, p. 241

14 NA, 79, 77, p. 40, passim.

15 OER regulation.

16 NA, 79, 65, p. 401.

17 Ibid., 360.

18 NA, 79, 83, pp.. 1-120.

19 Black, Anciennität und Beförderung, p. 142.

20 Model, Deutsche Generalstabsoffizier, App. C, D, E; Keilig, Generalität des Heeres in 2. Weltkrieg.

21 Rangliste, 1924-1932.

22 Hossbach, Die Entwicklung des Oberbefehls, pp. 138-139; Kauffmann, "Offizierkorps und Offiziernachwuchs," pp. 30-31.

23 See the following Militär-Wochenblatt articles: "Erwiderung zu Gedanken uber die Beförderungsverhältnissen in Reichsheer," December 4, 1928, pp. 834-835; December 25, 1928, p. 963; January 25, 1929, pp. 1131-1134; February 4, pp. 1171-1173.

24 Gordon, Reichswehr and German Republic, p. 446; Gordon Papers, Reichswehr Testimony Folder, 1919-1926.

25 Gordon Papers, Liebmann: Reichswehr Testimony Folder, 1919-1926.

26 Otto-Ernst Schüddekopf, Das Heer und die Republik: Quellen zur Politik der Reichswehrführung 1918 bis 1933 (Hannover: Norddeutsche Verlagsanstalt O. Goedel, 1955), p. 295ff.

27 Gen. Rudolf Hofmann (ret.), "German Efficiency Report System," MS#P-134, n.d., Foreign Military Studies Series, Modern Military Records Division, Record Group 338, National Archives, Washington, D.C., p. 37.

28 Stülpnagel, 75 Jahre, pp. 241-242.

CHAPTER 7

1 Wehrgesetz, 23.3.21, Article 29.

2 The best general work remains Gordon, Reichswehr and German Republic.   However, only the Seeckt period is examined, and

officer dismissal receives little attention (p. 295). Carsten's Reichswehr and Politics, while dealing with the entire Weimar period, is very sketchy on this subject, Also see Wohlfeil, Handbuch, pp. 202-212; Black, Anciennität und Beförderung, pp. 142-144.

3 NA, 79, 73, pp. 530-532.

4 Ibid., p. 500, passim.

5 OER regulation, sec. 11, 26.

6 NA, 79, 73, pp. 270-271.

7 Ibid., pp. 223-523.

8 NA, 79, 56, p. 3, passim; NA, 79, 65, p. 400, passim.

9 OER regulation, sec. 2.

10 Salary and pension amounts corresponded to categories dealing with Patent seniority within each grade. See Wohlfeil, Handbuch, pp. 180-181.

11 NA, 79, 77, pp. 147-148.

12 Stülpnagel, 75 Jahre, pp. 223-224; Stülpnagel to Gordon, November 9, 1959, Gordon Papers; Gordon, Reichswehr and German Republic, p. 259.

13 Stülpnagel, 75 Jahre, pp. 223-258; Erfurth, Geschichte des deutschen Generalstabes, pp. 119-126.

14 Ibid.; Wohlfeil, Handbuch, pp. 127-128; Rosinski, German Army, p. 113.

15 Stülpnagel, 75 Jahre, p. 242.

16 NA, 79, 77, pp. 129-133.

17 Ibid.

18 NA, 79, 56, pp. 782-785.

19 Ibid.

20 NA, 79, 77, pp. 74-80.

21 Ibid., pp. 49-51.

22 Stülpnagel, 75 Jahre, pp. 241-245.

23 See Schüddekopf, Heer und Republik, pp. 295-297.

24 NA, 79, 52, pp. 709-720; NA, 79, 76, pp. 1330-1331.

25 NA, 79, 76, pp. 1350-1361.

26 NA, 79, 52, pp. 709-720; NA, 79, 82, pp. 33-35.

27 Thilo Vogelsang, Reichswehr, Staat, und NSDAP: Beiträge zur deutschen Geschichte 1930-1933 (Stuttgart: Deutsche Verlagsanstalt, 1962), pp. 484-485.

28 U.S., Department of State, The Treaty of Versailles and After, pp. 356-359; Wohlfeil, Handbuch, pp. 188-194.

29 Radlmaier is listed in the 1929 Rangliste but not in the 1930 and 1931 Rangliste. In the 1930 Rangliste he is shown as dismissed, but from 1929-1931 he was a station leader in Russia. See Nehring, Geschichte der deutschen Panzerwaffe, p. 44.

30 Stulpnagel, 75 Jahre, p. 245.

CHAPTER 8

1 See, for example, Craig, Politics of the Prussian Army, pp. 395-402; Carsten, Reichswehr and Politics, p. 209ff.

2 Sauer, "Reichswehr," in Auflosung, p. 273; Carroll, Design for Total War; Geyer, "Zweite Rüstungsprogramm."

3 See the Times (London), February 17, 1927, p. 13.

4 NA, 79, 56, pp. 451-453; NA, 79, 65, p. 5, passim.

5 Col. A. L. Conger, "Training Schedule of the Germany Army," M.A. Rpt. No. 2016-1014, June 15, 1926.

6 "Maneuvers of the 2nd Group Command 1926," M.A. Rpt. No. 2016-1007(30), October 1926; Militär-Wochenblatt, October 11, 1926, pp. 473-475.

7 NA, 79, 64, p. 1187; NA, 79, 56, p. 1131.

8 NA, 79, 65, pp. 150-153; Gen. Waldemar Erfurth (ret.), "Training and Development of German General Staff Officers," MS# -031b, 1950, Foreign Military Studies Series, Modern Military Records, Record Group 338, National Archives, Washington, D.C.

9 See Seeckt's comments in Messerschmidt and Gersdorff, Offiziere im Bild, pp. 224-226; Rosinski, German Army. p. 129.

10 B. H. Liddell Hart, The German Generals Talk (New York: William Morrow & Co., 1948), pp. 1-19.

11 "Comments of the Commanding General of the German Army Based on His Inspections During the Years 1920-1926," M.A. Rpt. No. 2016-935, n.d. [1927].   R. G. No. 165 contains translated copies of Seeckt's yearly training critiques and Heye's consolidated version.   Seeckt's comments cited here are from sec. 1 of the consolidated version.   Subsequent references will cite the critique, year, and section only.

12 "Seeckt Tng Critique 1921," sec. 19.

13 "Seeckt Tng Critique 1924," sec. 10.

14 "Seeckt Tng Critique 1925," sec. 3.

15 Ibid.

16 "Seeckt Tng Critique 1921," sec. 18.

17 "Seeckt Tng Critique 1925," sec. 44.

18 "Seeckt Tng Critiques 1920-1926," sec. 7.

19 NA, 79, 64, p. 990.

20 NA, 79, 56, p. 456.

21 Ibid., pp. 1088-1091.

22 Erfurth, Geschichte des deutschen Generalstabes, p. 142.

23 Rabenau, Seeckt, pp. 481-483, 505-507.

24 Ibid., pp. 481-483; Schuddekopf, Heer und Republik, pp. 199-200; Carsten, Reichswehr and Politics, pp. 258-260; Hans Meier-Welcker, Seeckt (Frankfurt am Main: Bernard & Graefe Verlag für Wehrwesen, 1967), pp. 531-532.

25 Rabenau, Seeckt, pp. 481-483.

26 Ibid.

27 Ibid.

28 NA, 79, 64, pp. 1328-1329.

29 For Schleicher's memorandum, see Vogelsang, Reichswehr, Staat und NSDAP, pp. 409-413.

30 For Heye's plan, see NA, 79, 64, pp. 1171-1207.   The following description of the plan's objectives is based on this material.

31 See, for example, NA, 78, 278, pp. 6225384-6225386, 6225517-6225519.

32 Gaines Post, The Civil-Military Fabric of Weimar Foreign Policy (Princeton University Press, 1973), pp. 159-238.

33 NA, 79, 56, p. 916.

34 Militär-Wochenblatt, October 11, 1930; NA, 79, 30, pp. 264-275.

35 Theodor Heuss, Soldatentum in unsere Zeit (Tubingen: Rainer Wunderlich Verlag, 1959), pp. 26-28. For more on the program, see NA, 79, 64, p. 875; NA, 78, 278, p. 6226310; NA, 78, 279, p. 6226899; Otto Gessler, Reichswehrpolitik in der Weimarer Zeit (Stuttgart: Deutsche Verlags-Anstalt, 1958), p. 510; Fritz Ernst, "Aus dem Nachlass Gen. Walther Reinhardt, "Die Welt als Geschichte 18 (1958): 1-20; Fritz Ernst, "Walther Reinhardt (1872 bis 1930), "Zeitschrift für Württembergische Landesgeschichte 16 (1957):346-360.

36 Speidel, Aus unserer Zeit, p. 42; Bujard to Gordon, February 1978, Gordon Papers.

37 NA, 79, 30, pp. 198-211, 193-197; NA, 79, 62, pp. 522-537; NA, 78, 299, p. 485, passim.

38 Gordon A. Craig, "Reichswehr and National Socialism: The Policy of Wilhelm Groener, 1928-1932," Political Science Quarterly 63 (June 1948): 194-229; Heinz Brauweiler, Generale in der Deutschen Republik (Berlin: Tell-Verlag, 1932), p. 31. For a defense of Schleicher, see Erich von Manstein, Aus einem Soldatenleben, 1887-1939 (Bonn: Athenaum-Verlag, 1958), pp. 199-208.

39 Stulpnagel, 75 Jahre, p. 280.

40 Carsten, Reichswehr and Politics, pp. 300-302.

41 Ibid., pp. 309-338; Craig, Politics of the Prussian Army, pp. 228-233; Sauer, "Reichswehr," in Auflösung, pp. 268-284; Geyer, "Zweite Rüstungsprogramm," pp. 125-127.

42 Ibid.; Wohlfeil, Handbuch, pp. 228-233.

CONCLUSION

1 Rosinski, German Army, p. 112.

2 Wheeler-Bennett, Nemesis of Power.

[3] See especially Carsten, Reichswehr and Politics, pp. 253-308.

[4] Col. Truman Smith, "The German Officer Corps," M.A. Rpt. No. 2016-1260, May 28, 1936, Navy and Old Army Branch, Military Archives Division, Record Group 165, National Archives, Washington, D.C.

[5] Dupuy, Genius for War.

[6] Gordon, Reichswehr and German Republic, p. 166.

[7] See, for example, Carsten, Reichswehr and Republic, pp. 400-405.

[8] Liddell Hart, German Generals Talk, p. 18.

Bibliography

This bibliography is divided into two parts each consisting of several categories. A number of references are accompanied by explanatory notes because of the nature of the sources and the way they are used in this study.

I. Primary Sources

A. Manuscript Collections

Washington, D.C. National Archives. American Historical Association -- National Archives (AHA-NA) Microfilm Materials.
> Portions of this collection of captured German military records from the Second World War provide the basic documentation for this study. Materials cited from this series are keyed to it. References begin with the National Archives abbreviation (NA), followed by the file group number, the roll number, and the page (frame) number. For example, the citation NA, 79, 56, 250 referes to National Archives, file group T-79, Roll 56, page (frame) 250. The microfilm materials used include: T-78, Records of Headquarters, German Army High Command; T-79, Records of Germany Army Areas: Wehrkreis VII.

Washington, D.C. National Archives. Navy and Old Army Branch. Military Archives Division, Record Group 165, Records of the Military Intelligence Division.

> This file group contains the reports of American military attaches stationed in Germany during the Weimar period. Due to the large number of reports used for this study, specific reports are cited in the footnote references only. References

begin with the author (if known), followed by the report title, report number, and date of report. An example is: Col. Creed F. Cox, "Notes on the Education of Officers of the Reichswehr," M.S. Rpt. No. 2016-960(2), December 11, 1924. Because all attache reports are contained in Record Group 165, the record group number is omitted from the citation. Record Group 165 files used for this work include: File 2016, [Army Field Operations]; File 2277, [Army Education Activities]. However, as the above example illustrates, file contents do not always appear to reflect the nature of the particular file.

Washington, D.C. National Archives. Modern Military Records Division, Record Group 338. Foreign Military Studies Series.

This series contains manuscripts prepared by German generals interviewed following the Second World War. Materials used for this study include: Blumentritt, Gen. Gunther (ret.). "Instruction at Military Schools," MS#B-322, 1947; Blumentritt, "Training Regular Officers in Peacetime," MS#B-651, 1947; Erfurth, Gen. Waldemar (ret.). "Training and Development of German General Staff Officers," MS#P-031b; Hofmann, Gen. Rudolf (ret.). "German Efficiency Report System," MS#P-134.

Washington, D.C. Department of the Army. Office of the Chief of Military History.

On file in this office is an untitled, unnumbered gathering of German General Staff officer personnel records. The following folder from this collection is included in this work:

Jodl, Ferdinand [Personnel Folder] in what I have titled [General Staff Officer Personnel File].

Washington, D.C. National Archives, Microcopy 6, No. 137. Groener Papers, Roll 25, Stuck 225.

Freiburg, Germany. Bundesarchiv-Militararchiv.

The Federal Republic of Germany's federal and military archives houses a number of important Reichswehr regulations as well as an extensive if incomplete collection of Reichswehr-Wehrmacht personnel folders. For this study, the two key folders, on Eduard Zorn and Ferdinand Jodl, are cited as follows: BA-MA, Pers 6/2091 (Eduard Zorn); BA-MA, Pers 6/203 (Ferdinand Jodl).

B. Published Documents

Germany. Reichsministerium des Innern, eds. Reichs-Gesetzblatt. March 31, 1921.

Germany. Reichswehrministerium, eds. Bestimmungen fur Ubungsreisen, Ubungsritte, und Besprechungen im Gelände. Berlin, 1924.

Germany. Reichswehrmininsterium, eds. Bestimmungen uber Aufstellung und Vorlage der Offizierbeurteilungen. Berlin, 1921.

Germany. Reichswehrmininsterium, eds. Bestimmungen uber die Entlassung von Offizieren des Reichsheeres u.d. Reichsmarine. Berlin, July 28, 1930.

Germany. Reichswehrministerium, eds. Dienstältersliste der Hauptleute und Rittmeister, so wie der Oberleutnante und Leutnante des Reichsheeres. Stand vom 1.Juli 1922.

Germany. Reichswehrministerium, eds. Die Fähnrichs-Prüfung 1922. Berlin, 1922.

Germany. Reichswehrministerium, eds. Die Offizieranwärter-Prüfung 1922. Berlin, 1922.

Germany. Reichswehrministerium, eds. Offizier-Ergänzungsbestimmungen des Reichsheeres. Berlin 1928.

Germany. Reichswehrministerium, eds. Richtlinien fur die Ausbildung der als Führergehilfen in Aussicht genommen Offiziere. Berlin, 1922.

Germany. Reichswehrministerium, eds. Rangliste des deutschen Reichsheeres. Berlin, 1923ff.

>   The Rangliste lists every officer in the Reichswehr by position
>   in the Stellenbesetzung (table of organization) for his unit.
>   It was published by the Defense Ministry yearly from 1923-
>   1932. For the 1923 and 1924 lists, the effective date (Stand
>   or Stichtag) is April 1. Beginning in 1925, the Rangliste ef-
>   fective date is May 1. The Rangliste for the years 1924-1932
>   is available on microfilm from the National Archives (NA, 78,
>   509). The 1923 Rangliste is available in published form only.
>   For this study, citations include: the Rangliste, followed by
>   the particular year(s). For example, Rangliste 1924-1932 re-
>   fers to the Rangliste for the years 1924-1932 inclusive.

U.S. Department of State. The Treaty of Versailles and After: Annotations of the Text of the Treaty. Conference Series Pubn. No. 92 (1947); reprint ed., New York: Greenwood Press, Publishers, 1968.

C. Published Memoirs

Braun, Otto. Von Weimar zu Hitler. New York: Europa Verlag, 1940.

Choltitz, Dietrich von. Soldat unter Soldaten: Die deutsche Armee im Frieden und im Krieg. Konstanz, Zurich, Wien: Europa Verlag, 1951.

Faber du Faur, Moriz von. Macht und Ohnmacht: Erinnerungen eines alten Offiziers. Stuttgart: Gunther Verlag, 1953.

Gessler, Otto. Reichswehrpolitik in der Weimarer Zeit. Stuttgart: Deutsche Verlags-Anstalt, 1958.

Geyr von Schweppenburg, Leo Frhr. Gebrochenes Schwert. Berlin: Verlag Bernard & Graefe, 1952.

Guderian, Heinz. Panzer Leader. Translated by C. Fitzgibbon. London: Michael Joseph, 1952.

Heuss, Theodor. Soldatentum in Unsere Zeit. Tubingen: Rainer Wunderlich Verlag, 1959.

Kostring, Ernst. General Ernst Köstring: Der militärische Mittler zwischen dem Deutschen Reich und der Sowjetunion, 1921-1941. Frankfurt am Main: Mittler, 1966.

Manstein, Erich von. Aus Einem Soldatenleben, 1887-1939. Bonn: Athenaum-Verlag, 1958.

Ramcke, Hermann. Vom Schiffsjungen zum Fallschirmjaeger-General. Preussisch Oldendorf: Verlag K.W. Schutz KG, 1972.

Scheringer, Richard. Das grosse Los unter Soldaten, Bauern und Rebellen. Hamburg: Rowohlt Verlag, 1959.

Schwerin von Krosigk, Lutz Graf. Es Geschah in Deutschland: Menschenbilder unseres Jahrhunderts. Tubingen and Stuttgart: Ranier Wunderlich Verlag Hermann Leins, 1951.

Speidel, Hans. Aus unserer Zeit. Berlin: Propyläen Verlag, 1977.

Stulpnagel, Joachim von. 75 Jahre meines Lebens. Dusseldorf: By the Author, 1960.

Teske, Hermann. Die silbernen Spiegel: Generalstabdienst unter der Lupe. Heidelberg: K. Vowinckel, 1952.

D. Printed Contemporary Material

Brauweiler, Heinz. Generäle in der Deutschen Republik. Berlin: Tell-Verlag, 1932.

Cochenhausen, Friedrich von. Die Kriegswissenschaftlichen Fortbildung des Truppenoffiziers. Berlin: E. S. Mittler & Sohn, 1931.

_____. Die Truppenführung: Ein Handbuch für den Truppenführer und seine Gehilfen. Berlin: E. S. Mittler & Sohn, 1927.

Hossbach, Friedrich. Die Entwicklung des Oberbefehls Über das Heer in Brandenburg, Preussen und im Deutschen Reich von 1655-1945. Wurzburg: Holzner-Verlag, 1957.

> The author includes the text of a speech on officer career opportunities he gave to officers of II/I.R. 17 on January 15, 1932 (see pp. 135-149).

Kuhl, Gen. Heinrich von. Der deutsche Generalstab in Vorbereitung und Durchfuhrung des Weltkrieges. Berlin: Verlag Ernst Siegried Mittler & Sohn, 1920.

Kauffmann, Hauptmann [Gerhard]. "Offizierkorps und Offiziernachwuchs." Wissen und Wehr 12 (1931): 24-31.

Militar-Wochenblatt. Berlin, 1921ff.

> Due to the large number of articles used for this work, specific articles are cited in the footnote references.

Oertzen, Lt. Col. v. Deutsches Reichsheer-Handbuch. Berlin: Verlag OW Charlottenburg, 1922.

Times (London), February 21, 1927.

II. Secondary Sources

A. Monographs

Black, Hans; Wohlfeil, Ranier; Matuschka, Edgar Graf von: and Papke, Gerhard. Untersuchungen zur Geschichte des Offizierkorps: Anciennitat und Beforderung nach Leistung. Stuttgart: Deutsche Verlags-Anstalt, 1962.

Bond, Brian. The Victorian Army and the Staff College, 1854-1914. London: Eyre Meuthen Ltd, 1972.

Carroll, Berenice A. Design for Total War: Arms and Economics in the Third Reich. The Hague and Paris: Mouton, 1968.

Carsten, F.L. The Reichswehr and Politics, 1918-1933. Berkeley: University of California Press, 1966.

Challener, Richard D. The French Theory of the Nation in Arms, 1866-1939. New York: Columbia University Press, 1955.

Cosmos, Graham A. An Army for Empire: The United States Army in the Spanish-American War. Columbia, Missouri: University of Missouri Press, 1971.

Craig, Gordon A. Germany 1866-1945. New York: Oxford University Press, 1978.

_____. The Politics of the Prussian Army, 1640-1945.
New York: Oxford University Press, 1964.

Demeter, Karl. Das deutsche Offizierkorps in Gesellschaft und
Staat, 1650-1945. Frankfurt am Main: Bernard & Graefe Verlag fur
Wehrwesen, 1964.

Dupuy, Col. T. N. A Genius for War: The German Army and General
Staff, 1807-1945. Englewood Cliffs, N.J.: Prentice-Hall, Inc.,
1977.

Eberhardt, Fritz. Mititärisches Wörterbuch. Stuttgart: Alfred
Kroner Verlag, 1940.

Epstein, Klaus. The Genesis of German Conservatism. Princeton:
Princeton University Press, 1966.

Erfurth, Waldemar. Die Geschichte des deutschen Generalstabes von
1918 bis 1945. Berlin and Frankfurt: Musterschmidt-Verlag, 1957.

Falls, Cyril. A Hundred Years of War. London: Gerald Duckworth &
Co. LTD, 1953.

Fried, Hans. The Guilt of the German Army. New York: Macmillan,
1942.

Geyer, Michael. Aufrustung oder Sicherheit. Die Reichswehr in der
Krise der Machtpolitik, 1924-1936. Wiesbaden: Franz Steiner
Verlag GMBH, 1980.

Goerlitz, Walter, Der deutsche Generalstab: Geschichte und
Gestalt, 1657-1945. Frankfurt: Verlag der Frankfurter Hefte,
1951.

_____. History of the German General Staff, 1657-1945.
Translated by Brian Battershaw. New York: Frederick A. Praeger
Publishers, 1953.

_____. Generalfeldmarschall Keitel: Verbrecher oder
Offizier? Gottingen: Musterschmidt-Verlag, 1961.

Gordon, Harold J., Jr. Hitler and the Beer Hall Putsch.
Princeton: Princeton University Press, 1972.

_____. The Reichswehr and the German Republic,
1919-1926. Princeton: Princeton University Press, 1957.

Groener-Geyer, Dorothea. General Groener: Soldat und Staatsmann.
Frankfurt am Maim: Societats-Verlag, 1955.

Hackett, General Sir John Winthrop. The Profession of Arms.
London: Times Publishing Co. Ltd., 1970.

Homze, Edward L. Arming the Luftwaffe: The Reich Air Ministry and the German Aircraft Industry 1919-1939. Lincoln and London: University of Nebraska Press, 1976.

Howard, Michael. The Continental Committment. London: Maurice Temple Smith Ltd, 1972.

Huntington, Samuel P. The Soldier and the State: The Theory and Politics of Civil-Military Relations. Cambridge, Mass.: Harvard University Press, 1957.

Janowitz, Morris. The Professional Soldier. Glencoe, Ill.: Free Press, 1960.

Keilig, Wolf. Das Deutsche Heer 1939-1945. Part II: Die Generalitat des Heeres im 2. Weltkrieg 1939-1945. Bad Nauheim: Podzun-Verlag, 1956.

Kitchen, Martin. A Military History of Germany: From the Eighteenth Century to the Present Day. Bloomington: Indiana University Press, 1975.

Kramarz, Joachim. Claus Graf Stauffenberg, 15 Nov 1907-20 Juli 1944: Das Leben eines Offiziers. Frankfurt am Main: Bernard & Graefe, 1965.

Liddell Hart, B. H. The German Generals Talk. New York: W. Morrow and Co., 1948.

_____. Strategy, 2nd rev. ed. New York: Frederick A. Praeger, Publishers, 1967.

Macksey, Kenneth. Guderian: Creator of the Blitzkrieg. New York: Stein and Day, Publishers, 1975.

Meier-Welchker, Hans, and Groote, Wolfgang von., gen. eds. Handbuch zur deutschen Militargeschichte, 1648-1939, 7 vols. Frankfurt am Main: Bernard & Graefe Verlag fur Wehrwesen, 1970. Vol. 6: Reichswehr und Republik (1918-1933), by Ranier Wohlfeil.

Meier-Welcker, Hans. Seeckt. Frankfurt am Main: Bernard & Graefe Verlag fur Wehrwesen, 1967.

Messerschmidt, Manfred, and Gersdorff, Ursula von. Offiziere im Bild von Dokumenten aus drei Jahrhunderten. Stuttgart: Deutsche Verlags-Anstalt, 1964.

Meyer, Georg, ed. Generalfeldmarschall Wilhelm Ritter von Leeb: Tagebuchaufzeichnungen und Lagebeurteilungen aus zwei Weltkriegen. Stuttgart: Deutsche Verlags-Anstalt, 1976.

Model, Hansgeorg. Der deutsche Generalstabsoffiziere: Seine Auswahl und Ausbildung in Reichswehr, Wehrmacht und Bundeswehr.

Frankfurt am Main: Bernard & Graefe Verlag fur Wehrwesen, 1968.

Morgan, John H. Assize of Arms: Disarmament of Germany and Her Rearmament, 1919-1939. New York: Oxford University Press, 1946.

Muller, Christian. Oberst i.G. Stauffenberg: Eine Biographie. Dusseldorf: Droste Verlag, 1970.

Nehring, Walther. Die Geschichte der deutschen Panzerwaffe, 1916 bis 1945. Berlin: Propylaen Verlag, 1969.

The Officer's Guide. A Ready Reference on Customs of the Service and Correct Procedure in All Situations. Hamsburg, Pa.: The Military Service Publishing Company, 1936.

O'Neil, Robert. "Doctrine and Training in the German Army." In The Theory and Practice of War. pp. 143-165. Edited by Michael Howard. London: Cassell & Co. Ltd., 1965.

Paret, Peter. Clausewitz and the State. London: Oxford University Press, 1976.

Post, Gaines. The Civil-Military Fabric of Weimar Foreign Policy. Princeton: Princeton University Press, 1973.

Rabenau, Friedrich von. Seeckt: Aus seinem Leben, 1918-1936. Leipzig: von Hase and Koehler Verlag, 1940.

Ropp, Theodore. War in the Modern World. New York: Collier, 1973.

Rosinski, Herbert. The German Army. Washington, D.C.: The Infantry Journal, 1944.

Sauer, Wolfgang. "Die Reichswehr," In Die Auflösung der Weimarer Republik, pp. 229-284. Edited by Karl Dietrich Bracher. Stuttgart: Ruig Verlag, 1955.

Schmidt-Richberg, Wiegand. Die Generalstabe in Deutschland 1871-1945. Stuttgart: Deutsche Verlags-Anstalt, 1962.

Schuddekopf, Otto-Ernst. Das Heer und die Republik: Quellen zur Politik der Reichswehrfuhrung 1918 bis 1933. Hannover: Norddeutsche Verlags-anstalt O. Goedel, 1955.

Siegler, Fritz Frhr. von. Die Hoheren Dienststellen der Deutschen Wehrmacht 1933-1945. Munich: Institut fur Zeitgeschichte, 1953.

Speidel, Hans, ed. Ludwig Beck: Studien. Stuttgart: K.F. Koehler Verlag, 1955.

Taylor, Telford. Sword and Swastika: Generals and Nazis in the Third Reich. Chicago: Quadrangle Paperbacks, 1952.

Tessin, Georg. Deutsche Verbände und Truppen, 1918-1939.
Osnabrück: Biblio Verlag, 1974.

U.S. War Department, Military Intelligence Division, eds. German
Training Methods: A Study of German Military Training.
Washington, D.C.: GMDS, 1946.

U.S. War Department, Military Intelligence Division, eds. The
German General Staff Corps: A Study of the Organization of the
German General Staff. Washington, D.C.: Government Printing
Office, 1946.

Vagts, Alfred. A History of Militarism. New York: The Free
Press, 1959.

Völker, Karl-Heinz. Die Entwicklung der militärischen Luftfahrt in
Deutschland, 1920-1933: Planung und Massnahmen zur Schaffung einer
Fliegertruppe in der Reichswehr. Stuttgart: Deutsche
Verlags-Anstalt, 1962.

Vogelsang, Thilo. Reichswehr, Staat, und NSDAP: Beitrage zur
deutschen Geschichte 1930-1932. Stuttgart: Deutsche
Verlags-Anstalt, 1962.

Young, Warren L. Minorities and the Military: A Cross National
Study in World Perspective. Westport, CT.: Greenwood Press, 1982.

Watt, Donald C. Too Serious a Business: European Armed Forces and
the Approach to the Second World War. Berkeley and Los Angeles:
University of California Press, 1975.

Weigley, Russell F. History of the United States Army. New York:
Macmillan, 1967.

Wheeler-Bennett, John W. The Nemesis of Power: The German Army in
Politics, 1918-1945. New York: St. Martin's Press, 1967.

B. Articles and Newspapers

Blumentritt, Gunther. "Militärisches Schulsystem und Hochschule."
Wehrkunde 8 (1959): 670-672.

Craig, Gordon A. "Reichswehr and National Socialism: The Policy
of Wilhelm Groener, 1928-1932." Political Science Quarterly 63
(June 1948): 194-229.

Doepner, Friedrich. "Zur Auswahl der Offizieranwärter im
100000-Mann Heer." Wehrkunde 22 (1973): 200-204; 259-263.

Ernst, Fritz. "Aus dem Nachlass Gen. Walther Reinhardt." Die Welt
als Geschichte 18 (1958): 1-20.

_____. "Walther Reinhardt (1872 bis 1930)."

Zeitschrift für Würtembergische Landesgeschichte 16 (1957): 236-260.

Geyer, Michael. "Das zweite Rustungsprogramm (1930-1934)." Militärgeschichtliche Mitteilungen. no. 1 (1975), pp. 125-172.

Gillessen, Gunther. "Wie man Generalstäbler heranbildet." Frankfurter Allgemeine Zeitung, May 6, 1967, sec. Bilder und Zeiten.

Meier-Welcker, Hans. "Der Weg zum Offizier im Reichsheer der Weimarer Republik." Militärgeschichtliche Mitteilungen. no. 1 (1976), pp. 147-167.

Messerschmidt, Manfred. "Militar und Schule in der wilhelminischen Zeit." Militärgeschichtliche Mitteilungen. no. 1 (1978), pp. 51-77.

Preradovich, Nicholas von. "Die soziale Herkunft der Reichswehr-Generalitat 1930." Vierteljahrschrift für Sozial und Wirtschaftsgeschichte 54 (December 1967): 481-486.

Teske, Hermann. "Analyse eines Reichswehr-Regiment." Wehrwissenschaftliche Rundschau 12 (May 1962): 252-269.

Thilo, Karl Wilhelm. "Generalstabsreisen." Wehrkunde 13 (1964): 516-520.

Weckmann, Kurt. "Führergehilfenausbildung." Wissenschaftliche Rundschau 6 (1954): 268-277.

C. Unpublished Material

Harold J. Gordon, Jr., personal letter to Author, December 3, 1976.

Ibid., January 7, 1977.

Ibid., February 22, 1977.

Ibid., July 17, 1977.

Ibid., October 1, 1977.

Ibid., October 22, 1977.

Ibid., January 8, 1978.

Ibid., January 28, 1978.

Ibid., March 5, 1978.

Ibid., December 4, 1978.

Appendix 1.
Officer Candidate Selection

TABLE 1

1921 BRANCH AND UNIT QUOTAS FOR OFFICER CANDIDATES

Number per Branch		Number per Unit	
Infantry. 129	Infantry Regiment (I.R.).	6
Cavalry 40	Cavalry Regiment (R.R.)	2
Artillery 44	Artillery Regiment (A.R.)	6
Engineering 11	Engineering Battalion (P.B.).	1-2
Signals 8	Signals Battalion (N.A.).	1
Motorized Transport . . . 8	Motorized Transport Battalion (K.A.). . .	1
Supply (Horse-drawn). . . 10	Supply Battalion (Horse-drawn) (F.A.) . .	1-2
TOTAL 250		

SOURCE: NA, 79, 56, p. 261.

TABLE 2

REPRESENTATION OF NOBLES AMONG GROUPS OF NEWLY-

COMMISSIONED LIEUTENANTS

Year	Branch				Total
	Inf.	Kav.	Art.	Tech.	
1921	30(4)-13%	5(2)-40%	6(1)-17%	5(0)-0%	46(7)-15%
1922	79(15)-19%	29(10)-35%	23(1)-4%	13(0)-0%	144(26)-18%
1923	53(6)-11%	18(9)-50%	7(0)-0%	3(0)-0%	81(15)-19%
1924	50(4)-8%	12(1)-9%	15(0)-0%	11(2)-18%	88(7)-8%
1925	77(6)-9%	30(17)-57%	37(2)-6%	16(1)-6%	160(26)-16%
1926	84(12)-14%	38(19)-50%	24(5)-16%	29(1)-3%	176(36)-20%
1927	66(9)-14%	29(16)-55%	37(7)-19%	13(0)-0%	145(32)-22%
1928	121(19)-16%	44(21)-48%	45(7)-16%	42(4)-10%	252(51)-20%
1929	98(23)-23%	33(17)-52%	36(3)-8%	28(3)-11%	195(46)-24%
1930	71(19)-27%	24(17)-71%	31(6)-19%	7(0)-0%	133(42)-32%
1931	70(21)-30%	36(27)-75%	35(4)-11%	30(5)-17%	171(57)-33%
1932	42(10)-24%	13(7)-54%	17(7)-41%	2(0)-0%	74(27)-34%

SOURCE: Dienstaltersliste der Hauptleute u. Rittmeister, soweit sie seit dem 1 Februar 1922 zu diesem Dienstgrade befördert sind, sowie der Oberleutnante u. Leutnante des Reichsheeres, Stand vom 1 July 1922 (Berlin: Reichswehrministerium, 1922); Rangliste 1923-1932.

NOTE: Statistics are current as of Rangliste publication date. The total number of new Lts. is represented by the first of the three entries in each column. Nobles in the particular group are designated by the number in parenthesis and the percentage figure.

Appendix 2.
Officer Candidate Training

TABLE 1

EDUARD ZORN'S INFANTRY SCHOOL CURRICULUM (FIRST YEAR COURSE)

Subject	Average Number of Hours per Week
A. Theoretical (Scientific) Instruction	
Tactics	6
Terrain Study	2
Military Science.	3
Engineering Service	3
Air Defense	1
Signals Service	1
Motor Transport Service	1
Military Affairs.	2
Civil Government.	2
Military Administration	1/3
Physiology.	2/3
Calisthenics.	1
TOTAL.	23
B. Practical Instruction	
Infantry Service.	4
Machine Gun Service	1
Trench Mortar Service . . . . 2/3 ⎤	
Artillery Service . . . . 2/3 ⎬ 2-1/3	
Signals Service 1	
Motor Transport Service . . . . 1/3 ⎦	
Calisthenics.	3-2/3
Horsemanship.	3
TOTAL.	14

SOURCE: "Regulations Governing Instruction and Examination for the Service Schools," M.A. Rpt. No. 2277-B-18, Jul 1923, Navy and Old Army Branch, Military Archives Division, Record Group 165, National Archives, Washington, D.C.

TABLE 2

EDUARD ZORN'S INFANTRY SCHOOL CURRICULUM (SECOND YEAR COURSE)

Subject	Average Number of Hours per Week
A. Theoretical (Scientific) Instruction	
Tactics and Terrain Study	5
Military History.	3
Military Science.	1
Engineering Service	1/3
Air Defense	1
Knowledge and Care of Field Equipment, Theory of Driving	1/3
Military Affairs.	1
Care of the Horse	1/3
TOTAL.	12
B. Practical Instruction	
Infantry Service.	7
Machine Gun Service	6
Trench Mortar Service	5
Calisthenics.	3
Horsemanship: Driving Instruction.	3
Signals Service	1
TOTAL.	25

SOURCE: "Regulations Governing Instruction and Examination for the Service Schools," M.A. Rpt. No. 2277-B-18, Jul 1923, Navy and Old Army Branch, Military Archives Division, Record Group 165, National Archives, Washington, D.C.

Appendix **3.**
General Staff Candidate Selection

TABLE 1

FERDINAND JODL'S 1927 DISTRICT EXAMINATION SCHEDULE AND RESULTS

SCHEDULE

Day	Time	Subject
21.2.27	2½ hrs./0830-1100	Applied Tactics No. 1
	2 hrs./1130-1330	History
	2 hrs./1500-1700	Weapons Science
22.2.27	2½ hrs./0800-1030	Applied Tactics No. 2
	2 hrs./1100-1300	Civics
	2 hrs./1500-1700	Foreign Language
23.2.27	2½ hrs./0800-1030	Applied Tactics No. 3
	2 hrs./1100-1300	Engineering Service for All Weapons
	2 hrs./1500-1700	Economic Geography
24.2.27	2 hrs./0800-1000	Field Reconnaissance
	½ hrs./1005-1035	Map Sketch
	2 hrs./1100-1300	Formal Tactics
	1 hr./1400-1500	Physical Training (Theoretical)
	as required from 1530	Physical Training (Practical)

SOURCE: NA, 78, 370, p. 6332543.

RESULTS

Subject	Raw Score	Multiplier	Total	Scoring Scale
Applied Tactics #1	6	3	18	9 - superior
Applied Tactics #2	6	3	18	8 - very good
Formal Tactics	7	3	21	7 - good
Weapons Science	7	2	14	6 - above average
Field Reconnaissance	7	3	21	5 - satisfactory
Map Sketch	8	1	8	4 - fair
Engineering Service	5	2	10	3 - weak
English	5	2	10	2 - poor
Economic Geography	6	2	12	1 - unsatisfactory
History	8	2	16	
Civics	6	2	12	
Physical Training	8	2	16	
			197	

SOURCE: NA, 78, 370, p. 6332542.

TABLE 2

YEARLY NUMBER OF GENERAL STAFF SELECTEES

Year	Number From Bavaria	Number From Entire Reichswehr
1921	9	
1922	7	
1923	2	
1924	20	
1925	0	
1926	9	
1927	13	37
1928	1	33
1929	2	30
1930	4	35
1931	4	39
1932	6	38

SOURCE: NA, 78, 278, p. 6225745; NA, 78, 299, pp. 6250933-6250938; NA, 79, 73, pp. 607-609, 826-828, 954-955; NA, 79, 81, pp. 933-938.

NOTE: Accurate Reichswehr figures were not available for the first six years.

TABLE 3

BAVARIAN GENERAL STAFF SELECTEES, 1927

Order of Merit	Name	Lt. Patent	1Lt. Patent	Assignment	Location
1	Kathmann	1.9.15(128)	1.4.25(103)	5/A.R.7	Würzberg
2	Kaiser	1.9.15(247)	1.4.25(206)	Adj.III/A.R.7	Nürnberg
3	Winter	1.2.17(4)	1.4.25(495)	Adj./N.A.7	Munich
4	Cuno	1.9.14(2)	1.4.25(7)	3/K.A.7	Fürth
5	Preu	1.1.16(3)	1.4.25(340)	11/I.R.20	Passau
6	Jodl	1.9.15(240)	1.4.25(202)	Adj./F.A.7	Munich
7	Kittel	1.6.16(4)	1.4.25(397)	6/I.R.19	Augsburg
8	Herold	1.2.16(13)	1.4.25(367)	7/A.R.7	Nürnberg
9	Rasp	1.10.16(1)	1.4.25(455)	Adj.II/I.R.19	Augsburg
10	Schricker	1.9.15(60)	1.4.25(38)	Adj.II/A.R.7	Landsberg
11	Wittstatt	19.9.14	1.5.24(7)	Adj.III/I.R.21	Bayreuth
12	Rupprecht	1.9.15(273)	1.4.25(230)	9/I.R.21	Bayreuth
13	Chorbacher	1.9.15(44)	1.4.25(22)	A/A.R.7	Erlangen

SOURCE: NA, 78, 370, p. 6332541.

TABLE 4

COMPOSITE OF GENERAL STAFF CANDIDATE SELECTEES, 1928-1932

Year of Selection	Number That Passed District Examination	Number of Nobles That Passed District Examination	Branch of Service				Assignment				Number Stationed in a large city/University City	Number of Years Commissioned Service	
			Inf.	Art.	Kav.	Tech.	Staff	Adj.	Service School	M.G.Kp.		More Than 10	Less Than 10
1928	33	10	17	6	6	4	2	5	3	9	17	32	1
1929	30	4	21	6	2	1	2	9	0	5	11	30	0
1930	26	11	23	4	5	4	3	8	5	9	19	35	1
1931	39	8	21	8	7	3	5	7	2	10	17	38	1
1932	40	10	23	3	8	6	0	8	5	6	20	40	0

NOTE: Figures are current as of time of selection for training.

169

TABLE 5

GENERAL STAFF CANDIDATE SELECTEES, 1928-1932

1928

Name	Patent			Assignment	Location
	Lt.	1Lt.	Capt.		
v. Kurowski	1.9.15(110)	1.4.25(89)	. . . . .	1/I.R.9	Potsdam
v. Krosigk	1.7.16(12)	1.4.25(413)	. . . . .	8(M.G.)/I.R.9	Berlin-Lichterfelde
Jeschonneck	9.4.16(1)	1.4.25(386)	. . . . .	2/R.R.11	Loebschütz
Liss.	1.7.16(14)	1.4.25(415)	. . . . .	3/A.R.6	Münster
Skowronski.	1.4.14(44)	1.10.23(4)	1.4.28(41)	Adj./R.R.2	Allenstein
Zanssen	1.9.15(189)	1.4.25(156)	. . . . .	Adj./F.A.5	Ludwigsburg
Gittner	1.2.17(8)	1.4.25(499)	. . . . .	A/A.R.2	Schwerin
Prüter.	1.9.15(222)	1.4.25(185)	. . . . .	2/P.B.4	Magdeburg
Otzen	1.9.15(318)	1.4.25(270)	. . . . .	4/F.A.6	Hannover
Radziej	1.11.15(5)	1.4.25(311)	. . . . .	4(M.G.)/I.R.3	Martenwerder
Priess.	1.9.15(162)	1.4.25(134)	. . . . .	16/I.R.16	Osnabrück
Crisolli.	1.9.15(60)	1.4.25(39)	. . . . .	3/R.R.5	Stolp
Schwartzkopf. . . .	1.11.15(2)	1.4.25(308)	. . . . .	St.I/I.R.6	Schwerin
Dewitz.	1.7.16(6)	1.4.25(408)	. . . . .	16/I.R.4	Neustettin
v. Kirchbach. . . .	1.9.15(209)	1.4.25(171)	. . . . .	12(M.G.)/I.R.10	Dresden
v. Vormann.	1.8.19(4)	1.4.25(564a)	. . . . .	8(M.G.)/I.R.12	Quedlinburg
Frhr. v. Bodenhausen	1.10.15(30)	1.4.25(303)	. . . . .	Adj./R.R.16	Cassel
Steinmeister. . . .	1.9.15(68)	1.4.25(48)	. . . . .	Kdtr.Lötzen	Lötzen
Becker.	1.10.15(11)	1.4.25(289)	. . . . .	8(M.G.)/I.R.17	Göttingen
Kattmann.	1.9.15(155)	1.4.25(128)	. . . . .	2/F.A.5	Ludwigsburg
Graf v. Sponeck . .	1.4.15(14)	1.11.24(13)	. . . . .	13(M.W.)/I.R.14	Konstanz
Kurz.	11.10.18	1.11.25(4)	. . . . .	12.St./I.R.13	Ludwigsburg
Speth	1.7.16(32)	1.4.25(431)	. . . . .	Adj.III/A.R.6	Hannover
Reinshagen.	1.9.15(258)	1.4.25(218)	. . . . .	4(M.G.)/I.R.18	Paderborn
Frhr. v. Falkenstein	1.9.15(193)	1.4.25(160)	. . . . .	4(M.G.)/I.R.10	Dresden
Rohrbach.	1.9.15(106)	1.9.25(85)	. . . . .	8(M.G.)/I.R.14	Tübingen
Reussner.	1.9.15(321)	1.4.25(274)	. . . . .	Adj.IV(r.)/A.R.6	Verden
v. Bernuth.	1.9.15(297)	1.4.25(252)	. . . . .	11/I.R.15	Cassel
v. Bentivegni . . .	1.8.16(10)	1.4.25(442)	. . . . .	8/IIIA.R.3	Jüterbog
Hoffmann v. Waldau .	1.1.17(1)	1.4.25(487)	. . . . .	2/R.R.8	Oels
Hoppe	1.9.15(22)	1.4.25(2)	. . . . .	13(M.W.)/I.R.18	Paderborn
Berghammer.	18.10.18	1.10.23(3)	1.4.28(40)	1/R.R.18	Ludwigsburg
Raithel	1.9.15(268)	1.4.25(226)	. . . . .	12(M.G.)/I.R.20	Passau

SOURCE: NA, 78, 278, p. 6225745.

TABLE 5 - Continued

1929

Name	Patent		Assignment	Location
	Lt.	1Lt.		
Linstow	1.9.17(3)	1.4.25(590)	St.A/I.R.9	Wünsdorf
Dürking	1.9.15(151)	1.4.25(125)	15/I.R.18	Detmold
Linde	1.9.15(127)	1.4.25(102)	1/I.R.2	Ortelsburg
Feyerabend.	1.5.17(7)	1.4.25(535)	7/A.R.1	Allenstein
Walther	1.8.17(8)	1.4.25(571)	1/A.R.1	Insterburg
Pohlmann.	1.5.17(8)	1.4.25(537)	Adj.I/I.R.6	Schwerin
Schnepper	1.9.16(4)	1.4.25(454)	4(M.G.)/I.R.6	Lübeck
Volckheim	1.4.16(4)	1.4.25(382)	Kr./S.A.2	Stettin
Pruck	1.3.16(2)	1.4.25(371)	8(M.G.)/I.R.7	Hirschberg
Stadthagen.	1.9.15(162)	1.4.25(135)	5/I.R.7	Glatz
Busse	1.12.16(10)	1.4.25(480)	Adj.II/I.R.8	Liegnitz
Eberdring	1.3.18(6)	1.4.25(664)	10/I.R.7	Breslau
Schmundt.	1.9.15(212)	1.4.25(176)	R.Adj./I.R.9	Potsdam
Herfurth.	1.9.15(3)	1.2.25(23)	St.II/I.R.8	Liegnitz
Palm.	1.7.17(7)	1.4.25(555)	1/I.R.7	Oppeln
Hauck	1.9.15(319)	1.4.25(212)	16(r.)/A.R.3	Sagan
v. Reuss.	1.9.15(239)	1.4.25(201)	1/A.R.3	Schweidnitz
v. Mellenthin	1.2.16(8)	1.4.25(361)	Adj.IV(r.)/A.R.3	Potsdam
v. Raczeck.	1.1.19(4)	1.12.25(5)	4(M.G.)/I.R.14	Meiningen
Scherff	1.1.17(3)	1.4.25(489)	8(M.G.)/I.R.14	Ludwigsburg
Lange	1.5.16(7)	1.4.25(393)	Adj.I/I.R.13	Stuttgart
Herrmann.	1.7.17(14)	1.4.25(563)	Adj.III/I.R.15	Cassel
Geissler.	1.6.18(7)	1.6.25(4)	Adj.A/I.R.15	Marburg
Adam.	1.7.16(6)	1.4.25(407)	5/A.R.5	Wiblingen
Domizlaff	1.10.16(6)	1.4.25(461)	1/I.R.18	Paderborn
Glasl	1.5.17(1)	1.4.25(531)	Adj.III/I.R.20	Passau
Goth.	1.7.17(2)	1.4.25(549)	Adj.II/I.R.20	Ingolstadt
Schoepf	1.5.17(5)	1.4.25(533)	12(M.G.)/I.R.20	Passau
Lungershausen	1.9.15(205)	1.4.25(169)	3/R.R.16	Langensalza
Hasse	1.11.15(13)	1.4.25(315)	3/R.R.10	Züllichau

SOURCE: NA, 79, 73, pp. 954-955.

TABLE 5 - Continued

1930

Name	Patent		Assignment	Location
	Lt.	1Lt.		
Bork.	1.18.17(17)	1.4.25(518)	Adj.I/I.R.3	Martenwerder
Siewert	1.2.18(9)	1.4.25(650)	Adj.III/I.R.5	Rostock
Blümke.	1.12.17(5)	1.4.25(623)	4(M.G.)/I.R.6	Bremen
v. Waldenberg	1.6.19(2)	1.4.25(617a)	A/R.R.11	Ohlau
v. Hünersdorf	1.9.16(2)	1.4.25(452)	Adj./R.R.11	Neustadt
Frhr. v. Strachwitz . .	1.8.17(11)	1.4.25(575)	2/R.R.7	Breslau
Schniewind.	1.9.15(305)	1.4.25(258)	Adj.IV(r.)/A.R.3	Potsdam
v. Kries.	1.5.16(3)	1.4.25(389)	R.St./I.R.9	Potsdam
Sauberzweig	1.10.17(7)	1.4.25(606)	4(M.G.)/I.R.8	Frankfurt/Oder
Babel	1.3.18(5)	1.4.25(663)	12(M.G.)/I.R.7	Breslau
v. Lossberg	1.18.17(12)	1.4.25(576)	Kdtr.Berlin	Berlin
v. d. Burg.	1.2.18(8)	1.4.25(649)	Adj./IIIA.R.3	Jüterbog
Sperl	1.4.17(9)	1.4.25(525)	3/IIIA.R.3	Jüterbog
Bucher.	1.3.17(5)	1.4.25(511)	4(M.G.)/I.R.10	Dresden
Pampel.	1.6.17(5)	1.4.25(545)	12(M.G.)/I.R.11	Leipzig
Reuss	1.2.23(26)	1.5.25(15)	12(M.G.)/I.R.12	Magdeburg
Dorn	1.1.17(4)	1.4.25(490)	T.V.P.Attengrabow	Attengrabow
Schöne.	1.10.17(6)	1.4.25(605)	4/R.R.12	Grossenhain
Loechel	1.10.15(13)	1.4.25(291)	Inf.Sch.	Dresden
v. Thadden.	1.7.16(5)	1.4.25(406)	16/I.R.8	Lübben
Tschirdewahn.	1.7.17(6)	1.4.25(554)	2/I.R.2	Allenstein
Kühne	1.4.18(2)	1.4.25(607)	3/I.R.10	Dresden
v. Pfuhlstein	1.4.18(16)	1.4.25(685)	Inf.Sch.	Dresden
Pemsel.	1.5.17(2)	1.4.25(532)	1/I.R.20	Regensburg
Lamey	1.1.18(5)	1.4.25(465)	4(M.G.)/I.R.14	Meiningen
Frhr v. Liebenstein . .	1.1.18(5)	1.4.25(639)	2/R.R.18	Stuttgart
Klosterkemper	1.9.17(1)	1.4.25(588)	Adj.I/I.R.16	Bremen
Heinemann	1.4.17(7)	1.4.25(522)	4(M.G.)/I.R.17	Braunschweig
Wagner.	1.7.17(13)	1.4.25(562)	13(M.W.)/I.R.17	Braunschweig
Sieberg	1.9.15(157)	1.4.25(130)	Adj./K.A.6	Münster
Schwarz	1.9.15(285)	1.4.25(242)	2/F.A.5	Ludwigsburg
Schoch.	1.9.17(10)	1.4.25(598)	2/F.A.7	Munich
Degen	1.10.17(3)	1.4.25(601)	7/I.R.20	Ingolstadt
v. Le Suire	1.12.17(16)	1.4.25(633)	8(M.G.)/I.R.19	Augsburg
Frhr. v. Malsen-Ponickau.	1.2.18(11)	1.4.25(651)	Adj.I/A.R.7	Würzburg

SOURCE: NA, 79, 73, pp. 826-828.

172

TABLE 5 - Continued

1931

Name	Patent		Assignment	Location
	Lt.	1Lt.		
Frhr. Treusch V.				
Buttlar-Brandenfels	1.7.18(4)	1.7.25(5)	3/R.R.3	Stendel
Clausius	1.7.18(10)	1.8.25(6)	St./R.R.3	Rathenow
Voelter	1.1.18(6)	1.4.25(460)	1/N.A.5	Stuttgart
Hassenstein	1.4.20(1)	1.2.26(43)	1/I.R.17	Braunschweig
Munzel	1.9.18(1)	1.10.25(1)	3/R.R.4	Potsdam
Herhudt v. Rohden	1.10.18(1)	1.11.25(1)	A/R.R.8	Bernstadt
v. d. Borne	1.4.21(3)	1.6.26(6)	4(M.G.)/I.R.12	Dessau
Zitzewitz	1.7.18(15)	1.9.25(1)	3/A.R.1	Insterburg
Baurmeister	1.9.18(4)	1.10.25(8)	Adj.V(r.)/A.R.3	Sagan
Theilacker	1.2.18(3)	1.4.25(625)	Adj.III/I.R.13	Ulm
Ochsner	1.10.16(2)	1.4.25(456)	R.St./I.R.19	Munich
Bader	1.5.18(5)	1.5.25(8)	Adj.III/I.R.19	Kempten
Frhr. v. Elverfeldt	1.4.19(4)	1.1.26(7)	13(M.W.)/I.R.9	Potsdam
Korten	1.10.15(1)	1.4.25(280)	2/P.B.1	Königsberg
Gade	1.7.20(3)	1.4.26(11)	Adj.I/A.R.2	Stettin
Kühl	1.8.17(9)	1.4.25(573)	4/R.R.8	Namslau
Biermann	1.2.21(2)	1.5.26(10)	13(M.W.)/I.R.6	Ratzeburg
v. Gyldenfeldt	1.7.18(9)	1.8.25(5)	8/A.R.2	Itzehoe
Steffler	1.7.18(8)	1.8.25(4)	13(M.W.)/I.R.4	Kolberg
Blaurock	1.4.18	1.4.25(613)	7/A.R.7	Nürnberg
Rossmann	1.5.21(3)	1.7.26(5)	4(M.G.)/I.R.19	Munich
Löhr	1.3.19(2)	1.12.25(11)	12(M.G.)/I.R.6	Flensburg
Pfafferott	1.4.20(4)	1.3.26(2)	Kdtr.Berlin	Berlin
Kratzer	1.10.21(1)	1.9.26(1)	1/R.R.16	Hofgeismar
Deich	1.4.17(8)	1.4.25(524)	1/I.R.1	Königsberg
Dietlen	1.7.19(5)	1.2.26(14)	12(M.G.)/I.R.14	Konstanz
v. Collani	1.3.20(1)	1.12.24(6a)	2/R.R.3	Rathenow
Lyncker	1.5.18(4)	1.5.25(7)	4(M.G.)/I.R.21	Würzberg
Doerr	1.9.19(3)	1.2.26(21)	8/IIIA.R.3	Jüterbog
Hölter	1.12.18(1)	1.11.25(6)	St.GP.1	Berlin
R. u. Edler v. Dawans	1.1.22(17)	1.2.27(1)	8(M.G.)/I.R.14	Tübingen
Schmidt	1.11.21(2)	1.11.26(2)	8(M.G.)/I.R.17	Göttingen
Friebe	1.2.19(3)	1.12.25(9)	(Kr.)/S.A.1	Königsberg
Hoepke	1.4.19(10)	1.2.26(1)	Adj.A/I.R.4	Neustettin
Ehlert	1.7.17(10)	1.4.25(558)	7/A.R.2	Itzehoe
Feist	1.10.21(2)	1.9.26(2)	Adj.A/I.R.7	Schweidnitz
Kriescke	1.4.20(5)	1.3.26(3)	Adj.III/A.R.2	Itzehoe
Ehrig	1.10.18(4)	1.11.25(3)	14/I.R.11	Döbeln
Holle	1.12.16(8)	1.4.25(477)	12(M.C.)/I.R.16	Oldenburg

SOURCE: NA, 79, 73, pp. 607-609.

173

TABLE 5 - Continued

1932

Name	Patent		Assignment	Location
	Lt.	1Lt.		
Frhr. v. Schleinitz	1.2.21(1)	1.5.26(9)	10/I.R.17	Goslar
Stieff	1.4.22(4)	1.2.27(20)	16(r.)/A.R.3	Sagan
Kühn	1.2.20(7)	1.2.26(38)	Kdtr. Lötzen	Lötzen
Bayerlein	1.1.22(13)	1.1.27(2)	Adj.I/I.R.21	Würzburg
Gundelach	1.7.18(14)	1.8.25(10)	2/P.B.2	Stettin
Reinhardt	1.4.22(1)	1.2.27(16)	9/I.R.13	Ulm
Vollhase	1.10.21(15)	1.10.26(12)	2/N.A.6	Hannover
Brücker	1.4.22(8)	1.2.27(24)	16/I.R.5	Greifswald
Münch	1.7.18(6)	1.8.25(1)	4(M.G.)/I.R.15	Giessen
v. Woedtke	1.5.22(17)	1.3.27(22)	3/R.R.2	Allenstein
Groscurth	1.8.20(3)	1.4.26(15)	13(M.W.)/I.R.6	Ratzeburg
Kossmann	1.4.22(3)	1.2.27(18)	2/I.R.16	Bremen
Christ	1.4.22(2)	1.2.27(17)	4/F.A.4	Dresden
Foertsch	1.4.22(19)	1.2.27(33)	12(M.G.)/I.R.17	Goslar
Wentzell	1.11.21(4)	1.11.26(4)	6/A.R.2	Schwerin
Radke	1.10.21(19)	1.10.26(15)	1/I.R.1	Königsberg
Hildebrand	1.12.22(35)	1.12.27(3)	Adj./R.R.16	Cassel
Moeller	1.12.21(5)	1.12.26(2)	Adj.II/I.R.1	Tilsit
v. Quast	1.5.22(6)	1.3.27(11)	6/R.R.6	Demmin
Koerner	1.5.22(8)	1.3.27(14)	Adj.III/I.R.7	Breslau
Frhr.v. Imhof	1.4.22(46)	1.12.27(21)	1/R.R.13	Hannover
Frhr.v. Hanstein	1.10.19(7)	1.2.26(28)	2/A.R.5	Fulda
v. Watzdorf	1.10.20(1)	1.4.26(19)	4(M.W.)/I.R.10	Dresden
Oeltze	1.12.22(13)	1.9.27	3/I.R.8	Frankfurt/Oder
Schmoeger	1.8.19(3)	1.2.26(17)	12(M.G.)/I.R.21	Bayreuth
Jank	1.4.17(2)	1.4.25(516)	Adj.II/I.R.19	Augsburg
Schipp v. Branitz	1.4.22(21)	1.2.27(35)	Adj.I/I.R.2	Ortelsburg
v. Grolmann	1.8.20(2)	1.4.26(14)	Adj./R.R.9	Fürstenwalde
Schäfer	1.12.22(12)	1.8.27(5)	Adj.A/I.R.15	Marburg
Westphal	1.12.22(14)	1.11.27(1)	1/R.R.16	Hofgeismar
Schmidt(Hans)	1.4.22(6)	1.2.27(22)	13(M.W.)/I.R.21	Fürth
Siebert	1.12.19(1)	1.2.26(30)	5/I.R.2	Rastenburg
Macher	1.5.22(2)	1.3.27(7)	1/F.A.7	Munich
Höfle	1.10.17(8)	1.4.25(607)	1/K.A.7	Munich
v. Schaewen	1.4.22(17)	1.2.27(31)	4(M.G.)/I.R.1	Königsberg
Schwatlo-Gesterding	1.12.22(5)	1.7.27(1)	12(M.G.)/I.R.5	Rostock
Hirsch	1.6.22(14)	1.6.27(5)	A/R.R.8	Bernstadt
Schoder	1.12.22(20)	1.11.27(7)	1/N.A.5	Stuttgart
Issmer	1.2.18(14)	1.4.25(654)	13(M.W.)/I.R.8	Frankfurt/Oder
Munzel	1.8.18(1)	1.10.25(1)	3/R.R.4	Potsdam

SOURCE: NA, 78, 299, pp. 6250933-6250938.

Appendix **4.**
General Staff Candidate Training

TABLE 1

FERDINAND JODL'S FIRST YEAR CURRICULUM (D1)
OCTOBER 1927-MAY 1928

Subject	Number of Hours
Tactics (reinforced infantry regiment)	6 per week
Military History	4 per week
Supply and Quartering of Combat Troops (with tactical problems)	1 per week
Air Defense	1 every 2 weeks
Technical Instruction in Various Arms	1 every 2 weeks
Special Artillery Instruction	1 every 2 weeks
Engineering Service	1 every 2 weeks
Motor Transport Service	1 per week
Signals Service	1 per week
Sanitary Service and Care of Troops	10 total
Veterinary Service	10 total
Judge Advocate Department	8 total
Foreign Languages	2 per week
Physical Training	2 per week
Horsemanship	3 per week

SOURCE: Col. A. L. Conger, "Third Division Officers' Schools," M.A. Rpt. No. 2016-1004 (25), April 1928, Navy and Old Army Branch, Military Archives Division, Record Group 165, National Archives, Washington, D.C.

NOTE: Instruction averaged 22 hours per week. Additionally, one day per week was reserved for a wargame or map exercise.

TABLE 2

FERDINAND JODL'S SECOND YEAR CURRICULUM (D2)
OCTOBER 1928–MAY 1929

Subject	Number of Hours
Tactics (division)	6 per week
Military History	4 per week
Technique of Command	2 per week
Army Organization	1 per week
Supply and Quartering of Combat Troops	1 per week
Army Transport Service	1 every 2 weeks
Air Defense	1 every 2 weeks
Special Artillery Service (chemical warface)	8 total
Motor Transport Service	1 every 2 weeks
Signals Service	1 every 2 weeks
Army Administration	12 total
Foreign Languages	2 per week
Physical Training	2 per week
Horsemanship	3 per week

SOURCE: Col. A. L. Conger, "Third Division Officers' Schools," M. A. Rpt. No. 2016-1004 (25), April 1928, Navy and Old Army Branch, Military Archives Division, Record Group 165, National Archives, Washington, D.C.

NOTE: Instruction averaged 24 hours per week. Additionally, one day per week was reserved for a wargame or map exercise.

TABLE 3

FERDINAND JODL'S THIRD YEAR CURRICULUM (<u>LEHRGANG R</u>)
OCTOBER 1929-MAY 1930

Tactics (reinforced infantry division)

Military History

General Staff Service

Army Organization

Organization and Leadership in Foreign Armies

Counterintelligence

Supply and Quartering of Combat Troops

Army Transport Service

Military Technology

Naval War Leadership

Air Defense

External and Internal Political Situation

Economic Situation

Foreign Languages

Physical Training

SOURCE: Waldemar Erfurth, <u>Die Geschichte des deutschen
Generalstabes von 1918 bis 1945</u> (Berlin and Frankfurt:
Musterschmidt-Verlag, 1957), pp. 139-140.; NA, T-78, 375,
pp. 6349194-6349216.

NOTE: The number of hours for the third year curriculum
were unavailable.

TABLE 4

FERDINAND JODL'S GENERAL STAFF TRAINING CLASS
1927-1929

Name	Patent			Assignment				
	Lt.	1Lt.	Capt.	1923	1924	1925	1926	1927
Gerlach*	1.9.15(31)	1.4.25(11)	1.10.29(19)	14(r.)/A.R.3	4/A.R.3	.....	.....	R.St./A.R.3
Hüther	1.9.15(58)	1.4.25(36)	1.12.29(4)	5/A.R.3	A/R.R.7	4/R.R.7	.....	7/A.R.3
Hildebrandt*	1.9.15(190)	1.4.25(157)	1.1.31(1)	Adj./K.A.3	.....	7/I.R.7	.....	.....
Friede	1.11.15(1)	1.4.25(307)	1.2.32(1)	12(M.W.)/I.R.7	.....	.....	.....	.....
Heistermann v. Ziehlberg*	10.12.15(1)	1.4.25(334)	1.2.32(27)	Adj.I/I.R.5	.....	4(M.G.)/I.R.5	.....	14/I.R.5
Badenhop	1.1.16(6)	1.4.25(345)	.....	1/P.B.4	2/P.B.4	6/A.R.4	.....	1/P.B.3
Knesch	1.11.16(6)	1.4.25(466)	.....	Kdtr.Zötzen	.....	2/P.B.3	.....	.....
Traut	1.9.15(63)	1.5.25(13)	1.2.30(4)	R.St./I.R.3	Adj.I/I.R.3	.....	8(M.G.)/I.R.3	.....
v. Wagner*	1.7.16(23)	1.4.25(683)	.....	A/R.R.10	1/R.R.10	A/R.R.10	.....	St.R.R.10
Steuber*	1.4.18(140)	20.6.18(41)	.....	3/A.R.1	4/A.R.1	4/A.R.1	.....	.....
Kirschner		1.11.23(18)	1.2.27(26)	4(M.G.)/I.R.13	Adj.I/I.R.13	.....	.....	4(M.G.)/I.R.13
Flörke	1.4.14(77)	1.4.25(206)	.....	6/I.R.12	Adj.II/I.R.12	.....	.....	.....
Kaiser*	1.9.15(247)	1.4.25(340)	1.2.31(40)	9/A.R.7	Adj.III/A.R.7	.....	.....	.....
Preu	1.1.16(3)	1.4.25(367)	.....	10/I.R.20	.....	11/I.R.20	.....	.....
Herold	1.2.16(13)	1.4.25(417)	.....	R.St./A.R.7	.....	7/A.R.7	.....	.....
Heusinger	1.7.16(17)	1.4.25(455)	1.4.32(18)	Adj.III/I.R.15	.....	.....	.....	12(M.G.)/I.R.15
Rasp	1.10.16(1)	18.10.18(32)	.....	1/I.R.19	8(M.G.)/I.R.19	.....	.....	Adj.II/I.R.19
Koelitz		1.4.25(167)	1.2.28(45)	11/I.R.14	9/I.R.14	12(M.G.)/I.R.14	.....	.....
Cramer	1.9.15(202)	1.4.25(215)	.....	St./R.R.13	A/R.R.13	3/R.R.13	.....	.....
Ottens	1.9.15(255)	20.6.18(69)	.....	6/I.R.15	Adj.A/I.R.15	.....	9/I.R.15	.....
Leistikow		1.7.23(7)	1.4.27(12)	13(M.W.)/I.R.16	.....	.....	.....	.....
Bäntsch	1.4.14(28)	1.4.24(7)	1.4.28(24)	11/I.R.17	12(M.G.)/I.R.17	.....	.....	.....
Cuno		1.5.24(7)	1.2.29(12)	3/K.A.7	.....	.....	.....	.....
Wittstadt	19.9.14	1.4.25(22)	1.2.29(21)	9/I.R.21	10/I.R.21	Adj.III/I.R.21	.....	.....
Chorbacher	1.9.15(44)	1.4.25(102)	1.10.29(29)	A/A.R.7	8/A.R.7	.....	A/A.R.7	.....
Jodl*	1.9.15(240)	1.4.25(230)	1.2.31(36)	6/A.R.7	.....	.....	.....	.....
Rupprecht	1.9.15(273)	1.4.25(495)	1.4.31(6)	11/I.R.21	.....	.....	.....	Adj./F.A.7
Winter*	1.2.17(4)	1.4.25(155)	.....	1/N.A.7	Adj./N.A.7	.....	.....	9/I.R.21
Bauer*	1.9.15(195)	1.4.25(409)	.....	2/I.R.21	1/I.R.16	4(M.G.)/I.R.16	.....	.....
Niehoff	1.7.16(8)	1.4.24(8)	.....	15/I.R.17	1/I.R.21	.....	.....	.....
Beutler	2.9.14(1)	1.4.25(331)	1.2.29(13)	1/R.R.12	.....	St.II/I.R.13	8(M.G.)/I.R.13	Adj./R.R.12
Speidel*	1.12.15(10)	.....	1.2.33(24)	7/I.R.13	.....	5/I.R.13	R.Adj./I.R.13	.....
Schneckenburger			1.12.22(6)	12(M.G.)/I.R.13	St.III/I.R.13	.....	.....	.....

SOURCE: NA, T-78, 371, pp. 6333676-6333677.; *Rangliste* 1923-1932.

NOTE: Assignments are current as of *Rangliste* publication date. Where no assignment is listed for the particular year, the previous year's assignment or status applies.

*These officers represent brother combinations in the Reichswehr.

TABLE 4 – Continued

Name	1928	1929	Assignment 1930	1931	1932
Gerlach*	St.1.DIV.	. . . . .	1/A.R.3	7/A.R.2	W
Hüther	St.1.DIV.	. . . . .	5/A.R.2	1/K.A.1	. . . . .
Hildebrandt*	St.1.DIV.	. . . . .	St.4.DIV	. . . . .	. . . . .
Friede	St.1.DIV.	. . . . .			. . . . .
Heistermann v. Ziehlberg*					
Badenhop	St.1.DIV.	. . . . .	4/R.R.2	T1	3/P.B.4
Knesch	St.1.DIV.	. . . . .	St.3.DIV.	St.Inf.Kdr.4	. . . . .
Traut	St.1.DIV.	8(M.G.)/I.R.2	St.II/I.R.2	St.Kav.Div.2	14/I.R.2
v. Wagner*	St.1.DIV.	. . . . .	4/R.R.10	A/R.R.10	3/R.R.8
Steuber*	St.1.DIV.	. . . . .	2/A.R.1	St.4.DIV.	. . . . .
Kirschner	St.5.DIV.	. . . . .			. . . . .
Flörke	St.5.DIV.	. . . . .	K.Adj./I.R.12		. . . . .
Kaiser*	St.5.DIV.	. . . . .			. . . . .
Prue	St.5.DIV.	. . . . .	R.St./I.R.20		R.Adj./A.R.7
Herold	St.5.DIV.	. . . . .	Adj.III/A.R.7		. . . . .
Heusinger	St.5.DIV.	. . . . .	St.3.DIV.	St.Inf.Kdr.2	T1
kasp	St.5.DIV.	. . . . .	St.7.DIV.	2/N.A.5	. . . . .
Koelitz	St.5.DIV.	. . . . .	St.I/I.R.14	3/K.A.5	. . . . .
Cramer	St.5.DIV.	. . . . .	A/R.R.13	1/R.R.13	. . . . .
Ottens	St.5.DIV.	. . . . .	8(M.G.)/I.R.15	Gest.	. . . . .
Leistikow	St.6.DIV.	. . . . .	3/I.R.18		St.3.DIV.
Bantsch	St.6.DIV.	. . . . .		3/K.A.7	. . . . .
Cuno	St.6.DIV.	. . . . .	15/I.R.20		. . . . .
Wittstadt	St.6.DIV.	. . . . .	St.III/A.R.7		. . . . .
Chorbacher	St.6.DIV.	. . . . .	1/A.R.6	4/A.R.6	T3
Jodl*	St.6.DIV.	. . . . .	14/I.R.20		. . . . .
Rupprecht	St.6.DIV.	. . . . .	St.7.DIV.		. . . . .
Winter*	St.6.DIV.	. . . . .	8(M.G.)/I.R.21		. . . . .
Bauer*	St.6.DIV.	. . . . .	8(M.G.)/I.R.16	a.D.	. . . . .
Niehoff	St.6.DIV.	. . . . .	St.Kav.Div.3		St.II/I.R.16
Beutler	. . . . .	. . . . .		T2	. . . . .
Speidel*	. . . . .	13(M.W.)/I.R.13		T3	. . . . .
Schneckenburger	. . . . .		St.Inf.Kdr.3	St.5.DIV.	St.Inf.Kdr.3

SOURCE: NA, T-78, 371, pp. 6333676-6333677.; Rangliste 1923-1932.

NOTE: Assignments are current as of Rangliste publication date. Where no assignment is listed for the particular year, the previous year's assignment or status applies.

*These officers represent brother combinations in the Reichswehr.

180

TABLE 5

OFFICERS ASSIGNED TO LEHRGANG R, 1929-1932

Lehrgang R, 1929-1930			Lehrgang R, 1930-1931			Lehrgang R, 1931-1932		
Rank	Name	Unit	Rank	Name	Unit	Rank	Name	Unit
Capt.	Büntsch	I.R.17	Capt.	Böhme**	I.R.11	Capt.	Röhricht**	I.R.3
Capt.	Beutler**	I.R.2	Capt.	Gause**	P.B.1	Capt.	Holm*,**	I.R.4
Capt.	Cuno	K.A.7	Capt.	Koehler**	R.R.17	1Lt.	Adam*	I.R.5
Capt.	Kirschner	I.R.13	Capt.	Krebs**	I.R.17	1Lt.	Busse*	I.R.8
Capt.	Schneckenburger**	I.R.13	Capt.	Rottiger**	A.R.4	1Lt.	Domizlaff	I.R.18
1Lt.	Gerlach*	A.R.2	Capt.	Tschache**	R.R.2	1Lt.	Feyerabend*	A.R.1
1Lt.	Heistermann v. Ziehlberg*	I.R.5	1Lt.	Steinmetz*,**	A.R.6	1Lt.	Glasl	I.R.20
1Lt.	Heusinger*	I.R.15	1Lt.	v. Bentivegni	III/A.R.3	1Lt.	Goth	I.R.20
1Lt.	Hildebrandt*	K.A.3	1Lt.	v. Bernuth	I.R.15	1Lt.	Hauck*	A.R.3
1Lt.	Jodl*	A.R.7	1Lt.	Gittner	A.R.2	1Lt.	Herfurth*	I.R.8
1Lt.	Kaiser	A.R.7	1Lt.	Hoffman v. Waldau	R.R.8	1Lt.	Herrmann*	I.R.15
1Lt.	Knesch	P.B.3	1Lt.	Jeschonnek	R.R.11	1Lt.	Lange*	I.R.13
1Lt.	Rasp	I.R.19	1Lt.	v. Krosigk*	I.R.9	1Lt.	Linstow	I.R.9
1Lt.	Dr. Speidel*,**	I.R.13	1Lt.	v. Kurowski	I.R.9	1Lt.	Lungershausen	R.R.16
1Lt.	Winter*	N.A.7	1Lt.	Liss	A.R.6	1Lt.	Pohlmann	I.R.6
			1Lt.	Priess	I.R.16	1Lt.	v. Reuss	A.R.3
			1Lt.	Prüter	P.B.4	1Lt.	Scherff	I.R.13
			1Lt.	Speth	A.R.6	1Lt.	Schmundt	I.R.9
			1Lt.	Graf v. Sponeck*	I.R.14	1Lt.	Schnepper	I.R.6
			1Lt.	v. Vormann	I.R.12	1Lt.	v. Wedel**	R.R.16

SOURCE: NA, T-79, 73, pp. 929, 73, 722-723, 591.

*These officer's represent brother combinations.

**These officers were assigned to Lehrgang R directly from the field. They had completed the first two years of General Staff training earlier in their careers.

TABLE 6

COMPOSITE OF OFFICERS ASSIGNED TO LEHRGANG R, 1929-1932

Class Year	Class Size	Number Assigned Directly From D2	Number Assigned Directly From Field Units	Nobles	Brother Combinations	Rank			Branch				Geographic Area					
						Lt.	1Lt.	Capt.	Inf.	Kav.	Art.	Tech.	Pr.	Bav.	Wü.	Bad.	Sax.	Other
1929-1930	15	12	3	1	7	0	10	5	5	0	3	4	6	5	3	0	0	1
1930-1931	20	13	7	7	3	0	15	5	8	4	6	2	17	0	0	1	2	0
1931-1932	20	17	3	3	10	0	14	6	15	1	4	0	15	2	2	1	0	0

TABLE 7

OFFICERS ASSIGNED TO GENERAL STAFF TRAINING, 1924-1925

Rank	Name	Unit	Rank	Name	Unit	Rank	Name	Unit	Rank	Name	Unit
Capt.	Volkmann*	St.5.DIV.	Capt.	Scheller	I.R.16	Capt.	Wisselinck	R.R.9	1Lt.	Wuthmann	A.R.2
Capt.	v. Ludwig	I.R.2	Capt.	Brennecke	I.R.17	1Lt.	v. Gersdorff*	R.R.9	Capt.	Duvert	A.R.3
Capt.	Nehring	I.R.2	Capt.	Keitel*	I.R.17	1Lt.	Hesse	R.R.9	Capt.	Lindemann*	A.R.3
1Lt.	Berthold	I.R.2	Capt.	Rupp	I.R.17	1Lt.	Herr	R.R.9	1Lt.	Baier*	A.R.3
1Lt.	Röhricht	I.R.3	1Lt.	Hossbach	I.R.17	1Lt.	v. Wolff	R.R.9	1Lt.	Bamler*	A.R.3
Lt.	Meister	I.R.4	1Lt.	Koch*	I.R.17	1Lt.	v. Greiffenberg*	R.R.10	1Lt.	Noeldecken	A.R.3
1Lt.	Braun*	I.R.5	1Lt.	Ruccius	I.R.17	1Lt.	Drum	R.R.12	1Lt.	v. Rost	A.R.3
1Lt.	Hoffmeister	I.R.5	1Lt.	Utsch	I.R.17	1Lt.	Versock	R.R.12	1Lt.	Schlemm	A.R.3
1Lt.	Michelmann	I.R.6	Capt.	Rhode*	I.R.18	1Lt.	Müller	R.R.13	Capt.	Burdach	A.R.4
1Lt.	Pflugradt	I.R.6	Capt.	Stapf	I.R.19	Capt.	Grossmann	R.R.14	Capt.	Matzky	A.R.4
Lt.	Burgdorff*	I.R.8	Capt.	Zorn*	I.R.19	1Lt.	Schwabedissen	R.R.14	Lt.	Rottiger	A.R.4
1Lt.	Diestel*	I.R.9	Capt.	Dostler	I.R.20	1Lt.	Rabe v. Pappenheim	R.R.15	1Lt.	Bessel*	A.R.5
Capt.	Richter*	I.R.10	Capt.	Müller*	I.R.20	1Lt.	Frhr. v. Stein	R.R.15	1Lt.	Foertsch*	A.R.5
Capt.	Schoenknecht	I.R.10	Capt.	Forster	I.R.21	Capt.	Kittel*	R.R.17	1Lt.	Heim*	A.R.5
1Lt.	Frhr.v.Falkenstein	I.R.10	1Lt.	R. v. Kanitz	R.R.2	1Lt.	Hübner*	R.R.17	1Lt.	Schunck*	A.R.5
Lt.	Heygendorff	I.R.10	1Lt.	Tschache	R.R.2	1Lt.	Schoerner	R.R.17	1Lt.	Wagner*	A.R.5
1Lt.	v. Groeling	I.R.11	1Lt.	Weckmann*	R.R.2	Capt.	Allmendinger	R.R.18	1Lt.	Beisswanger*	A.R.6
Capt.	Graessner	I.R.12	Capt.	Hauffe	R.R.3	1Lt.	Hecker	R.R.18	1Lt.	Praun	A.R.6
Capt.	Hellmich*	I.R.12	1Lt.	Rawald	R.R.4	1Lt.	Henn	R.R.18	1Lt.	Schröder*	A.R.6
1Lt.	Buhle	I.R.13	Capt.	v. Wulisch	R.R.5	1Lt.	Vockammer v. Kirchensittenbach	R.R.18	1Lt.	Steinmetz	A.R.6
1Lt.	Merker	I.R.13	1Lt.	v. Horn	R.R.5	1Lt.	John*	A.R.1	1Lt.	Warlimont	A.R.6
1Lt.	Beutter	I.R.13	1Lt.	Schilling*	R.R.5	Capt.	Osterkamp	A.R.1	Capt.	Brandenberger	A.R.7
1Lt.	Speidel, W.*	I.R.13	1Lt.	Schmidt*	R.R.5	1Lt.	Haessler	A.R.1	Capt.	Jodl*	A.R.7
1Lt.	Speidel, H.*	I.R.13	Lt.	v. Ahlfen*	R.R.5	1Lt.	Prange	A.R.1	Capt.	Metz*	A.R.7
1Lt.	Henke*	I.R.14	1Lt.	Lob	R.R.6	1Lt.	Stuckenschmidt	A.R.1	Capt.	Müller*	A.R.7
1Lt.	Jost	I.R.14	1Lt.	v. Witzleben*	R.R.6	Lt.	Scheffler	A.R.1	Capt.	Ochsner*	A.R.7
1Lt.	Ullmer	I.R.14	Capt.	Schaefer*	R.R.7	Capt.	Schlieper*	A.R.2	Capt.	R. v. Pohl	A.R.7
Capt.	Blumentritt*	I.R.15	Lt.	Kohler	R.R.7	1Lt.	Schieb	A.R.2	1Lt.	Mayer*	A.R.7
Lt.	v. Herff*	I.R.15	Capt.	Engelbrecht	R.R.8	1Lt.	Waeger	A.R.2	Capt.	Wollmann	P.B.3
1Lt.	Wöhler	I.R.15	Lt.	Krebs	R.R.8				1Lt.	v. Pfetten	S.A.7

SOURCE: Col. Creed F. Cox, "Notes on Education of Officers of the Reichswehr," M. A. Rpt. No. 2016-960(2), 11 December 1924, Navy and Old Army Branch, Military Archives Division, Record Group 165, National Archives, Washington, D.C.

*These officers represent brother combinations.

Appendix 5.
Officer Assignments

TABLE 1

1932 DIVISION VII OFFICER STELLENBESETZUNG

Unit	Number of Authorized Officers	Number of Assigned Officers
Div. Kdr. + St.	21	21
Inf. Kdr. + St.	4	4
Art. Kdr. + St.	4	4
I.R.19	74	73
I.R.20	71	71
I.R.21	71	71
R.R.17	38	38
A.R.7	76	76
P.B.7	11	11
N.A.7	11	11
F.A.7	16	13
K.A.7	10	12
S.A.7	9	9
Kdtr. Munich	5	5
Kdtr. Ingolstadt	4	4
T.U.P. Grafenwöhr	7	7
	432	430

SOURCE: NA, 79, 83, p. 28; Rangliste 1923-1932.

NOTE: I.R.19 was authorized 3 more officers than the other 2 infantry regiments because of its additional responsibility for high mountain operations.

TABLE 2

1932 DIVISION VII STELLENBESETZUNG BY UNIT

DIVISION HEADQUARTERS STELLENBESETZUNG

```
        Kdr.       - 1 Maj. Gen.
        C. St.     - 1 Col.

        St.        - 1 Lt. Col.
                   - 5 Majs.
                   - 1 Capt. (W)
                   - 2 Capts.
                   - 9 1Lts.

        Inf. Kdr.  - 1 Col.
        St.        - 2 Majs.
                   - 1 Capt.

        Art. Kdr.  - 1 Brig. Gen.
        St.        - 1 Lt. Col.
                   - 1 Maj.
                   - 1 Capt.
```

1932 I.R.19 STELLENBESETZUNG

```
        Kdr.       - 1 Col.
        R. St.     - 1 Lt. Col.
                   - 2 1 Lts.
        R. Adj.    - 1 Capt.
```

I. Btl.	1. Kp.	2. Kp.	3. Kp.	4.(M.G.) Kp.
Kdr.-1 Lt.Col.	Kdr.-1 Maj.	Kdr.-1 Capt.	Kdr.-1 Capt.	Kdr.-1 Capt.
St.I-1 Maj.	Offz.-2 Lts.	Offz.-2 Lts.	Offz.-1 1Lt.	Offz.-3 1Lts.
Adj.I-1 1Lt.			1 Lt.	

II. Btl.	5. Kp.	6 Kp.	7 Kp.	8.(M.G.) Kp.
Kdr.-1 Lt.Col.	Kdr.-1 Capt.	Kdr.-1 Capt	Kdr.-1 Capt.	Kdr.-1 Capt.
St.II-1 Maj.	Offz.-1 1Lt.	Offz.-2 Lts.	Offz.-2 1Lts.	Offz.-1 Capt.
Adj.II-1 1Lt.	-1 Lt.			2 1Lts.

III. Btl.	9. Kp.	10 Kp.	11 Kp.	12.(M.G.) Kp.
Kdr.-1 Maj.	Kdr.-1 Capt.	Kdr.-1 Capt.	Kdr.-1 Capt.	Kdr.-1 Capt.
St.III-1 Maj.	Offz.-3 Lts.	Offz.-1 1Lt.	Offz.-2 1Lts.	Offz.-3 1Lts.
Adj.III-1 1Lt.		2 Lts.	1 Lt.	

TABLE 2 – <u>Continued</u>

<u>13.(M.W.) Kp</u>.
Kdr.-1 Capt.
Offz.-1 Capt.
      4 1Lts.

<u>A. Btl.</u>	<u>14. Kp.</u>	<u>15. Kp.</u>	<u>16. Kp.</u>
Kdr.-1 Maj.	Kdr.-1 1Lt.	Kdr.-1 Capt.	Kdr.-1 1Lt.
St.A-1 Capt.	Offz.-2 1Lts.	Offz.-2 Lts.	Offz.-1 1Lt.
Adj.A-1 1Lt.			

1932 R.R.17 <u>STELLENBESETZUNG</u>

Kdr. - 1 Col.
St. - 1 Maj.
     - 3 Capts.
     - 1 1Lt.
Adj. - 1 1Lt.

<u>1. Esk.</u>	<u>2. Esk.</u>	<u>3. Esk.</u>
Kdr.-1 Capt.	Kdr.-1 Capt.	Kdr.-1 Capt.
Offz.-2 1Lts.	Offz.-2 1Lts.	Offz.-2 Capts.
-2 Lts.	-2 Lts.	-2 1Lts.
		-1 Lt.

<u>4. Esk.</u>	<u>5.(A.)Esk.</u>	<u>6. Esk.</u>
Kdr.-1 Capt.	Kdr.-1 Capt.	Kdr.-1 Capt.
Offz.-1 Capt.	Offz.-2 1Lts.	Offz.-2 Capts.
-2 1Lts.	-1 Lt.	-1 1Lt.
-1 Lt.		-2 Lts.

1932 A.R.7 <u>STELLENBESETZUNG</u>

Kdr.   - 1 Col.
R.St. - 2 Lt.Cols.
       - 1 Maj.
       - 1 1Lt.
R.Adj. - 1 Capt.

<u>I. Abt. (Btl.)</u>	<u>1. Battr.</u>	<u>2. Battr.</u>	<u>3. Battr.</u>
Kdr.-1 Lt.Col.	Kdr.-1 Capt.	Kdr.-1 Capt.	Kdr.-1 Capt.
St.I-2 Capts.	Offz.-1 Capt.	Offz.-1 Capt.	Offz.-1 Capt.
	-2 1Lts.	-1 1Lt.	-3 1Lts.
Adj.I-1 1Lt.	-2 Lts.	-1 1Lt.(W)	-1 Lt.
		-2 Lts.	

TABLE 2 – Continued

II. Abt. (Btl.)	4. Battr.	5. Battr.	6. Battr.
Kdr.-1 Lt.Col.	Kdr.-1 Capt.	Kdr.-1 Capt.	Kdr.-1 Capt.
St.II-2 Capts.	Offz.-1 Capt.	Offz.-2 Capts.	Offz.-2 Capts.
Adj.II-1 1Lt.	-2 1Lts.	-2 1Lts.	-1 1Lt.
	-1 Lt.	-1 Lt.	-2 Lts.
	-1 Lt.(W)		

III. Abt. (Btl.)	7. Battr.	8. Battr.	9. Battr. (kw)
Kdr.-1 Lt.Col.	Kdr.-1 Capt.	Kdr.-1 Capt.	Kdr.-1 Capt.
St.III-1 Maj.	Offz.-1 Capt.	Offz.-1 Capt.	Offz.-1 Capt.(W)
-1 Capt.	-2 1 Lts.	-2 1Lts.	-3 1Lts.
Adj.III-1 Lt.	-2 Lts.	-2 Lts.	-2 Lts.

10.(A.) Battr.
Kdr.-1 Capt.
Offz.-1 1Lt.
-1 Lt.

SOURCE: Rangliste 1932; Georg Tessin, Deutsche Verbande und Truppen, 1918-1939 (Osnabrück: Biblio Verlag, 1974), pp. 187-188.

NOTE: 13(M.W.)/I.R.19 and 10/A.R.7 were subordinated directly to their regimental staffs rather than to one of the battalions. 6/R.R.17 was subordinated to the division staff. Approximate NCO and enlisted strength numbered 2,300 for the infantry regiment, 800 for the cavalry regiment, and 1,300 for the artillery regiment.

188

TABLE 3

FIELD COMMANDERS IN THE BAVARIAN REGIMENTS, 1923-1932

I.R.19-Munich

Unit/Location	1923	1924	1925	1926	1927
A. Btl.Landshut	Lt.Col.Hofmann 1.2.23(10)	...	...	Maj.Hoffmann 1.4.21(3)	...
I. Btl.Munich	Maj.Frhr.Loeffel-holz v.Colberg 15.7.18(15)	Lt.Col.Frhr.v.Berchem 1.10.20(122)	Lt.Col.Gaul 1.2.25(12)	...	...
II. Btl.Augsburg	Lt.Col.R.v.Pflügel 1.10.20(77)	...	Lt.Col.v.Hösslein* 15.2.23(1)	...*	Lt.Col.Bauer* 1.2.27(5a)
III. Btl.Kempten	Maj.List* 27.1.18(15)	Lt.Col.List* 15.11.22(6a)	Lt.Col.Wenk 1.4.24(4)	...	...
1. Kp.Munich	Capt.Dietl 22.3.18(15)	Capt.Nissl 18.4.17(7)	Capt.Graf* 18.6.15(28)	...*	...*
2. Kp.Munich	Capt.Wilger* 8.10.14(58)	1Lt.Braun 18.4.17(31)	Capt.Braun 1.1.25(3)	...	Capt.Volckamer v. K. 1.11.26(4)
3. Kp.Munich	Capt.v.Schacky auf Schönfeld 18.12.15(17)	...	...	...	...
4. (M.G.)Kp.	Capt.Kniess 18.12.15(16)	...	Capt.Deboi 1.2.25(3)	...	Capt.Stapf* 18.10.18(9)
5. Kp.Augsburg	Capt.Krampf 18.4.17(26)	...	Maj.Reinwald 1.11.23(1)	Capt.Krampf	...
6. Kp.Augsburg	Capt.Stapf* 18.10.18(9)	Capt.Haverkamp	...	...	...
7. Kp.Augsburg	Capt.Heberlein 18.8.16(15)	...	...	...	Capt.Neumayr
8. (M.G.)Kp.	Capt.Schwub 18.8.16(23)	...	...	...	...
9. Kp.Lindau	Capt.Krafft* 18.8.15(19)	Capt.Stapf*	1Lt.Kaiser 27.3.18(27)	Capt.Wimmer 22.8.18(8)	Capt.Kress 1.7.26(4)
10. Kp.Kempten	Capt.Graf v. Bothmer 27.1.18(19)	...	...	...	...

TABLE 3 - Continued

I.R.19-Munich

Unit/Location	1928	1929	1930	1931	1932
A. Btl.Landshut	Lt.Col.Hoffmann 1.3.27(3)	Maj.Graf* 1.2.28(27)	Maj.Dietl 1.2.28(42)	Maj.Heberlein 1.10.29(1)	...
I. Btl.Munich	Lt.Col.Schwandner* 1.2.28(10)	Lt.Col.Wäger* 1.2.29(7)	...*	no listing	Lt.Col.Kübler* 1.4.32(18)
II. Btl.Augsburg	Lt.Col.Bauer*	Lt.Col.R.v.Schobert 1.4.29(14)	...	Lt.Col.Müller* 1.2.31(19)	...*
III. Btl.Kempten	Lt.Col.Schindler* 1.2.27(7a)	...*	Col.Schindler* 1.2.30(5)	Maj.Dietl	...
1. Kp.Munich	Capt.Thoma	...	...	...	Maj.Thoma 1.4.32(14)
2. Kp.Munich	Capt.Volckamer v. K.	...	Capt.Blumentritt* 1.4.26(7)	...*	...*
3. Kp.Munich	Capt.Jais 1.2.27(4)	1Lt.Streil 1.2.25(10)	Capt.Streil 1.6.29(5)	...	Capt.Hoffmeister* 1.12.26(11)
4. (M.G.)Kp. Munich	Capt.Stapf*	...*	Capt.Zorn* 1.12.22(8)	...*	Capt.Streil 1.6.29(5)
5. Kp.Augsburg	Capt.Krampf	Capt.Rorich 1.2.23(17)	...	...	...
6. Kp.Augsburg	Capt.Haverkamp	Capt.Eberth 1.5.29(1)	...	...	...
7. Kp.Augsburg	Capt.Neumayr	...	...	...	Capt.Hofmann* 1.6.28(4)
8. (M.G.)Kp. Augsburg	Capt.Schwub	Capt.Forster 1.2.23(19)	Capt.Deboi	...	...
9. Kp.Lindau	Capt.Kress	...	...	...	...
10. Kp.Kempten	Capt.Graf v. Bothmer	Capt.Schörner	...	...	Capt.Stettner R.v.

TABLE 3 - Continued

I.R.19-Munich

Unit/Location	1923	1924	1925	1926	1927
11. Kp.Lindau	Capt.Karl 18.8.16(10)	...	Maj.R.v.Schobert 1.1.24(4)	ILt.Utz 18.4.18(21)	Capt.Utz 1.11.26(2)
12. (M.G.)Kp. Kempten	Capt.Frhr.v.Mauchenheim* 18.8.16(20)	...*	...*	...*	Capt.Weisenberger* 18.4.17(28)
13. (M.W.)Kp. Munich	Capt.Heyl 5.9.14(7)	Lt.Col.Wenk 1.4.24(4)	Capt.Daser 28.11.14(64)	Capt.Gollwitzer 15.4.17(2)	Capt.Frhr.v. Mauchenheim*
14. Kp.Landshut	Capt.Thoma 18.10.18(25)				...
15. Kp.Landshut	Capt.Haverkamp 18.10.18(12)	ILt.Kress 22.3.18(34)	Capt.v.Marees 28.11.14(41)	Capt.Braunhofer 1.2.25(12)	Capt.Deboi 1.2.25(3)
16. Kp.Landshut	Capt.Neumayr 1.2.23(24)	...	...	...	Capt.Schoerner 1.7.26(8)

I.R.20

Unit/Location	1923	1924	1925	1926	1927
A. Btl.Amberg	Lt.Col.Fischer 1.2.23(12)	...	Lt.Col.Geis	...	Lt.Col.Schönhärl
I. Btl.Regensberg	Lt.Col.v.Unruh 1.10.20(90)	...	Maj.Baumann* 18.5.20(6)	...*	Lt.Col.Baumann* 1.2.26(17)
II. Btl.Ingolstadt	Maj.Haselmayr* 22.3.18(27)	Maj.R.v.Kieffer 18.5.18(8)	...	...	Lt.Col.Mehler 1.2.26(18)
III. Btl.Passau	Lt.Col.Adam* 1.2.23(6)	...*	Lt.Col.R.v.Fuchtbauer 1.2.24(2)	...	...
1. Kp.Regensberg	Lt.Col.Geis 1.4.23(6)	Capt.Dehner 22.3.18(12)	...	Capt.Danhauser 1.2.23(8)	...
2. Kp.Regensberg	Capt.Sintzenich 18.4.17(27)	Capt.Fürst 22.3.18(10)	...	...	...
3. Kp.Regensberg	Capt.Lang 18.8.16(22)	Capt.Dostler 18.10.18(29)	ILt.Huber 18.4.18(29)	Capt.Sintzenich 18.4.17(27)	Capt.Huber 1.12.26(3)
4. (M.G.)Kp Regensberg	Capt.Siebert 18.8.16(17)	...	...	...	Capt.Dipl.Ing.R.v. Weber 1.2.23(23)

TABLE 3 - Continued

I.R.19-Munich

Unit/Location	1928	1929	1930	1931	1932
11. Kp.Lindau	Capt.Utz	...	...	Capt.Vogl* 1.4.28(30)	... *
12. (M.G.)Kp. Kampten	Capt.Weisenberger*	Maj.Weisenberger* 1.2.28(19a)	...	lLt.Pürckauer 1.4.25(221) Capt.Pürckauer 1.3.31(4)	...
13. (M.W.)Kp.	Capt.Frhr v. Mauchenheim*	Maj.Kohl 1.4.29(13)	Capt.Jais	...	Capt.Utz
14. Kp.Landshut	lLt.Greiner 1.10.23(18)	Capt.Greiner 1.6.28(2)	...	...	lLt.Gloss 1.4.25(441)
15. Kp.Landshut	Capt.Deboi	...	Capt.Maier* 1.4.28(38)	lLt.Christl 1.4.25(377)	Capt.Christl 1.4.32(27)
16. Kp.Landshut	Capt.Schoerner	lLt.Stettner R.v. Grabenhofen 1.4.25(53)	Capt.Stettner R.v.Grabenhofen 1.2.30(15)	...	lLt.Vogler 1.4.25(396)

I.R.20

Unit/Location	1928	1929	1930	1931	1932
A. Btl.Amberg	Lt.Col.Schonhärl	...	Maj.Deyrer 1.3.27(12)	...	Maj.Gollwitzer 1.3.30(2)
1. Btl.Regensberg	Maj.Otto* 1.11.23(6)	Lt.Col.Otto* 1.4.29(11)	Lt.Col.Heins* 1.10.29(26)	... *	... *
II. Btl.Ingolstadt	Lt.Col.Mehler	...	Maj.Daser 1.12.26(3)	Maj.v.Mauchenheim* 1.10.29(3)	... *
III. Btl.Passau	Maj.Frhr.v.Lutz 1.12.26(2)	...	...	Maj.Kohl 1.4.29(13)	...
1. Kp.Regensberg	Capt.Danhauser	...	Capt.Hauser 1.2.30(29)	...	...
2. Kp.Regensberg	Capt.Haban 1.2.27(31)	...	Capt.Meyerhöfer 1.11.28(19)	...	...
3. Kp.Regensberg	Capt.Huber	lLt.Heikaus 1.4.25(94)	Capt.Heikaus 1.4.30(3)	...	Capt.Döpping 1.6.26(3)
4. (M.G.)Kp	Capt.Dipl.Ing.R.v. Weber	...	lLt.Hörder 1.4.25(207)	Capt.Hörder 1.2.31(41)	...

TABLE 3 - Continued

I.R.20

Unit/Location	1923	1924	1925	1926	1927
5. Kp.Ingolstadt	Capt.Dippold 15.4.17(3)	Capt.Strasser 1.2.23(25)	...	...	...
6. Kp.Ingolstadt	Capt.Häckel 22.3.18(14)	...	...	...	...
7. Kp.Ingolstadt	Capt.Bickel 1.1.23(7)	...	...	...	...
8. (M.G.)Kp. Ingolstadt	Maj.Taufkirch 1.10.20(47)	Capt.Kohl 18.4.16(36)	...	...	Capt.Dippold 15.4.17(3)
9. Kp.Passau	Capt.Zimmermann 1.2.23(11)	...	...	...	Capt.Amann 1.10.26(12)
10. Kp.Passau	Capt.Deyrer 27.1.15(11)	...	Maj.Hoffmann 1.4.21(3)	1Lt.Mayr(Leo) 20.6.18(14)	Capt.Mayr 1.2.27(3)
11. Kp.Passau	Capt.Sitzler 18.8.16(19)	...	1Lt.Streit 22.3.18(35)	...	Capt.Streit 1.7.26(5)
12. (N.G.)Kp. Passau	Capt.Kittel 1.2.23(6)	Capt.Müller 1.1.23(1)	...	...	Capt.Evtl 1.2.25(25)
13. (M.W.)Kp. Regensberg	Capt.Danhauser 1.2.23(8)	Capt.Golwitzer 15.4.17(2)	...	Capt.Kittel 1.2.23(6)	...
14. Kp.Amberg	Capt.Strasser 1.2.23(25)	Maj.Taufkirch	1Lt.Düpping 22.3.18(28)	Capt.Wachter 1.1.23(2)	Capt.Schmitt 1.2.27(7)
15. Kp.Amberg	Capt.Lippmann 22.3.18(16)	...	Maj.Nepf 18.5.20(1)	1Lt.Haban 20.6.18(47)	Capt.Burger 1.2.25(1)
16. Kp.Amberg	Capt.Heiss 28.11.14(62)	1Lt.Amann 18.4.18(18)	...	...	1Lt.Weber 1.4.23(7)
I.R.21-Nürnberg					
A. Btl.Erlangen	Lt.Col.Glasser 1.4.22(1)	...	...	Maj.Schwandner* 1.7.21(20v)	...*
I. Btl.Würzburg	Lt.Col.R.v.Höfl 1.6.21(2)	Lt.Col.Höfl 1.4.24(2)	...	...	...

193

TABLE 3 - Continued

I.R.20

Unit/Location	1928	1929	1930	1931	1932
5. Kp.Ingolstadt	Capt.Strasser 1.2.27(7)	...	...	...	...
6. Kp.Ingolstadt	Capt.Krakau 1.4.28(35)		1Lt.Hofmeister 1.4.25(279)	...	Capt.Hofmeister 1.10.31(3)
7. Kp.Ingolstadt	Capt.Picker 1.5.28(3)	...	...	...	...
8. (M.G.)Kp. Ingolstadt	Capt.Dippold	...	Maj.Dippold 1.3.30(3)	Capt.Krakau 1.4.28(35)	...
9. Kp.Passau	Capt.Amann	...	Capt.Rupp* 1.2.22(7)	...*	...*
10. Kp.Passau	Capt.Mayr	...	...	Capt.Dipl.Ing. Riesch 1.4.28(14)	...
11. Kp.Passau	Capt.Streit	Capt.Burger	...	...	...
12. (M.G.)Kp. Passau	Capt.Muller		Capt.Amann	...	...
13. (M.W.)Kp. Regensberg	Capt.Kittel	...	...	...	Capt.Weber
14. Kp.Amberg	Capt.Schmitt	Capt.Strasser	1Lt.Rupprecht 1.4.25(230)	Capt.Rupprecht 1.4.31(6)	...
15. Kp.Amberg	Capt.Burger	Capt.Streit	Capt.Wittstatt 1.2.29(21)		...
16. Kp.Amberg	Capt.Weber 1.4.28(9)	...	1Lt.Kullmer 1.4.25(182)	Capt.Kullmer 1.2.31(18)	...

I.R.21-Nürnberg

Unit/Location	1928	1929	1930	1931	1932
A. Btl.Erlangen	Maj.Daser 1.12.26(3)	...	Maj.Kniess 1.12.28(2)	...	...
I. Btl.Würzburg	Maj.Karmann* 1.4.23(31)	Lt.Col.Karmann* 1.2.29(27)	...*	Maj.Siebert 1.10.29(2)	...

TABLE 3 - Continued

I.R.21-Nürnberg

Unit/Location	1923	1924	1925	1926	1927
II. Btl.Nürnberg	Lt.Col.Dümlein* 1.4.23(4)	Lt.Col.Kalbfus 15.11.22(9b)	...	Lt.Col.Hansen 1.2.26(7)	...
III. Btl.Bayreuth	Lt.Col.R.v.Mittelberger* 15.11.22(3)	..*	Maj.R.v.Reitzenstein 1.10.20(25)	...	Lt.Col.R.v.Reitzenstein 1.2.27(18)
1. Kp.Würzburg	Maj.Mehler 18.5.20(9)	Capt.Görlitz 27.1.18(21)	...	Capt.Lippmann 22.3.18(16)	...
2. Kp.Würzburg	Capt.Kirch 18.8.16(11)	...	Capt.Engelhardt 1.11.24(4)	...	...
3. Kp.Würzburg	Capt.Funke 18.10.18(11)	...	...	...	...
4. (M.G.)Kp. Würzburg	Capt.Geuder 18.8.16(21)	...	...	1Lt.Klüg 20.6.18(27)	Capt.Klüg 1.2.27(13)
5. Kp.Nürnberg	Capt.Toussaint 1.2.23(5)	...	...	Capt.Körbitz 27.1.18(16)	...
6. Kp.Nürnberg	Capt.R.v.Mann 1.2.23(22)	...	...	...	Capt.Müller 1.1.23(1)
7. Kp.Nürnberg	Capt.Fleissner 18.10.18(44)	...	Maj.Schuster 1.2.25(10)	Capt.Dostler* 18.10.18(29)	Capt.Reichert
8. (M.G.)Kp. Nürnberg	Capt.Schwarz 18.10.18(32)	...	...	...	Capt.Nebauer 1.2.27(17)
9. Kp.Bayreuth	Capt.Köppel 18.10.18(30)	...	...	...	...
10. Kp.Bayreuth	Capt.Blümm 18.8.15(4)	...	...	Maj.v.Marées 1.5.26	...
11. Kp.Bayreuth	Capt.Döderlein 28.11.14(65)	Capt.Pflaum 18.10.18(41)	...	...	...
12. (M.G.)Kp. Bayreuth	Capt.Veith 27.1.18(18)	...	Capt.Adlhoch 1.2.25(4)	...	...
13. (M.W.)Kp. Fürth	Capt.Reichert 18.10.18(28)	...	...	...	Capt.Bodenschatz

195

TABLE 3 - Continued

I.R.21-Nürnberg

Unit/Location	1928	1929	1930	1931	1932
II. Btl.Nürnberg	Lt.Col.Hansen	Maj.Friedrichs* 1.3.27(11)	..*	Maj.Lang 1.10.29(4)	...
III. Btl.Bayreuth	Lt.Col.R.v.Reitzen- stein	Maj.Graf*	..*	Maj.Karl	...
1. Kp.Würzburg	1Lt.Schneider (Karl) 1.10.23(21)	Capt.Schneider 1.7.28(1)	...	1.6.29(1)	.
2. Kp.Würzburg	Capt.Engelhardt	...	...	...	Capt.Schmidt(Hans)
3. Kp.Würzburg	Capt.Roth 1.2.27(19)	...	...	...	Capt.Full 1.5.32
4. (M.G.)Kp. Würzburg	Capt.Klüg	...	...	...	...
5. Kp.Nürnberg	Capt.Oller " 1.2.27(15)	...	...	...	...
6. Kp.Nürnberg	Capt.Dostler*	...	...	...	Capt.Hammerschmidt 1.2.29(44)
7. Kp.Nürnberg	Capt.Reichert	Capt.Bürcky 1.11.28(20)	...	...	...
8. (M.G.)Kp. Nürnberg	Capt.Nebauer	...	...	...	...
9. Kp.Bayreuth	Capt.Hülttner	...	...	...	...
10. Kp.Bayreuth	Capt.Schilffarth 1.2.27(24)	...	...	Capt.Adlhoch	...
11. Kp.Bayreuth	Capt.Pflaum	1Lt.Eckart 1.4.25(14)	Capt.Eckart 1.10.29(22)	...	...
12. (M.G.)Kp. Bayreuth	Capt.Adlhoch	...	...	Capt.Schilffarth	...
13. (M.W.)Kp.Fürth	Capt.Korbitz	Capt.Bodenschatz	...	1Lt.Maisel 1.4.25(352)	Capt.Maisel 1.4.32(7)

TABLE 3 - Continued

I.R.21-Nürnberg

Unit/Location	1923	1924	1925	1926	1927
14. Kp.Erlangen	Capt.Graf* 18.-.15(28)	...	Capt.Meyer 1.4.23(15)	...	Capt.Schwarz
15. Kp.Erlangen	Maj.Thüter 1.10.22(2)	...	...	Capt.Hüttner 1.2.25(5)	...
16. Kp.Erlangen	Capt.Bodenschatz 18.10.18(31)	...	...	1Lt.Öller 20.6.18(29)	Capt.R.v.Mann

R.R.17-Bamberg

Unit/Location	1923	1924	1925	1926	1927
1. Esk.Bamberg	Capt.Frhr.v. Schaezler 5.9.14(8)	...	Capt.Wallner	...	...
2. Esk.Ansbach	Capt.Frhr.v. Speidel 27.1.15(5)	Capt.Winkels-Herding	...	...	Capt.Walther 18.10.18(46)
3. Esk.Ansbach	Maj.v.Tannstein 1.10.20(6)	...	Capt.Desseloch 18.10.18(45)	...	Capt.Wimmer 22.3.18(8)
4. Esk.Straubing	Capt.Frhr.v.Perfall 8.11.14(43)	...	Capt.Renz 28.11.14(59)	...	...
5. (A)Esk. Bamberg	Capt.Wallner 28.11.14(66)	...	Maj.Taufkirch 1.10.20(47)	Maj.Frhr.v. Perfall 1.1.26(2)	Maj.Frhr.v. Speidel 1.3.27(8)
6. Esk.Straubing	Capt.Winkels-Herding 18.12.15(21)	Capt.Koch* 28.11.14(68)	Maj.Koch* 1.3.24(2)	...*	Capt.Frhr.v. Thüngen 1.2.25(15)

A.R.7-Nürnberg

Unit/Location	1923	1924	1925	1926	1927
I. Abt.Würzburg	Lt.Col.Feeser 1.10.20(67)	Lt.Col.Kaupisch 15.11.22(4a)	...	Lt.Col.Vogl* 15.2.23(1a)	...*
II. Abt.Landsberg	Lt.Col.Mack 1.3.21(2)	...	Col.R.v.Leeb* 1.2.25(6)	Maj.Wolf 1.10.22(1)	...
III. Abt.Nürnberg	Lt.Col.Eberth* 1.6.21(4)	Lt.Col.Meier 1.7.21(8)	Lt.Col.Curtze 1.5.24(1)	Maj.Grün 1.7.21(208)	...

197

TABLE 3 - Continued

I.R.21-Nürnberg

Unit/Location	1928	1929	1930	1931	1932
14. Kp.Erlangen	Capt.Schwarz	...	Capt.Kohler 1.11.28(4)	...	...
15. Kp.Erlangen	Capt.Schmidt 1.5.28(5)	...	Capt.Schmidt (Hans) 1.5.28(5)	...	1Lt.Kütt 1.4.25(419)
16. Kp.Erlangen	Capt.R.v.Mann	...	Capt.Schmid (Martin) 1.10.29(1)	...	...
R.R.17-Bamberg					
1. Esk.Bamberg	Capt.Luz 1.9.24(4)	Capt.Harteneck* 1.4.28(11)	...*	Maj.v.Tettau 1.11.30(13)	Capt.Walzer
2. Esk.Ansbach	Maj.Fehn 1.4.27(1)	Capt.Rodt	...	...	...
3. Esk.Ansbach	Capt.Dessloch	Maj.Fehn	...	Capt.Dessloch	Capt.Hübner (Kurt) 1.2.23(12)
4. Esk.Straubing	Capt.Dipl.Ing. Fritsch 1.4.26(5)	Capt.Hübner (Dietrich) 1.2.28(49)	Capt.Becker 1.5.27(10)	...	...
5. (A)Esk.Bamberg	Capt.Winkels-Herding	Capt.Luz	...	...	...
6. Esk.Straubing	Capt.Frhr.v. Thüngen	...	Capt.Schoepke	Capt.Rübsam 1.10.29(16)	Capt.Leuze 1.2.23(10)
A.R.7-Nürnberg					
I. Abt.Würzburg	Lt.Col.Dollmann* 1.4.27(3)	...*	Maj.vanGinkel 1.2.26(13)	...	Lt.Col.R.v.Speck* 1.2.32(1)
II. Abt.Landsberg	Lt.Col.Wolf 1.4.28(2)	Maj.Zwengauer 1.2.25(3)	...	Maj.Fahrmbacher	...
III. Abt.Nürnberg	Lt.Col.Auer 1.2.27(30)	...	Maj.Hirschauer 1.2.26(14)	...	...

TABLE 3 - Continued

A.R.7-Nürnberg

Unit/Location	1923	1924	1925	1926	1927
1. Battr.Würzberg	Capt.Siry 18.10.18(14)	...	Maj.Rüdel* 1.4.23(26)	..*	Maj.Hengen 1.4.26(4a)
2. Battr.Würzberg	Capt.Steinbauer 22.3.18(13)	...	...	Capt.Frhr.v.Roman 1.6.24(11)	...
3. Battr.Würzberg	Capt.Hengen 18.8.15(5)	Capt.Köhl 28.11.14(69)	...	...	Capt.Müller(Eugen)* 18.10.18(8)
4. Battr.Landsberg	Capt.Jodl* 18.10.18(15)	Maj.Halder* 1.4.23(26a)	..*	Capt.Ochsner 1.12.22(9)	...
5. Battr.Munich	Capt.Hartmann* 8.11.14(59)	..*	Capt.Metz 1.7.24(1)	Capt.Kraus 1.7.24(2)	...
6. Battr.Landsberg	Capt.Wintergerst 1.2.23(21)	...	...	...	Capt.Braun 1.4.26(4)
7. Battr.Nürnberg	Capt.Leeb* 8.10.14(56)	Capt.Breith 1.1.23(5)	...	...	...
8. Battr.Erlangen	Capt.Zenetti 28.11.14(60)	Capt.v.Schallern 8.11.14(60)	...	Capt.Meiler 1.2.25(22)	...
9. Battr.Nürnberg	Capt.Sturm 28.11.14(63)	Capt.Heilingbrunner 18.10.18(13)	Capt.Zenetti	Capt.Heilingbrunner	...
10. (A)Battr. Nürnberg	Capt.Bergmann 8.11.14(49)	Capt.Aschenbrandt 8.11.14(55)	Capt.vanGinkel 8.11.14(56)	Maj.Aschenbrandt 1.2.26(12)	Capt.R.v.Pohl* 1.6.24(12)

199

TABLE 3 - Continued

A.R.7-Nürnberg

Unit/Location	1928	1929	1930	1931	1932
1. Battr.Würzberg	Maj.Hengen	...	Capt.Siry	...	Capt.Zutavern 1.7.24(3)
2. Battr.Würzberg	Capt.Raithel 1.6.26(6)	...	...	...	Capt.Müller* 1.2.23(7)
3. Battr.Würzberg	Capt.Müller(Eugen)*	...*	Capt.Seywald 1.4.28(43)	Capt.Neuffer 1.5.28(6)	Capt.Wagner* 1.11.24(1)
4. Battr.Landsberg	Maj.Fahrmbacher 1.11.27(4a)	Capt.Betzel 1.5.28(7)	...	Capt.Dipl.Ing. Schlemmer 1.7.26(6)	Capt.Lichtenberger 1.8.29(6)
5. Battr.Munich	Maj.Heyl 1.11.23(2)	Capt.Brandenberger* 1.1.23(3)	...*	Capt.Winter* 1.6.24(10)	...*
6. Battr.Landsberg	Capt.Wintergerst	Capt.Ochsner	Capt.Wintergerst	...	Capt.Breith
7. Battr.Nürnberg	Capt.Steinbauer	...	...	Capt.Mesmer 1.7.26(3)	...
8. Battr.Erlangen	Capt.Kraus	...	Capt.Walther 1.2.27(20)	...	Capt.v.Arthelm
9. Battr.Nürnberg	Capt.Heilingbrun-ner	...	Capt.v.Axthelm 1.10.26(6)	...	Capt.Steinwachs 1.5.31(1)
10. (A)Battr. Nürnberg	Capt.R.v.Pohl* 1.7.24(1)	Capt.Metz 1.7.24(1)	Capt.Feuchtinger 1.11.29(1)	...	...

SOURCE: Rangliste 1923-1932; NA, 79, 83, pp. 1-120.

NOTE: Assignments are current as of Rangliste publication date. Where no assignment is listed for the particular year, the previous year's assignment or status applies.

*General Staff Officers.

200

TABLE 4

SENIOR BAVARIAN OFFICERS, 1923-1932

DIV.VII-Munich

	1923	1924	1925	1926	1927
Kdr.7.DIV.	Maj.Gen.v.Lossow 1.7.21(3)	Maj.Gen.Frhr.Kress v.K. 1.10.23	...	...	...
Chief of Staff	Lt.Col.Frhr.v.Berchem 1.10.20(122)	Lt.Col.R.v.Leeb* 1.10.20(216)	Col.v.Wenz zu N. 1.11.23(1)	Lt.Col.Adam*	Col.Adam* 1.2.27(17)
Senior St. Officer	Lt.Col.Endres* 15.11.22(2)	...*	Lt.Col.List* 15.11.22(6a)	...*	Lt.Col.R.v.Kieffer 1.5.24(2)
Inf.Kdr.	Brig.Gen.R.v.Epp 1.7.21(2)	Brig.Gen.R.v.Ruith	...	Maj.Gen.R.v.Ruith 1.4.26	....
Art.Kdr.	Brig.Gen.Frhr.Kress v.K.* 1.7.21(5)	Col.Frhr.Loeffelholz v.Colberg	....	Col.Theysohn 1.1.24(1)	....
Kdt.Ingolstadt	Lt.Col.Hofmann 1.4.22(2)	..	...		
Kdt.Munich	Brig.Gen.R.v.Danner 1.7.21(8)	..	...	Brig.Gen.R.v.Beckh 1.4.26	Col.R.v.Sauer 1.11.23(3)
Kdt.Grafenwöhr	Lt.Col.Krummel 1.4.22(4)	...	...	Lt.Col.Curtze 1.5.24(1)	
Kdr.I.R.19	Col.R.v.Ruith 16.6.20(4)	Col.R.v.Dittelberger	Col.R.v.Prager* 1.7.22(1)	..*	Col.R.v.Pflügel
R.St.OfficerI.R.19	Lt.Col.v.Wenz zu Niederlahnstein 1.10.20(66)	...	Col.R.v.Pflügel 1.2.24(1)	...	Lt.Col.C.v.Hösslin 15.2.23(1)
Kdr.I.R.20	Brig.Gen.Herrgott 1.2.23(6)	Col.R.v.Schmidtler 1.10.23(6)		...	Col.vonWenz zu N.
R.St.OfficerI.R.20	Col.Etzel 1.4.22(3)	Lt.Col.Geis 1.4.23(6)	Col.v Unruh 1.4.24(2)	Col.v.Wenz zu N. 1.11.23(1)	Lt.Col.Lüst 1.2.23(17)

TABLE 4 - Continued

	1923	1924	1925	1926	1927
Kdr.I.R.21	Col.R.v.Bekh 1.7.21(8)	. .	. .	Col.R.v.Sauer	Col.Schemmel 1.11.24(3)
R.St.OfficerI.R.21	Lt.Col.R.v.Schmidtler 1.10.20(64)	Col.R.v.Sauer 1.11.23(3)	. .	Col.R.v.Hörauf 1.2.26(3)	
Kdr.R.R.17	Col.Zürn 1.4.22(1)	. .	. .	. .	Lt.Col.Frhr.v. Hirschberg 1.3.25
St.OfficerR.R.17	Col.Frhr.v.Bibra 1.2.23(8)	Maj.Frhr.v.Hirschberg 15.7.18(17)	. .	. .	Maj.Frhr.v.Lotzbeck 1.2.26(15)
Kdr.A.R.7	Col.Frhr.Loeffelholz v. Colberg 1.10.20(28)	Col.Theysohn 1.1.24(1)	. .	Col.R.v.Leeb* 1.2.25(6)	. . .*
R.St.OfficerA.R.7	Lt.Col.Theyson 1.10.20(74)	Lt.Col.Eberth* 1.6.21(4)	. . .*	Col.Eberth* 1.2.26(4)	. . .*
Kdr.P.B.7	Lt.Col.Königsdorfer	Maj.Kuprion 1.4.21(4)	. .	. .	Maj.Vara 1.3.23(2)
Kdr.N.A.7	Lt.Col.Schubert 1.4.23(5)	Maj.Prügel 15.7.18(14)	Lt.Col.Prügel 1.2.25(10)	. .	. . .
Kdr.K.A.7	Lt.Col.Lutz 1.2.23(8)	Maj.Fessmann 1.3.23(1)	. .	. .	. . .
Kdr.F.A.7	Lt.Col.Deuringer 1.3.23(3)	. . .	Maj.Frhr.v.Pechmann 1.10.20(8)	. . .	Lt.Col.Frhr.v.P. 1.2.27(9)
Kdr.S.A.7	Maj.Dihm 1.5.22(3)	Maj.Frhr.v.Pechmann 1.10.20(8)	Capt.Nüsslein 27.1.15(37)	Maj.Dihm	. . .

TABLE 4 - Continued

	1928	1929	1930	1931	1932
Kdr.I.R.21	Col.Schemmel	Col.Dumlein* 1.2.28(19)	. . .*	Col.R.v.Reitzenstein	.
R.St.OfficerI.R.21	Lt.Col.R.v.Füchtbauer 1.2.24(2)	Lt.Col.R.v.Reitzenstein 1.2.27(18)	Col.R.v.Reitzenstein 1.2.30(16)	Lt.Col.Frhr.v.Lutz 1.2.31(30)	Lt.Col.Frhr.v.Lutz
Kdr.R.R.17	Lt.Col.Frhr.v. Hirschberg	Col.Frhr.v.H 1.3.29(1)	Lt.Col.Koch* 1.10.29(3)	. . .*	Col.Koch* 1.4.32(7)
St.OfficerR.17	Col.R.v.Leeb*	Lt.Col.Mauck 1.2.27(7)	Maj.Renz 1.11.26	Maj.Winkels- Herding 1.1.29(3)	Maj.Sintzenich 1.8.30
Kdr.A.R.7	Col.Eberth*	Col.Vogl*	. . .*	Col.Brandt 1.11.30(4)	. .
R.St.OfficerA.R.7	Col.Vogl* 1.2.28(5)	Lt.Col.Auer 1.2.27(30)	Lt.Col.Leeb* 1.12.29(2)	. . .*	. . .*
Kdr.P.B.7	Maj.Vara	Maj.Jacob 1.2.26(11)	. . .	Maj.Dennerlein 1.2.28(30)	. . .
Kdr.N.A.7	Maj.Rust 1.2.25(8)	. . .	Lt.Col.Rust 1.2.30(1)	Maj.Löwenick 1.4.29(12)	. . .
Kdr.K.A.7	Maj.Fessmann	Lt.Col.Fessmann 1.11.28(10)	Maj.Wagner 1.1.29(1)	Lt.Col.Krafft* 1.2.31(14)	Maj.Kempf* 1.2.29(1)
Kdr.F.A.7	Lt.Col.Dihm 1.2.28(26)	Lt.Col.Heinemann		Lt.Col.Bergmann 1.11.30(2)	. . .
Kdr.S.A.7	Lt.Col.Heinemann 1.4.28(16)	Capt.Fichtner 1.5.26(4)	Maj.Pirner 1.4.30(13)	Capt.R.v.Thoma 1.2.25(2)	. . .

SOURCE: Rangliste 1923-1932; NA, 79, 83, pp.1-120.

NOTE: Assignments are current as of Rangliste publication date. Where no assignment is listed for the particular year, the previous year's assignment or status applies.

*General Staff Officers.

TABLE 5

CAREER PROFILES OF BAVARIAN OFFICERS WHO HELD COMMAND ASSIGNMENTS IN 1932

I.R.19

Name 1932	1931	1930	1929	1928	1927
A.Btl.Kdr. Maj. Heberlein 1.10.29(1)	A.Btl.Kdr.	WehrA.-Vers.	WehrA.-Vers. Capt.18.8.16(15)	St.II/I.R.19	St.II/I.R.19
I.Btl.Kdr. Lt.Col.Kübler* 1.4.32(18)	St.1.DIV. Maj.1.2.28(12a)	St.1.DIV.	St.1.DIV.	St.1.DIV. Capt.15.4.17(1)	St.GP.1
II.Btl.Kdr. Lt.Col.Müller* 1.2.31(19)	Kdr.II/I.R.19	St.Inf.Kdr.1 Maj.1.5.26(3)	St.Inf.Kdr.1	St.Inf.Kdr.1	T3
III.Btl.Kdr. Maj.Dietl 1.2.28(42)	Kdr.III/I.R.19	Kdr.A./I.R.19	#2 R.St.O. I.R.19 Capt.22.3.18	Inf.Sch. Instructor	Inf.Sch. Instructor
1.Kp.Kdr. Maj.Thoma 1.4.32(14)	Kdr.1/I.R.19 Capt.18.10.18(25)	Kdr.1/I.R.19	Kdr.1/I.R.19	Kdr.1/I.R.19	Kdr.14/I.R.19
2.Kp.Kdr. Capt.Blumentritt* 1.4.26(7)	Kdr.1/I.R.19	Kdr.1/I.R.19	St.6.DIV.	St.6.DIV.	St.6.DIV.
3.Kp.Kdr. Capt.Hoffmeister* 1.12.26(11)	3.Kdr./I.R.19	T3	T3	#2 Officer 6/R.4	T3 1Lt.1.2.23(2)
4.(M.G.)Kp.Kdr. Capt.Streil 1.6.29(5)	Kdr.3/I.R.19	Kdr.3/I.R.19	Kdr.3/I.R.19	#2 Officer 4(M.G.)/I.R.19	#2 Officer 4(M.G.)/I.R.19
5.Kp.Kdr. Capt.Rorich 1.2.23(17)	Kdr.5/I.R.19	Kdr.5/I.R.19	Kdr.5/I.R.19	#2 Officer 5/I.R.19	Kdr.2/I.R.12
6.Kp.Kdr. Capt.Eberth 1.5.29(1)	Kdr.6/I.R.19	Kdr.6/I.R.19	Kdr.6/I.R.19	1Lt.1.2.25(3) #2 Officer 8(M.G.)/I.R.19	#2 Officer 8(M.G.)/I.R.19

TABLE 5 - Continued

I.R.19

Name 1932	1923	1924	1925	1926
A.Btl.Kdr. Maj. Heberlein 1.10.29(1)	Kdr.7/I.R.19	Kdr.7/I.R.19	Kdr.7/I.R.19	Kdr.7/I.R.19
I.Btl.Kdr. Lt.Col.Kübler* 1.4.32(18)	T1	T1	T1	Gen.St.GP.1
II.Btl.Kdr. Lt.Col.Müller* 1.2.31(19)	T3	T3	T3	T3
III.Btl.Kdr. Maj.Dietl 1.2.28(42)	Kdr.1/I.R.19	St.A.Btl./ I.R.19	Inf.Sch. Instructor	Inf.Sch. Instructor
1.Kp.Kdr. Maj.Thoma 1.4.32(14)	14.Kp.Kdr./I.R.19	14.Kp.Kdr./I.R.19	14.Kp.Kdr./I.R.19	14.Kp.Kdr./I.R.19
2.Kp.Kdr. Capt.Blumentritt* 1.4.26(7)	#2 Officer 11/I.R.15	#2 Officer 14/I.R.15	#2 Officer 5.1/R.R.19	Gen.St.6.DIV.
3.Kp.Kdr. Capt.Hoffmeister* 1.12.26(11)	#2 Officer 5/R.R.7	#2 Officer 3/I.R.5	#5 St. Officer R.R.10	#4 St. Officer R.R.10
4.(M.G.)Kp.Kdr. Capt.Streil 1.6.29(5)	#4 Officer 4(M.G.)/I.R.19	#2 Officer 4(M.G.)/I.R.19	#2 Officer 4(M.G.)/I.K.19	#2 Officer 4(M.G.)/I.R.19
5.Kp.Kdr. Capt.Rorich 1.2.23(17)	Kdr.2/I.R.12	Kdr.2/I.R.12	Kdr.2/I.R.12	Kdr.2/I.R.12
6.Kp.Kdr. Capt.Eberth 1.5.29(1)	7/I.R.19 #2 Officer Lt.11.5.15(2)	#2 Officer 7/I.R.19	#2 Officer 7/I.R.19	#2 Officer 6/I.R.19

205

TABLE 5 - Continued

Name 1932	1931	1930	1929	1928	1927
7.Kp.Kdr. Capt.Hofmann* 1.6.28(4)	T4	T2	T2	T4 1Lt.1.10.23(20)	#2 Officer 1/I.R.21
8.(M.G.)Kp.Kdr. Capt.Deboi 1.2.25(3)	Kdr.8(M.G.)/ I.R.19	Kdr.8(M.G.)/ I.R.19	Kdr.15/I.R.19	Kdr.15/I.R.19	Kdr.4(M.G.)/ I.R.19
9.Kp.Kdr. Capt.Kress 1.7.26(4)	Kdr.9/I.R.19	Kdr.9/I.R.19	Kdr.9/I.R.19	Kdr.9/I.R.19	Kdr.9/I.R.19
10.Kp.Kdr. Capt.Stetther R. v. Grabenhofer 1.2.30(15)	Kdr.16/I.R.19	Kdr.16/I.R.19	Kdr.16/I.R.19 1Lt.1.4.25(53)	#3 Officer 13(M.W.)/I.R.19	#3 Officer 13(M.W.)/I.R.19
11.Kp.Kdr. Capt. Vogel* 1.4.28(30)	Kdr.11/I.R.19	#2 Officer 13(M.W.)/I.R.19	St.7.DIV.	St.7.DIV.	St.7.DIV. 1Lt.1.8.23(3)
12.(M.G.)Kp.Kdr. Capt. Purckhauer 1.3.31(4)	Kdr.12(M.G.)/ I.R.19	1Lt.1.4.25(221) Kdr.12(M.G.)/ I.R.19	Adj.III/I.R.19	Adj.III/I.R.19	Adj.III/I.R.19
13(M.W.)Kp.Kdr. Capt. Utz 1.11.26(2)	#2R.St.Officer I.R.19	Kdr.11/I.R.19	Kdr.11/I.R.19	Kdr.11/I.R.19	Kdr.11/I.R.19
14.Kp.Kdr. 1Lt.Closs* 1.4.25(441)	#2 Officer 14/I.R.19	#2 Officer 11/I.R.19	#3 Officer 11/I.R.19	#2 Officer 12(M.G.)/I.R.19	#2 Officer 14/I.R.19
15.Kp.Kdr. Capt.Christl 1.4.32(27)	Kdr.15/I.R.19 1 Lt.4/25(337)	#2 Officer 16/I.R.19	#2 Officer 11/I.R.19	#2 Officer 11/I.R.19	#2 Officer 11/I.R.19
16.Kp.Kdr. 1Lt.Vogler 1.4.25(396)	#2 Officer 4(M.G.)/I.R.19	#2 Officer 4(M.G.)/I.R.19	#2 Officer 4(M.G.)/I.R.19	#3 Officer 4(M.G.)/I.R.19	#3 officer 4(M.G.)/I.R.19

TABLE 5 - Continued

R.R.17

Name 1932	1931	1930	1929	1928	1927
1.Esk.Kdr. Capt. Walzer 1.2.30(7) #3 Officer 4/R.R.17	#3 Officer 4/R.R.17	#3 Officer 4/R.R.17	1Lt.1.4.25(449) #2 Officer 4/R.R.17	#4 Officer 4/R.R.17	#5 Officer 4/R.R.17
2.Esk.Kdr. Capt. Rodt 1.8.28(2)	Kdr.2/R.R.17	Kdr.2/R.R.17	Kdr.2/R.R.17	#2 Officer 2/R.R.17 1Lt.1.1.23(4)	#3 Officer 2/R.R.17
3.Esk.Kdr. Capt.Hübner (Kurt)1.2.23(12) #3 Officer 3/R.R.17	#3 Officer 3/R.R.17	#3 Officer 3/R.R.17	#3 Officer 3/R.R.17	#2 Officer 3/R.R.17	#3 Officer 3/R.R.17
4.Esk.Kdr. Capt. Beeker .3.2.(10)	Kdr.4/R.R.17	Kdr.4/R.R.17	St.GP.1	St.GP.1	#3 Officer 9/A.R.2 1Lt.20.6.18(98)
5.(A)Esk.Kdr. Capt. Lu_ 1.9.24(4)	Kdr.5/R.R.17	Kdr.5/R.R.17	Kdr.5/R.R.17	Kdr.1/R.R.17	Adj./R.R.17
6.Esk.Kdr. Capt. Leuze 1.2.23(18) #2 Officer 3/R.R.17	#2 Officer 3/R.R.17	Kdr.4/R.R.8	Kdr.4/R.R.8	#2 Officer 4/R.R.8	Kdr.4/R.R.8

A.R.7

Name 1932	1931	1930	1929	1928	1927
I.Abt.Kdr. Lt.Col.R.v.Speck* 1.2.32(1)	St.7.DIV. Maj.1.11.27(1)	St.3.DIV.	St.3.DIV.	Adj.to CH	W Capt.18.8.16(14)
II.Abt.Kdr. Lt.Col.Fahrmbacher 1.2.32(3)	Kdr.II/A.R.7 Maj.1.1.27(4a)	Wa	Wa	Kdr.4/A.R.7	St.II/A.R.4 Capt.18.18.16(18)
III.Abt.Kdr. Lt.Col.Hirschauer 1.11.30(7)	Kdr.III/A.R.7	Kdr.III/A.R.7 Maj.1.2.26(14)	St.III/A.R.7	St.III/A.R.7	Kdt.Cuxhaven

TABLE 5 - Continued

R.R.17

Name 1932	1926	1925	1924	1923
1.Esk.Kdr. Capt.Walzer 1.2.30(7)	#4 Officer 4/R.R.17	#5 Officer 4/R.R.17	#6 Officer 4/R.R.17	Lt.18.8.16(5) #4 Officer 6/R.R.17
2.Esk.Kdr. Capt.Rodt 1.8.28(2)	#5 Officer 1/R.R.17	#4 Officer 2/R.R.17	#4 Officer 2/R.R.17	#4 Officer 2/R.R.17 Lt.1.4.14(64)
3.Esk.Kdr. Capt.Hübner (Kurt)1.2.23(12)	#2 Officer 3/R.R.17	#2 Officer 3/R.R.17	#2 Officer 3/R.R.17	#2 Officer 6/R.R.17
4.Esk.Kdr. Capt.Becker 1.5.21(10)	#2 Officer 2/N.A.2	#3St.Officer R.R.18	#4St.Officer R.R.18	#2 Officer 2/N.A.5
5.(A)Esk.Kdr. Capt.Luz 1.9.24(4)	Adj./R.R.17	Adj./R.R.17	#3St.Officer Adj./R.R.17	#4St.Officer R.R.17 Lt.18.4.17(18)
6.Esk.Kdr. Capt.Leuze 1.2.23(18)	Kdr.4/R.R.8	#2 Officer Kdr.4/R.R.8	#4 Officer 4/R.R.17	Inf.Sch. Instructor

A.R.7

Name 1932	1926	1925	1924	1923
I.Abt.Kdr. Lt.Col.R.v.Speck* 1.2.32(1)	W	T1	Gen.St.GP.2	Gen.St.GP.2
II.Abt.Kdr. Lt.Col.Fahrmbacher 1.2.32(3)	St.II/A.R.7	Kdr.4/F.A.7	Kdr.4/F.A.7	4/F.A.7
III.Abt.Kdr. Lt.Col.Hirschauer 1.11.30(7)	#2 Officer Cuxhaven	#2 Officer Cuxhaven	St.III/A.R.7	St.III/A.R.7

TABLE 5 - Continued

A.R.7

Name 1932	1931	1930	1929	1928	1927
1.Battr.Kdr. Capt.Zutavern 1.7.24(3)	St.I/A.R.7	St.GP.2	Kdr.2/F.A.5	Kdr.2/F.A.5	Kdr.:2/F.A.5
2.Battr.Kdr. Capt.Müller* (Angelo)1.2.23(7)	Kdr.2/F.A.7	Kdr.2/F.A.7	Kdr.2/F.A.7	Kdr.2/F.A.7	St.I/A.R.7
3.Battr.Kdr. Capt.Wagner* 1.11.24(1)	#2 Officer 1/A.R.7	#2 Officer 1/A.R.7	#2 Officer 1/A.R.7	#2 Officer 1/A.R.7	#2 Officer 1/A.R.7
4.Battr.Kdr. Capt.Lichtenberger 1.8.29(6)	#2 Officer 9/A.R.7	#2 Officer 9/A.R.7	1Lt.1.2.25(20a) #3 Officer 9/A.R.7	#3 Officer 9/A.R.7	#4 Officer 9/A.R.7
5.Battr.Kdr. Capt.Winter 1.6.24(10)	Kdr.5/A.R.7	St.Art.Kdr.7	St.Art.Kdr.7	St.Art.Kdr.7	R.Adj./A.R.7
6.Battr.Kdr. Capt.Wintergerst 1.2.23(21)	Kdr.6/A.R.7	Kdr.6/A.R.7	#2 Officer 6/A.R.7	Kdr.6/A.R.7	St.II/A.R.7
7.Battr.Kdr. Capt.Breith 1.1.23(5)	#2R.St.Officer A.R.7	R.Adj./A.R.7	R.Adj./A.R.7	R.Adj./A.R.7	Kdr.7/A.R.7
8.Battr.Kdr. Capt.v. Axthelm 1.10.26(6)	Kdr.9/A.R.7	Kdr.9/A.R.7	#2 Officer 9/A.R.7	#2 Officer 9/A.R.7	#2 Officer 9/A.R.7
9.Battr.Kdr. Capt.Steinwachs 1.5.31(1)	#2 Officer 9/A.R.1	1Lt.1.4.25(257) #2 Officer 9/A.R.1	#3 Officer 9/A.R.1	St.4.DIV.	St.4.DIV.
10.(A)Battr.Kdr. Capt.Feuchtinger 1.11.29(1)	Kdr.10/A.R.7	Kdr.10/A.R.7	1Lt.1.4.25(26) Kdr.10/A.R.7	#3 Officer 2/A.R.2	#3 Officer 2/A.R.2

TABLE 5 – Continued

A.R.7

Name 1932	1926	1925	1924	1923
1.Battr.Kdr. Capt.Zutavern 1.7.24(3)	Kdr.2/F.A.5	#2 Officer 5/A.R.5	#2 Officer 5/A.R.5	#2 Officer 5/A.R.5 1Lt.18.4.17(10)
2.Battr.Kdr. Capt.Müller* (Angelo)1.2.23(7)	T3	#2 Officer 1/A.R.7	#2 Officer 8/A.R.7	#2 Officer 1/F.A.7
3.Battr.Kdr. Capt.Wagner* 1.11.24(1)	#2 St.Officer III/A.R.3	#2 St.Officer III/A.R.3	1Lt.18.4.17(20) #2 Officer 3/A.R.7	#3 Officer 5/A.R.7
4.Battr.Kdr. Capt.Lichtenberger 1.8.29(6)	#4 Officer 9/A.R.7	#5 Officer 9/A.R.7	#5 Officer 9/A.R.7	9/A.R.7 #5 Officer Lt.23.12.16
5.Battr.Kdr. Capt.Winter 1.6.24(10)				#2 Officer 8/A.R.7 1Lt.8.4.17(4)
6.Battr.Kdr. Capt.Wintergerst 1.2.23(21)	R.Adj./A.R.7	R.Adj./A.R.7	R.Adj./A.R.7	Kdr.6/A.R.7
7.Battr.Kdr. Capt.Breith 1.1.23(5)	Kdr.7/A.R.7	Kdr.7/A.R.7	Kdr.6/A.R.7	#2 Officer 7/A.R.7
8.Battr.Kdr. Capt.v.Axthelm 1.10.26(6)	#2 Officer 9/A.R.7	#3 Officer 9/A.R.7	#3 Officer 5/A.R.7	Adj.III/A.R.7 1Lt.18.4.18(11)
9.Battr.Kdr. Capt.Steinwachs 1.5.31(1)	#4 Officer 4/A.R.4	#3 Officer 4/A.R.4	#4 Officer 6/A.R.5	Lt.1.9.15(304) #5 Officer 6/A.R.7
10.(A)Battr.Kdr. Capt.Feuchtinger 1.11.29(1)	#3 Officer 2/A.R.2	#5 Officer 8/A.R.2	#3 Officer 10/A.R.5	#3 Officer Lt.1.9.15(47) 10/A.R.5

TABLE 5 - Continued

DIV.VII

Name 1932	1931	1930	1929	1928	1927
Kdr.7.DIV. Maj.Gen.R.v.Leeb* 1.12.29	Kdr.7.DIV	Kdr.7.DIV	Art.Kdr.7 Brig.Gen. 1.2.29(2)	Art.Kdr.5	Kdr.Ar.7 Col.1.2.25(6)
C.St. Col.Wäger* 1.10.31(6)	C.St.7.DIV Lt.Col.1.2.29(7)	Kdr.1/I.R.19	Kdr.1/I.R.19 Lt.Col.1.2.29(7)	T1	T1
Senior Staff Officer Lt.Col.Doederlein 1.2.31(32)	Senior St. Officer	St.7.DIV.	#2R.St.Officer I.R.20	#2R.St.Officer I.R.20	St.Inf.Kdr.7 Maj.1.12.26(4)
Inf.Kdr. Col.Bauer* 1.2.30(2)	Inf.Sch. Class Kdr.	Inf.Sch. Class Kdr.	Inf.Sch. Class Kdr.	Kdr.II/I.R.19	Kdr.II/I.R.19 Lt.Col.1.2.27(15a)
Art.Kdr. Brig.Gen. Curtze 1.2.32(2)	Kdr.A.R.3	Kdr.A.R.3	R.St.Officer Col.1.2.29(8)	R.St.Officer	Kdt.Grafenwöhr
Kdt.Ingolstadt Lt.Col.Aschenbrandt 1.11.30(5)	Kdt.Ingolstadt	St.Art.Kdr.7	A.R.7	#2R.St.Officer Kdt.Borkum	Kdt.Emsmündung
Kdt.Munich Lt.Col.van Ginkel 1.11.30(6)	Kdr.I/A.R.7	Kdr.I/A.R.7	St.I/A.R.7	#2R.St.Officer A.R.4	St.I/A.R.7
Kdt. Grafenwöhr Lt.Col.Renz 1.2.31(28)	Kdt.Grafenwöhr	St.Officer R.R.17	#2St.Officer R.R.17	#2St.Officer R.R.17	Kdr.4/R.R.17 Maj.1.11.26
Kdr.I.R.19 Col.Schindler* 1.2.30(5)	Kdr.1.R.19	Kdr.III/I.R.19	Kdr.III/I.R.19	Kdr.III/I.R.19 Lt.Col.1.2.27(7a)	VH
R.St.OfficerI.R.19 Lt.Col. Graf* 1.11.30(3)	R.St.Officer I.R.19	Kdr.A./I.R.19	Kdr.A./I.R.19	St.A./I.R.9 Maj.1.2.28	Kdr.1/I.R.19
Kdr.I.R.20 Col.Schwandner* 1.2.31(1)	Kdr.I.R.20	R.St.Officer I.R.19	St.7.DIV.	Kdr.I/I.R.19 Lt.Col.1.2.28(10)	Kdr.A/I.R.20

TABLE 5 - Continued

DIV.VII

Name 1932	1926	1925	1924	1923
Kdr.7.DIV. Maj.Gen.R.v.Leeb* 1.12.29	Kdr.A.R.7	Kdr.A.R.7	C.St.7.DIV. Lt.Col.1.10.20	C.St.2.DIV
C.St. Col.Wäger* 1.10.31(6)	T1	T7	T7 Maj.1.4.23(14)	Kdr.2/I.R.19 Capt.8.10.14(58)
Senior Staff Officer Lt.Col.Doederlein 1.2.31(32)	Inf.Kdr.7	St.III/I.R.21	St.III/I.R.21	Kdr.11/I.R.21 Capt.28.11.14(65)
Inf.Kdr. Col.Bauer* 1.2.30(2)	Inf.Sch. Instructor	Inf.Sch. Instructor	Inf.Sch. Instructor	Kav.Sch. Instructor
Art.Kdr. Brig.Gen. Curtze 1.2.32(2)	Kdt.Grafenwöhr	KdrII/A.R.7 Lt.Col.1.5.24(1)	#2 Officer T.U.P.Ohrdruf	#2 Officer T.U.P.Ohrdruf
Kdt.Ingolstadt Lt.Col.Aschenbrandt 1.11.30(5)	Kdr.10/A.R.7 Maj.1.2.26(12)	Kdr.10/A.R.7 Capt.8.11.14(55)	Kdr.10/A.R.7 Capt.8.11.14(55)	#2R.St.Officer A.R.7
Kdt.Munich Lt.Col.van Ginkel 1.11.30(6)	St.I/A.R.7 Maj.1.2.26(13)	St.III/A.R.7	St.II/A.P.7	St.II/A.R.7
Kdt. Grafenwöhr Lt.Col.Renz 1.2.31(28)	Kdr.4/R.R.17	Kdr.4/R.R.17 Capt.28.11.14(59)	Kdtr.Munich	Kdtr.Munich
Kdr.I.R.19 Col.Schindler* 1.2.30(5)	T3	T3	T3	T3 Maj.1.7.21(200)
R.St.OfficerI.R.19 Lt.Col.Graf* 1.11.30(3)	Kdr.1/I.R.19	Kdr.1/I.R.19	Kdr.14/I.R.21	Kdr.14/I.R.21 Capt.18.6.15(28)
Kdr.I.R.20 Col.Schwandner* 1.2.31(1)	Kdr.A./I.R.21	Gen.St.Officer Art.Kdr.7	Gen.St.Officer Art.Kdr.7	Maj.1.7.21(20v) Gen.St.Officer Art.Kdr.7

212

TABLE 5 - Continued

DIV.VII

Name 1932	1931	1930	1929	1928	1927
R.St.Officer I.R.20 Col. Otto* 1.2.32(2)	R.St.Officer I.R.20	R.St.Officer I.R.20	Kdr.I/I.R.20 Lt.Col.1.4.29(1)	Kdr.I/I.R.20	St.2.DIV.
Kdr.I.R.21 Col.R.v.Reitzenstein 1.2.30(16)	Kdr.I.R.21	R.St.Officer I.R.21	R.St.Officer I.R.21	Kdr.III/I.R.21	Kdr.III/I.R.21 Lt.Col.1.2.27(18)
R.St.Officer I.R.21 Lt.Col.Frhr.v.Lutz 1.2.31(30)	R.St.Officer I.R.21	Kdr.III/I.R.20	Kdr.III/I.R.20	Kdr.III/I.R.20	In2 Maj.1.12.26(2)
Kdr.R.R.17 Col. Koch* 1.4.32(7)	Kdr.R.R.17	Kdr.R.R.17 Lt.Col.1.10.29(3)	St.Art.Kdr.7	St.7.DIV.	St.7.DIV.
St.Officer R.R.17 Maj. Sintzenich 1.8.30	St.Inf.Kdr.7	St.Inf.Kdr.7	St.Inf.Kdr.7	St.Inf.Kdr.7	#3St.Officer I.R.20
Kdr.A.R.7 Col. Brandt 1.11.30(4)	Kdr.7/A.R.7	St.Inf.Kdr.III	Kdr.IV(r.)/ A.R.3	Lt.Col.1.7.27(2) Kdr.IV(r.)/ A.R.3	In4
R.St.Officer A.R.7 Lt.Col. Leeb* 1.12.29(2)	R.St.Officer A.R.7	R.St.Officer A.R.7	St.II/A.R.7	St.7.DIV.	Sv.7.DIV.
Kdr.P.B.7 Maj.Dennerlein 1.2.28(30)	Kdr.P.B.7	St.P.B.3	St. P.B.5	St. P.B.5	Inf.Sch. Instructor
Kdr.N.A.7 Maj. Löwenick 1.4.29(12)	Kdr.N.A.7	Kdr.Munich	Kdr.Munich	Kdr.Munich	Kdr.2/N.A.7
Kdr.K.A.7 Maj. Kempf* 1.2.29(11)	In6	In6	In6	Kdr.2/K.A.1	Kdr.2/K.A.1
Kdr.F.A.7 Lt.Col.Bergmann 1.11.30(2)	Kdr.F.A.7	In4	In4	In4	#2R.St.Officer A.R.7
Kdr.S.A.7 Capt.R.v.Thoma 1.2.25(2)	Kdr.F.A.7	St.GP.2	Kdr.2/K.A.7	Kdr.2/K.A.7	Kdr.2/K.A.7

213

TABLE 5 - Continued
DIV.VII

Name 1932	1926	1925	1924	1923
R.St.Officer I.R.20 Col. Otto* 1.2.32(2)	Gen.St.2.DIV.	Gen.St.2.DIV.	Gen.St.2.DIV Maj.1.11.23(6)	Gen.St.2.DIV Capt.28.11.14(50)
Kdr.I.R.21 Col.R.v.Reitzensten 1.2.30(16)	Kdr.III/I.R.21	Kdr.III/I.R.21	Kdt.Munich	Kdt.Munich Maj.1.10.20(25)
R.St.Officer I.R.21 Lt.Col.Frhr.v.Lutz 1.2.31(30)	In2	In2	St.III/I.R.20	St.III/I.R.20 Capt.28.11.14(61)
Kdr.R.R.17 Col. Koch* 1.4.32(7)	Kdr.6/R.R.17	Kdr.6/R.R.17	Kdr.6/R.R.17 Maj.1.3.24(2)	T2 Capt.28.11.14(68)
St.Officer R.R.17 Maj. Sintzenich 1.8.30	Kdr.3/I.R.20	#2R.St.Officer I.R.20	#3R.St.Officer I.R.20	Kdr.2/I.R.20 Capt.18.4.17(27)
Kdr.A.R.7 Col. Brandt 1.1.30(4)	In4	In4	In4	Instr.Art.Sch, Maj.1.7.21(6)
R.St.Officer A.R.7 Lt.Col. Leeb* 1.12.29(2)	Gen.St.7.DIV.	Gen.St.7.DIV. Maj.1.2.25(3)	#2R.St.Officer A.R.7	Kdr.7/A.R.7 Capt.18.10.14(156)
Kdr.P.B.7 Maj.Dennerlein 1.2.28(30)	Inf.Sch. Instructor	Inf.Sch. Instructor	Inf.Sch. Instructor	Kdtr.Ingolstadt Capt.18.6.15(32)
Kdr.N.A.7 Maj. Löwenick 1.4.29(12)	Kdr.2/N.A.7	Kdr.2/N.A.7	In6	In6 Capt.18.4.16(35)
Kdr.K.A.7 Maj.Kempf* 1.2.29(11)	S.A.1	Gen.St.Inf. Kdr.2	Gen.St.Inf. Kdr.2	Gen.St.Inf. Kdr.2 Capt.27.1.16(20)
Kdr.F.A.7 Lt.Col.Bergmann 1.11.30(2)	#2R.St.Officer Maj.1.2.26	#2R.St.Officer	#3R.St.Officer A.R.7	Kdr.10/A.R.7 Capt.8.11.14(49)
Kdr.S.A.7 Capt.R.v.Thoma 1.2.25(2)	Kdr.2/K.A.7	Kdr.2/K.A.7	#2 Officer 2/K.A.7	Adj.K.A.7 1Lt.18.4.17(34)

TABLE 5 - Continued

SOURCE: _Rangliste_ 1923-1932; NA, 79, 83, pp. 1-120.

NOTE: Table 5 should be read from left to right beginning with the 1932 assignment. Assignments are current as of _Rangliste_ publication date.

*General Staff Officers.

215

TABLE 6

CAREER PROFILES OF OFFICERS WHO WERE DIVISION COMMANDERS AND CHIEFS OF STAFF IN 1932

Name 1932	1931	1930	1929	1928	1927
Kdr.1.DIV. Maj.Gen.v.Blomberg 1.10.29(3)	Kdr.1.DIV.	Kdr.1.DIV.	Kdr.TA	Kdr.TA Brig.Gen.1.4.28(3)	Kdr.TA
C.St.1.DIV. Col.v.Reichenau 1.2.32(11)	C.St.1.DIV.	C.St.In7	Kdr.N.A.5 Lt.Col.1.4.29(3)	Kdr.N.A.5	Kdr.N.A.5
Kdr.2.DIV. Maj.Gen.Bock 1.2.31(2)	Kdr.Kav.Div.1	Kdr.Kav.Div.1	Kdr.I.R.4 Brig.Gen.1.2.29(8)	Kdr.I.R.4	Kdr.I.R.4
C.St.2.DIV. Col.Liese	C.St.2.DIV.	C.St.2.DIV.	Kdr.III/I.R.9 Lt.Col.1.12.28(1)	Kdr.III/I.R.9	St.1.DIV.
Kdr.3.DIV. Maj.Gen.v.Rundstedt 1.3.29	Kdr.Kav.Div.2	Kdr.Kav.Div.2	Kdr.Kav.Div.2	C.St.GP2	C.St.GP2 Brig.Gen.1.11.27(1)
C.St.3.DIV. Col.v.Schwedler 1.2.32(1)	C.St.3.DIV. Lt.Col.1.2.29(32)		Kdr.II/I.R.9 Lt.Col.1.2.29(32)	Kdr.II/I.R.9	PA
Kdr.4.DIV. Maj.Gen.Frhr.v.Gienath 1.2.31(1)	Kdr.Kav.Div.3	Kdr.Kav.Div.3	Kdr.Kav.Div.3 Brig.Gen.1.2.29(7)	Kdr.I.R.6	Kdr.I.R.6
C.St.4.DIV. Lt.Col.v.Falkenhorst 1.1.30(1)	St.4.DIV.	Kdr.I/I.R.1 Lt.Col.1.1.30(1)	Kdr.I/I.R.1	Kdr.I/I.R.1	T1
Kdr.5.DIV. Maj.Gen.Liebmann 1.10.31(1)	C.St.GP2	C.St.GP2 Brig.Gen.1.10.29(6)	Kdr.I.R.5	Kdr.I.R.5	Kdr.T3
C.St.5.DIV. Col.Höring 1.10.31(5)	C.St.5.DIV.	Kdr.II/I.R.4	Kdr.II/I.R.4 Lt.Col.1.2.29(6)	St.2.DIV.	St.2.DIV.
Kdr.6.DIV. Maj.Gen.Fleck 1.3.30	Kdr.7.DIV.	Inf.Kdr.3	Inf.Kdr.3 Brig.Gen.1.2.29(6)	Kdr.I.R.9	C.St.5.DIV.
C.St.6.DIV. Col.Halder 1.12.31(2)	T4	T4	T4 Lt.Col.1.2.29(22)	St.7.DIV.	St.7.DIV.

TABLE 6 – Continued

Name 1932	1931	1930	1929	1928	1927
Kdr.7.DIV. Maj.Gen.R.v.Leeb 1.12.29	Kdr.7.DIV.	Kdr.7.DIV.	Art.Kdr.7 Brig.Gen.1.2.29(2)	Art.Kdr.5	Kdr.A.R.7
C.St.7.DIV. Col.Wäger 1.10.31(6)	C.St.7.DIV.	Kdr.I/I.R.19	Kdr.I/I.R.19 Lt.Col.1.2.29(7)	T1	T1
Kdr.Kav.Div.1 Brig.Gen.Frhr.v.Fritsch 1.11.30(3)	Art.Kdr.2	Art.Kdr.2	Kdr.A.R.2	Kdr.T1	Kdr.T1 Col.1.3.27(1)
C.St.Kav.Div.1 Col.Frhr.v.Weichs 1.11.30(18)	C.St.Kav.Div.1	C.St.Kav.Div.1	Kdr.R.R.18	Kdr.R.R.18 Lt.Col.1.2.28(6)	Inf.Sch. Instructor
Kdr.Kav.Div.2 Brig.Gen.v.Kleist Chav1.1.32	Kdr.I.R.9	C.St.3.DIV. Col.1.10.29(26)	C.St.Kav.Div.2	C.St.Kav.Div.2	Kav.Sch. Instructor
C.St.Kav.Div.2 Col.Frhr.Kress v. K. 1.11.30(19)	C.St.Kav.Div.2	Kdr.R.R.7	Kdr.R.R.7	St.Inf.Kdr.7 Lt.Col.1.2.28(7)	St.Inf.Kdr.7
Kdr.Kav.Div.3 Brig.Gen.Knochenhauer 1.10.31(2)	Kdr.R.R.16	Kdr.R.R.16	Kdr.R.R.16	C.St.Kav.Div.1 Col.1.2.28(11)	C.St.Kav.Div.1
C.St.Kav.Div.3 Lt.Col.v.Wietersheim 1.2.30(14)	Kdr.III/I.R.17	Kdr.III/I.R.17	Kdr.III/I.R.17	T4	T4

TABLE 6 – Continued

Name 1932	1926	1925	1924	1923
Kdr.1.DIV. Maj.Gen.v.Blomberg 1.10.29(3)	Kdr.T4	Kdr.T4	C.St.5.DIV.	C.St.5.DIV. Lt.Col.1.10.20(127)
C.St.1.DIV. Col.v.Reichenau 1.2.32(11)	Gen.St.3.DIV.	Gen.St.3.DIV.	Gen.St.3.DIV.	Kdr.8(M.G.)/I.R.8 Capt.28.11.14(33)
Kdr.2.DIV. Maj.Gen.Bock 1.2.31(2)	R.St.OfficerI.R.4 Col.1.5.25(1)	Kdr.II/I.R.4	Kdr.II/I.R.4	C.St.3.DIV. Lt.Col.1.10.20(140)
C.St.2.DIV. Col.Liese	Gen.St.1.DIV.	Gen.St.1.DIV.	Gen.St.1.DIV. Maj.1.4.23(3a)	Kdr.14/I.R.1
Kdr.3.DIV. Maj.Gen.v.Rundstedt 1.3.29	Kdr.I.R.18	Kdr.I.R.18	C.St.2.DIV.	C.St.Kav.Div.3 Col.1.2.23(12)
C.St.3.DIV. Col.v.Schwedler 1.2.32(1)	PA	Inf.Kdr.3	Kdr.13(M.W.)/I.R.15 Maj.1.6.23(1)	Kdr.13(M.W.)/I.R.15
Kdr.4.DIV. Maj.Gen.Frhr.v.Gienath 1.2.31(1)	C.St.In3	C.St.In3 Col.1.4.25(9)	Kdr.R.R.13	C.St.Kav.Div.2 Lt.Col.1.10.20(138)
C.St.4.DIV. Lt.Col.v.Falkenhorst 1.1.30(1)	T1	T1 Maj.1.2.25(6)	T1	T1 Capt.24.12.14(38)
Kdr.5.DIV. Maj.Gen.Liebmann 1.10.31(1)	Kdr.T3 Col.1.2.26(16)	Kdr.T3	Kdr.II/I.R.1	Kdr.II/I.R.1 Lt.Col.1.6.21(17)
C.St.5.DIV. Col.Höring 1.10.31(5)	St.2.DIV.	St.2.DIV.	St.2.DIV. Maj.1.4.23(13)	Inf.Sch. Instructor
Kdr.6.DIV. Maj.Gen.Fleck 1.3.30	C.St.5.DIV.	C.St.5.DIV. Col.1.4.25(7)	Kdr.II/I.R.7	Kdr.II/I.R.7 Lt.Col.1.10.20(136)
C.St.6.DIV. Col.Halder 1.12.31(2)	Gen.St.7.DIV.	Kdr.4/A.R.7	Kdr.4/A.R.7	Kdr.4/A.R.7

TABLE 6 – Continued

Name 1932	1926	1925	1924	1923
Kdr.7.DIV. Maj.Gen.R.v.Leeb 1.12.29	Kdr.A.R.7	Kdr.II/A.R.7 Col.1.2.25(6)	C.St.7.DIV.	C.St.2.DIV. Lt.Col.1.1.10.20(116)
C.St.7.DIV. Col.Wäger 1.10.31(6)	T2	T7	T7 Maj.1.4.23(4)	Kdr.2/I.R.19
Kdr.Kav.Div.1 Brig.Gen.Frhr.v.Fritsch 1.11.30(3)	Kdr.T1	C.St.1.DIV.	C.St.1.DIV.	Kdr.II/A.R.5 Lt.Col.15.11.22(5)
C.St.Kav.Div.1 Col.Frhr.v.Weichs 1.11.30(18)	Inf.Sch. Instructor	Inf.Sch. Instructor	Kdr.2/R.R.18	Kdr.2/R.R.18 Maj.1.7.21(20m)
Kdr.Kav.Div.2 Brig.Gen.v.Kleist Chav1.1.32	Kav.Sch. Instructor 1.12.26(5)	Kav.Sch. Instructor	Kav.Sch. Instructor	Kdr.1/R.R.13 1.7.21(20a)
C.St.Kav.Div.2 Col.Frhr.Kress v. K. 1.11.30(19)	Gen.St.Inf.Kdr.7	Kav.Div.2	Kav.Div.2 Maj.1.7.21(20n)	Kav.Div.2
Kdr.Kav.Div.3 Brig.Gen.Knochenhauer 1.10.31(2)	C.St.Kav.Div.1	C.St.Kav.Div.1	Kdr.II/I.R.3 Lt.Col.15.2.23(7)	Kdr.II/I.R.3 Maj.18.5.18(126)
C.St.Kav.Div.3 Lt.Col.v.Wietersheim 1.2.30(14)	T4	Kdr.6/I.R.15 Maj.1.4.25(1)	Kdr.6/I.R.15	Inf.Kdr.3 Capt.8.10.14(79)

SOURCE: Rangliste 1923-1932

NOTE: Table 6 should be read from left to right beginning with the 1932 assignment. Assignments are current as of Rangliste publication date.

TABLE 7

THE INFANTRY OFFICER'S LAUFBAHN

Rank	Line Assignment	Staff Assignment
Lt.	Company Officer	None
1 Lt.	Company Officer	Battalion Adjutant Regiment Staff Group Staff
Capt.	Company Commander	Regimental Adjutant Division Staff Group Staff Infantry School Defense Ministry
Maj.	Battalion Commander	Infantry Commander Staff Battalion Staff Group Staff Division Staff Defense Ministry Infantry School
Lt. Col.	Battalion Commander	Regimental Staff Officer Division Staff Group Staff Infantry School Defense Ministry Division Chief of Staff
Col.	Regiment Commander	Infantry School Group Staff Defense Ministry Branch Commander
Brig. Gen.	Division Infantry Commander Cavalry Division Commander	Group Staff Group Chief of Staff Defense Ministry Infantry School Commander
Maj. Gen.	Infantry Division Commander	Group Chief of Staff Defense Ministry

NOTE: The information in this table is based on an analysis of the data in Tables 3, 4, 5, and 6.

TABLE 8

ASSIGNMENT RECOMMENDATION LISTS

List II:	Defense Ministry
List III:	1) Field Unit Staffs (including General Staffs)
	2) Adjutant Service
List IV:	1) Munitions Service
	2) Technical Weapons Assignments
	3) Technical Colleges
List V:	Garrisons and Higher Staffs
List VI:	Weapons Schools
List VII:	Detached Duty with Other Branches

SOURCE: NA, 79, 52, pp. 715-716; OER regulation; Gen.
Rudolf Hofmann (ret.), German Efficiency Report System, Foreign
Military Studies Series MS#P-134 (Washington, D.C.: Department
of the Army, Office of the Chief of Military History, 1952), pp.
17-19.

Officer Promotions

TABLE 1

EDUARD ZORN'S LT. **PATENT** GROUP (1.12.24)

Name	Assignment	Patent
Berger	I.R.12	1.12.24 (1)
Zorn	I.R.19	" (2)
Knittel	A.R.5	" (3)
Kaulbach	I.R.9	" (4)
Buddee	K.A.1	" (5)
Litzmann	R.R.1	" (6)
Loebel	A.R.5	" (7)
Schmid (Joseph)	I.R.21	" (8)
Müller (Walter)	R.R.17	" (9)
Uber	R.R.8	" (10)
Franz	I.R.17	" (11)
Schneider	I.R.17	" (12)
Reinhard	K.A.4	" (13)
v. Kahlden	I.R.4	" (14)
Windisch	I.R.19	" (15)
Bürker	I.R.13	" (16)
Mantey	A.R.1	" (17)
Finke	I.R.2	" (18)
Sachs	A.R.6	" (19)
Balthasar	A.R.5	" (20)
Rauser	I.R.15	" (21)
Soehngen	I.R.1	" (22)
Macher	I.R.19	" (23)
Falkner	I.R.20	" (24)
Langhaeuser	I.R.20	" (25)
Föst	I.R.1	" (26)
Wagner	A.R.7	" (27)
Wupper	I.R.14	" (28)
Peltzer	I.R.12	" (29)
Stange	I.R.2	" (30)
Rohrbach	K.A.5	" (31)
Berchtenbreiter	I.R.20	" (32)
Pfafferott (Werner)	I.R.12	" (33)
Kober	I.R.14	" (34)
Wagener	R.R.11	" (35)
Langkau	A.R.3	" (36)
v. Both	K.A.3	" (37)
Reiss	R.R.9	" (38)
Maier	I.R.20	" (39)
Hellberg	A.R.7	" (40)
Clotz	I.R.15	" (41)
Wüller (Fritz)	N.A.4	" (42)
Schaefer (Otto)	I.R.21	" (43)
Laegeler	I.R.13	" (44)
Meess	R.R.18	" (45)

TABLE 1 - Continued

Name	Assignment	Patent
Deinhardt	R.R.18	1.12.24(46)
Engelke	I.R.21	" (47)
Merker	I.R.6	" (48)
Pannicke	R.R.2	" (49)
Raum	I.R.21	" (50)
Blässer	I.R.11	" (51)
Laacke	I.R.11	" (52)
Seitz	K.A.7	" (53)
Henning	I.R.6	" (54)
Baumann	I.R.15	" (55)
Renner	I.R.20	" (56)
Koch	I.R.20	" (57)
Bomend	P.B.1	" (58)
Keppel	R.R.4	" (59)
Peters	I.R.11	" (60)
Metzger	R.R.18	" (61)
Hoeffner	R.R.17	" (62)
Burmeister	R.R.14	" (63)
Laicher	A.R.5	" (64)
v. Merkatz	I.R.5	" (65)
Nielsen	I.R.6	" (66)
Kretschmer	K.A.5	" (67)
Nesper	N.A.5	" (68)
Hoebel	I.R.15	" (69)
v. d. Becke	I.R.16	" (70)
v. Stocki	R.R.15	" (71)
Koob	A.R.7	" (72)
Beseler	I.R.17	" (73)
Sosna	I.R.15	" (74)
Furbach	I.R.4	" (75)
Anders	A.R.3	" (76)
Boner	N.A.3	" (77)
v. Vallade	I.R.W	" (78)
Becher	I.R.1	" (79)
Jacobs	A.R.5	" (80)
Merz	I.R.15	" (81)
Feucht	A.R.5	" (82)
v. Sydow	K.A.2	" (83)
Lutz	A.R.5	" (84)
Wimmel	I.R.15	1.2.25
v. Xylander	I.R.19	1.3.25

SOURCE: Rangliste 1925.

224

TABLE 2

A COMPARISON BETWEEN FERDINAND JODL'S LT.

AND 1LT. PROMOTION GROUPS

Name	Assignment	Lt. Patent	1Lt. Patent
Rieke	I.R.16	1.9.15(21)	1.4.25(1)
Gerlach	A.R.3	" (31)	" (11)
Chorbacher	A.R.7	" (44)	" (22)
Burgdorf	I.R.8	" (66)	" (45)
v. Stangen	R.R.4	" (96)	" (75)
Doege	St.2.DIV.	" (125)	" (100)
Dürking	I.R.18	" (151)	" (125)
Bourquin	St.4.DIV.	" (182)	" (150)
Berger	I.R.2	" (211)	" (175)
Bleyer	I.R.15	" (238)	" (200)
v. Reuss	A.R.3	" (239)	" (201)
Jodl	A.R.7	" (240)	" (202)
Böhme	I.R.11	" (242)	" (203)
Krummacher	A.R.6	1.10.15(26)	" (300)
Scheider	I.R.2	6.6.16(1)	" (401)
Gittner	A.R.2	1.2.17(3)	" (499)
Degen	I.R.20	3.10.17(3)	" (601)
v. Pfuhlstein	I.R.9	1.4.18(16)	" (685)

SOURCE: Rangliste 1924-1926.

TABLE 3

OFFICERS ADDED TO FERDINAND JODL'S

1LT. PROMOTION GROUP AFTER 1.4.25

First Rangliste Appearance as 1Lt.	First Rangliste Appearance as Lt.	Name	Assignment when Awarded 1Lt. Patent	Lt. Patent	1Lt. Patent
1927	1923	Barsnick	A.R.1	1.4.22(13)	1.4.25(567a)
1927	1923	Tinzmann	A.R.3	1.4.22(5)	" (641a)
1928	1923	Johannesson	I.R.4	1.7.16(4)	" (405a)
1928	1923	Meier	I.R.16	1.2.22(6)	" (461a)
1928	1925	✠ v. Vormann	St.4.DIV.	1.8.19(1)	" (564a)
1929	1923	Fabiunke	A.R.3	25.11.16(1)	" (71a)
1929	1925	Golden	S.A.6	1.4.18(5a)	" (319a)
1929	1923	✠ v. Waldenburg	R.R.11	1.6.19(2)	" (617a)
1930	1924	✠ v. Scheven	R.R.3	18.2.17(6)	" (323a)
1930	1924	Eberding	St.1.DIV.	1.3.18(6)	" (418a)
1930	1924	Kelpe	S.A.6	1.1.19(2)	" (454b)
1930	1925	Burmeister	R.R.14	1.12.24(63)	" (567b)
1931	1923	✠ Stollbrock	R.R.3	1.7.17(18)	" (452a)
1931	1924	v. Raczeck	St.GP.2	1.1.19(4)	" (527a)

SOURCE: Rangliste 1923-1924.

226

TABLE 4

AUTHORIZED AND ASSIGNED OFFICER STRENGTH

OF THE REICHSWEHR, 1924-1932

Grade	Number of Authorized Officers	Number of Assigned Officers								
		1924	1925	1926	1927	1928	1929	1930	1931	1932
Lt. Gen.	3	3	3	3	3	3	3	3	3	3
Maj. Gen.	14	14	13	14	14	14	14	14	13	14
Brig. Gen.	25	25	26	25	26	24	27	25	25	27
Col.	105	106	121	105	105	109	105	106	107	104
Lt. Col.	190	190	192	189	194	192	192	192	191	191
Maj.	372	373	373	375	377	376	376	378	375	374
Capt.	1,098	1,089	1,096	1,098	1,100	1,101	1,100	1,098	1,098	1,095
1Lt.	1,306	625	632	1,275	1,283	1,274	1,279	1,332	1,276	1,274
Lt.	653	1,248	1,188	538	608	575	626	624	639	638
TOTAL	3,798	3,673	3,643	3,622	3,710	3,668	3,722	3,772	3,727	3,720

SOURCE: Hossbach, Die Entwicklung des Oberbefehls, p. 149; Kauffmann, "Offizier-korps und Offiziernachwuchs," p. 25; Hofmann, German Efficiency Report System, p. 62; Rangliste 1924-1932.

NOTE: The authorized figures for Lts. and 1Lts. apply to the years, 1926-1932. The total figures for authorized and assigned personnel do not include the (W), or munitions officers (80 authorized), and military officials (1,202 authorized) who are included in the 4,000 figure authorized by the Versailles Treaty. Figures for assigned personnel are current as of Rangliste publication date.

TABLE 5

NUMBER OF NEWLY-PROMOTED OFFICERS, 1924-1932

Grade	1924	1925	1926	1927	1928	1929	1930	1931	1932
Maj. Gen.	4	4	5	7	6	6	7	5	6
Brig. Gen.	13	8	10	15	15	17	19	17	19
Col.	33	31	29	34	45	40	46	55	45
Lt. Col.	43	30	43	59	68	71	70	84	65
Maj.	77	68	72	80	94	65	72	90	73
Capt.	102	125	112	121	140	127	129	121	96
1Lts.	107	151	780	148	203	188	168	121	241
Lts.	41	91	160	243	265	196	191	161	135

SOURCE: Rangliste 1924-1932.

NOTE: Figures are current as of Rangliste publication date.

228

TABLE 6

PROMOTION OPPORTUNITIES IN THE REICHSWEHR

Grade	Age at Time of Promotion (yrs.)			Projections based on 1931 Promotion Data (yrs.)		
	1913	1928	1931	Total Officer Time	Time in Grade	Age
Brig. Gen.	55 5/12	53 3/12	55	34 9/12	3	55-56
Col.	52 11/12	51 6/12	52 3/12 49 4/12*	31 10/12	3	52-53
Lt. Col.	50 4/12	48	47 5/12 43 7/12*	27 5/12	4 7/12	49-50
Maj.	45 6/12	42 7/12	41 1/12 37 9/12*	22 5/12	12 11/12	44-45
Capt.	35	32 7/12	34 6/12	14 6/12	4 11/12 (Jodl)	34
1Lt.	28 7/12	26 7/12	26 5/12	3 6/12	3 6/12	29

SOURCE: Hossbach, Die Entwicklung des Oberbefehls, p. 149; Kauffmann, "Offizierkorps und Offiziernachwuchs," p. 31; Rangliste 1923-1932.

NOTE: The time in grade figures refer to the previous grade. For example, 1Lts. in 1931 were being promoted after serving an average of 3 6/12 years as Lts.

*The lower figure applies to officers receiving preferential promotions.

229

TABLE 7

NEWLY-PROMOTED MAJORS, 1924-1932

Year	Name	Assignment	Capt. Patent	Maj. Patent	Time in Grade (yrs.)
1924	Dauber	Inf.Sch.	19.8.14(1)	1.5.23(1)	8 9/12
"	Barends	R.R.14	" (5)	1.7.23(1)	
"	Rühle v. Lilienstern	Kdtr.Stettin	" (10)	1.10.23(1)	
"	R. v. Molo	RWM	5.9.14(3)	" (5)	
"	Bodenstein	St.Kav.Div.3	" (14)	1.1.24(1)	
"	Strauss	St.GP.1	18.10.14(1)	" (5)	
"	Sorche	St.GP.1	" (2)	1.2.24(1)	
"	Bardt	Kdtr.Ulm	" (12)	1.2.24(9)	
"	v. Lowenich	R.R.1	" (16)	1.4.24(1)	
"	Steiglehner	A.R.5	" (22)	" (5)	9 6/12
1925	v. Sichart	St.Inf.Kdr.4	" (27)	1.6.24(1)	9 8/12
"	Bock v. Wülsingen	RWM	" (36)	" (6)	
"	Ziemer	St.GP.2	" (44)	1.9.24	
"	Frhr. v. Biegeleben	St.Kav.Div.1	" (46)	1.11.24(1)	
"	Glehrach	A.R.2	" (49)	" (3)	
"	Heidrich	St.Art.Kdr.3	" (52)	1.2.25(1)	
"	Haase	A.R.5	" (53)	" (2)	
"	Buchs	St.2.DIV.	" (70)	" (19)	
"	Neugebauer	I.R.5	" (82)	1.4.25(1)	
"	v. Keiser	St.GP.2	18.11.14(2)	" (8)	
"	Weste	I.R.11	" (15)	" (16)	
"	Warnebold	A.R.3	" (16)	1.5.25(1)	
"	Braumüller	A.R.6	" (23)	" (6)	10 6/12
1926	v. Priem	I.R.3	8.11.14(25a)	1.8.25(1)	10 9/12
"	Schade	St.GP.1	" (33)	" (4)	
"	Lucht	Gen.St.7.DIV.	" (41)	1.12.25(1)	
"	Quade*	I.R.2	18.4.15(6)	1.2.26(1)	

TABLE 7- <u>Continued</u>

Year	Name	Assignment	Capt. Patent	Maj. Patent	Time in Grade (yrs.)
1926	Heinrici*	I.R.13	18.6.15(13)	1.2.26(6)	
"	Beyer	I.R.9	18.11.14(65)	" (21)	
"	Schubert	I.R.8	28.11.14(11)	" (34)	
"	v. Vietinghoff*	I.R.9	24.7.15(3)	1.3.26(1)	
"	v. Kempski	Inf.Sch.	28.11.14(17)	" (6)	
"	v. Hanstein	St.2.DIV.	" (18)	1.4.26(1)	
"	Reischle	St.5.DIV.	" (40)	" (13)	
"	v. Marees	I.R.21	" (41)	1.5.26	11 6/12
1927	Hildebrand	I.R.6	28.11.14(49)	1.8.26	11 9/12
"	v. Viebahn*	RWM	18.10.15(7)	1.10.26(1)	
"	Stumme*	St.Kav.Div.3	" (12)	" (8)	
"	v. Krenzki*	Kdtr.Berlin	18.12.15(1)	1.2.27(1)	
"	Pfeffer	A.R.6	24.12.14(10)	" (12)	
"	Ludewig	RWM	" (14)	" (16)	
"	Volk	Kav.Sch.	" (16)	" (20)	
"	Veiel	St.Kav.Div.3	" (37)	" (32)	
"	Schley	T.U.P. Grafenwöhr	" (39a)	" (33)	
"	Fromm*	R.R.14	18.4.16(4)	1.3.27(1)	
"	Reinhardt*	R.R.12	" (19)	" (13)	
"	Bassoll	St.6.DIV.	27.1.15(19)	1.5.27(1)	
"	Haccius	RWM	" (27)	" (5)	12 4/12
1928	v. Faber du Faur	R.R.15	27.1.15(29)	1.6.27(2)	12 5/12
"	Holtz	St.Inf.Kdr.2	" (31)	" (4)	
"	R. v. Speck*	RWM	18.8.16(14)	1.11.27(1)	
"	Ebeling*	I.R.16	" (24)	" (8)	
"	Brand*	A.R.2	" (39)	1.2.28(1)	
"	Schneider	RWM	18.6.15(6)	" (10)	
"	Dransfeld	K.A.6	" (15)	" (16)	
"	Haubs	N.A.7	" (30)	" (29)	

TABLE 7 - <u>Continued</u>

Year	Name	Assignment	Capt. <u>Patent</u>	Maj. <u>Patent</u>	Time in Grade (yrs.)
1930	v. Alten	Kdtr.Berlin	18.4.17(25)	1.4.30(14)	13
1931	Sintzenich	St.Inf.Kdr.7	18.4.17(27)	1.8.30	13 4/12
"	Bielfeld	St.Inf.Kdr.1	20.5.17(7)	1.11.30(1)	
"	Krocker	Kdtr.Breslau	16.9.17(2)	" (14)	
"	Loehning	St.3.DIV.	28.11.17(3)	1.2.31(1)	
"	Naumann	RWM	18.12.17(12)	" (9)	
"	Linkenbach	R.R.14	27.1.18(9)	" (20)	
"	Dr. Meise	RWM	22.3.18(7)	" (34)	
"	Theune	RWM	" (16a)	" (40)	
"	Mittermaier	St.Kav.Div.3	18.4.18(3)	1.4.31(1)	
"	Jungeblodt	RWM	18.5.18(1)	" (6)	
"	Dormagen	T.U.P.Neuhammer	15.7.18(2)	" (18)	
"	Frhr. v. Kettler	I.R.6	" (3)	1.5.31(1)	
"	v. Kalm	Kdtr.Ulm	15.7.18(9)	" (6)	12 10/12
1932	Martin	RWM	18.8.18(2)	1.8.31	13
"	Böttger	I.R.11	" (4)	1.10.31(1)	
"	Schelle	St.2.DIV.	" (14)	" (8)	
"	Baltzer	St.3.DIV.	" (24)	" (13)	
"	Reinhardt	I.R.11	20.9.18(6)	1.2.32(1)	
"	Schroeder	K.A.5	" (12)	" (6)	
"	Just	Kdtr.Küstrin	18.10.18(1)	" (17)	
"	Wilke	RWM	" (3)	1.4.32(1)	
"	Haverkampf	I.R.19	" (12)	" (5)	
"	Cantzler	RWM	" (26)	" (15)	
"	Rommel	Inf.Sch.	" (34)	" (22)	
"	Schwartz	St.Inf.Kdr.4	" (38)	" (25)	13 6/12

SOURCE: <u>Rangliste</u> 1924-1932.

NOTE: Time in grade figures, which refer to the time served in the grade of Capt., are provided for the first and last new Major in each <u>Rangliste</u>.

*Officers so designated received a preferential promotion.

TABLE 8

COMPOSITE OF NEWLY-PROMOTED FIELD GRADE
AND GENERAL OFFICERS, 1924-1932

Grade	Year	Total	Branch of Service				Nobles	No. in Senior Staff Assign.
			Inf.	Kav.	Art.	Tech.		
New Majors								
	1924	73	41	8	19	5	12	8
	1925	68	30	7	23	8	16	34
	1926	74	28	17	21	8	19	24
	1927	81	43	20	11	7	17	39
	1928	93	46	12	18	17	27	41
	1929	65	28	9	13	15	16	25
	1930	66	34	15	13	4	10	24
	1931	90	44	22	8	16	17	29
	1932	73	37	10	12	14	5	29
New Lt. Cols.								
	1924	43	19	8	10	6	14	10
	1925	30	14	3	5	8	6	6
	1926	43	19	4	8	12	13	10
	1927	61	30	6	14	11	17	13
	1928	67	29	13	11	14	26	9
	1929	71	37	4	19	11	17	20
	1930	70	28	9	25	8	14	14
	1931	83	46	10	13	14	22	21
	1932	65	35	10	13	7	12	
New Cols.	1924	32	18	1	10	3	10	8
	1925	27	15	3	7	2	12	11
	1926	29	18	1	7	3	13	8
	1927	34	19	0	12	3	7	18
	1928	45	17	7	11	10	13	24
	1929	40	24	6	6	4	15	14
	1930	46	19	3	14	10	11	15
	1931	55	18	15	11	11	22	20
	1932	45	24	4	11	6	10	20
New Brig. Gens.								
	1924	13	4	2	7	0	7	
	1925	8	1	2	4	1	5	
	1926	10	5	1	3	1	5	
	1927	15	7	1	5	2	6	
	1928	16	11	0	5	0	9	
	1929	17	10	2	5	0	10	
	1930	19	12	0	7	0	6	
	1931	17	10	1	4	2	6	
	1932	19	11	2	6	0	8	

233

TABLE 8 – <u>Continued</u>

Grade	Year	Total	Branch of Service				Nobles	No. in Senior Staff Assign.
			Inf.	Kav.	Art.	Tech.		
New Maj. Gens.	1924	4	3	0	1	0	3	
	1925	4	2	1	1	0	2	
	1926	5	5	0	0	0	2	
	1927	7	4	1	2	0	5	
	1928	6	1	3	2	0	4	
	1929	6	3	1	2	0	5	
	1930	7	4	1	2	0	3	
	1931	5	3	1	1	0	2	
	1932	6	4	0	2	0	3	
New Lt. Gens.	1924	0	0	0	0	0		
	1925	2	1	1	0	0	1	
	1926	0	0	0	0	0		
	1927	2	1	0	1	0	1	
	1928	2	1	0	1	0	2	
	1929	1	1	0	0	0		
	1930	1	0	0	1	0	1	
	1931	1	1	0	0	0	1	
	1932	1	1	0	0	0	1	

TABLE 9

NEWLY-PROMOTED BRIGADIER GENERALS, 1924-1932

Year	Name	Assignment	Col. Patent	Brig. Gen. Patent	Time in Grade(yrs)
1924	Frhr. v. Forstner	Inf.Kdr.6	14.6.20(7)	1.5.23(1)	2 11/12
"	v. Kayser	Kdr.Kav.Sch.	1.10.20(2)	1.7.23	
"	Mand	Art.Kdr.6	" (7)	1.11.23(1)	
"	Schwager	Art'.Kdr.2	" (10)	" (3)	
"	Frhr. v. Esebeck	Kdr.I.R.8	" (14)	1.1.24	
"	v. Armsberg	Kdr.Inf.Sch.	" (16)	1.3.24	3 5/12
1925	v. Metzsch	Kdr.In1	1.10.20(19)	1.4.24	3 5/12
"	v. Natzmer	Kdr.In6	" (24)	1.3.25	
"	v. Graberg	St.3.DIV.	" (26)	1.4.25(1)	
"	v. Brandenstein	Inf.Kdr.4	1.10.20(31)	1.4.25(4)	4 6/12
1926	Fischer	St.GP.1	" (33)	" (5)	4 6/12
"	v. Dewitz	Kdr.Art.Sch.	" (38)	1.11.25	
"	v. Aigner	Art.Kdr.3	" (39)	1.2.26(1)	
"	Severin	Kdt.Berlin	1.4.21(4)	" (5)	
"	R. v. Beckh	Kdt.Munich	1.7.21(8)	1.4.26	4 9/12
1927	Poetter	Art.Kdr.1	1.7.21(13)	1.5.26	4 10/12
"	v. Stülpnagel	Inf.Kdr.5	1.1.22(1)	1.10.26	
"	v. Sommerfeld v. Falkenhayn	St.GP.2	1.2.22(1)	1.2.27(1)	
"	R. v. Prager	Kdr.In2	1.7.22(1)	" (5)	
"	Lorenz	Art.Kdr.6	1.12.22(3)	1.4.27	
"	Buchholz	RWM	1.8.22	1.5.27(2)	4 9/12
1928	Frhr. Seutter v. Lötzen	Inf.Kdr.7	1.2.23(11)	1.7.27	4 5/12
"	v. Rundstedt	C.St.GP.2	" (12)	1.11.27(1)	
"	v. Greiff	Kdr.In1	1.4.23(1)	" (4)	
"	v. Wenz zu Niederlahnstein	Kdr.I.R.20	1.11.23(1)	1.2.28(1)	
"	Theysohn	Art.Kdr.7	1.1.24(1)	" (3)	
"	Sehmsdorf	Kdr.In5	1.3.24(4)	1.4.28(1)	
"	v. Falkenhausen	Kdr.Inf.Sch.	1.4.24(3)	" (2)	4
"	v. Blomberg*	C.TA	1.4.25(8)	" (3)	3
"	v. Stülpnagel*	C.PA	1.8.25(4)	" (4)	2 8/12
1929	v. Schenckendorff	Inf.Kdr.6	1.5.24(2)	1.11.28(1)	4 6/12
"	Fleck	Inf.Kdr.5	1.2.25(5)	1.2.29(1)	
"	R. v. Leeb	Art.Kdr.7	" (6)	" (2)	
"	Fleck	Inf.Kdr.3	1.4.25(7)	" (6)	
"	v. Bock	Kdr.I.R.4	1.5.25(1)	" (8)	
"	Frhr. v. Hammerstein-Equord	C.St.3.DIV.	" (2)	" (9)	
"	v. Stülpnagel (Otto)	St.GP.1	1.8.25(4)	" (10)	
"	Eberth	Art.Kdr.5	1.2.26(4)	1.4.29(1)	
"	v. Platen	Kdr.I.R.16	" (6)	1.5.29	3 3/12

TABLE 9 - Continued

Year	Name	Assignment	Col. Patent	Brig. Gen Patent	Time in Grade(yrs)
1930	Waenker v. Dankenschweil	Inf.Kdr.5	1.2.26(8)	1.6.29	3 4/12
"	Halm	St.GP.1	" (9)	1.10.29(1)	
"	Liebmann	C.St.GP.2	" (16)	" (6)	
"	Frhr. v. d. Bussche	C.Wehr-A	1.3.26(1)	" (7)	
"	v. Schleicher	C.MinA	1.3.26(2)	" (8)	
"	Marx	Kdr.In4	1.2.27(1)	" (11)	
"	Streccius	Kdr.I.R.17	1.2.27(12)	1.2.30(1)	
"	Adam	C.St.GP.1	" (17)	" (5)	
"	R. v. Mittelberger	Kdr.In1	" (18)	1.3.30 (1)	
"	v. Cochenhausen	Kdr.A.R.4	" (19)	" (2)	3 1/12
1931	Kaupisch	Art.Kdr.5	1.2.27(20)	1.11.30(1)	3 9/12
"	Frhr. v. Fritsch	Art.Kdr.2	1.3.27(1)	" (3)	
"	List	Kdr.Inf.Sch.	" (3)	" (5)	
"	Held	Inf.Kdr.1	1.4.27(2)	1.12.30	
"	Koch	Kdt.Königsberg	1.5.27(3)	1.2.31(3)	
"	v. Roques	Inf.Kdr.6	1.1.28(1)	" (8)	
"	Lutz	Kdr.In6	" (2)	1.4.31(1)	
"	v. Hösslin	Inf.Kdr.7	1.2.28(4)	" (3)	
"	v. Bonin	Kdr.In7	" (6)	" (5)	3 2/12
1932	v. Roques	Inf.Kdr.1	1.2.28(7)	1.5.31	3 3/12
"	v. Boetticher	Kdr.Art.Sch.	" (9)	1.10.31(1)	
"	v. Brauchitsch	Kdr.In4	1.4.28(2)	" (8)	
"	Curtze	Art.Kdr.7	1.2.29(8)	1.2.32(2)	
"	Bitthorn	RWM	" (10)	" (4)	
"	Haenicke	Kdr.I.R.2	" (13)	1.4.32(1)	
"	Roese	Kdr.I.R.4	1.3.29(2)	" (3)	3 1/12

SOURCE: Rangliste 1924-1932.

NOTE: Time in grade figures, which refer to the time served in the grade of Col., are provided for the first and last new Brig.Gen. in every Rangliste with the exception of 1928.

*Officers so designated received a preferential promotion.

236

TABLE 10

REICHSWEHR GENERALS AS OF 1 MAY 1932

Name	Branch of Service	Promotion Data							
		Lt.Gen. Patent	Maj.Gen. Patent	Time in Grade (Brig.Gen.)	Brig.Gen. Patent	Time in Grade (Col.)	Col. Patent	Time in Grade (Lt.Col.)	Lt.Col. Patent
F. v. Hammerstein-Equord	Inf.	1.3.29	---	---	1.2.29(9)	3 9/12	1.5.25(2)	4 7/12	1.10.20(141)
Hasse	Inf.	1.4.29	1.2.26	3	1.2.23(3)	. : .	. : . : .	. . .	. . .
F. Seutter v. Lotzen	Inf.	1.12.31	1.2.29(2)	1 7/12	1.7.27	4 5/12	1.2.23(11)	. . .	. . .
v. Rundstedt	Inf.	. . .	1.3.29	1 4/12	1.11.27(1)	4 9/12	1.2.23(12)	. . .	. . .
v. Vollard-Bockelberg	Art.	. . .	1.4.29	1 5/12	1.11.27(3)	4 9/12	1.2.23(14)	. . .	. . .
v. Blomberg	Inf.	. . .	1.10.29(3)	1 6/12	1.4.28(3)	3	1.4.25(8)	4 6/12	1.10.20(137)
R. v. Leeb	Art.	. . .	1.12.29	10/12	1.2.29(2)	4	1.2.25(6)	4 4/12	1.10.20(116)
Fleck	Inf.	. . .	1.3.30	1 1/12	1.2.29(6)	3 10/12	1.4.25(7)	4 6/12	1.10.20(136)
F. v. Gienanth	Kav.	. . .	1.2.31(1)	2	1.2.29(7)	3 10/12	1.4.25(9)	4 6/12	1.10.20(138)
v. Bock	Inf.	. . .	1.2.31(2)	2	1.2.29(8)	3 9/12	1.5.25(1)	4 7/12	1.10.20(140)
Wachenfeld	Art.	. . .	1.4.31	1 6/12	1.10.29(2)	3 8/12	1.2.26(10)	4 8/12	1.6.21(11)
Liebmann	Inf.	. . .	1.10.31(1)	2	1.10.29(6)	3 8/12	1.2.26(16)	4 8/12	1.6.21(17)
F. v. d. Bussche-Ippenburg	Art.	. . .	1.10.31(2)	2	1.10.29(7)	3 7/12	1.3.26(1)	4 9/12	1.6.21(18)
v. Schleicher	Inf.	. . .	1.10.31(3)	2	1.10.29(8)	3 7/12	1.3.26(2)	4 9/12	1.6.21(20)
Adam	Inf.	. . .	1.12.31	1 10.12	1.2.30(5)	3	1.2.27(17)	4 3/12	15.11.22(2a)
R. v. Mittelberger	Inf.	. . .	1.1.32	1 10/12	1.3.30(1)	3 1/12	1.2.27(18)	4 3/12	15.11.22(3)
Kaupisch	Art.	. . .	1.3.32	1 4/12	1.11.30(1)	3 9/12	1.2.27(20)	4	1.2.23(19)
F. v. Fritsch	Art.	. . .	. . .	. . .	1.11.30(3)	3 8/12	1.3.27(1)	4 4/12	15.11.22(5)
List	Inf.	. . .	. . .	. . .	1.11.30(5)	3 8/12	1.3.27(3)	4 4/12	15.11.22(6a)
Boehm-Tettelbach	Art.	. . .	. . .	. . .	1.11.30(6)	3 7/12	1.4.27(1)	4 5/12	15.11.22(6b)
Beck	Art.	. . .	. . .	. . .	1.2.31(5)	3 3/12	1.11.27(2)	5	15.11.22(10)
v. Roques	Tech.	. . .	. . .	. . .	1.2.31(8)	3 1/12	1.1.28(1)	4 11/12	1.2.23(4)
Lutz	Tech.	. . .	. . .	. . .	1.4.31(1)	3 3/12	1.1.28(2)	4 11/12	1.2.23(8)
v. Bonin	Inf.	. . .	. . .	. . .	1.4.31(5)	3 2/12	1.2.28(6)	5	15.2.23(2)
v. Roques	Inf.	. . .	. . .	. . .	1.5.31	3 3/12	1.2.28(7)	5	15.2.23(3)
v. Boetticher	Arts.	. . .	. . .	. . .	1.10.31(1)	3 8/12	1.2.28(9)	5	15.2.23(5)
Knochenhauer	Inf.	. . .	. . .	. . .	1.10.31(2)	3 8/12	1.2.28(11)	5	15.2.23(7)
Schönheinz	Inf.	. . .	. . .	. . .	1.10.31(3)	3 8/12	1.2.28(12)	5	15.2.23(8)

TABLE 10 - Continued

Name	Branch of Service	Promotion Data						
		Brig. Gen. Patent	Time in Grade (Col.)	Col. Patent	Time in Grade (Lt.Col.)	Lt. Col. Patent	Time in Grade (Maj.)	Maj: Patent
Muff	Inf.	1.10.31(4)	3 8/12	1.2.28(13)	5	15.2.23(9)	. . .	. . .
Kühlenthal	Art.	1.10.31(6)	3 7/12	1.3.28(4)	4 9/12	1.6.23(2)	. . .	. . .
Feige	Inf.	1.10.31(7)	3 6/12	1.4.28(1)	4 10/12	1.6.23(3)	. . .	. . .
v. Brauchitsch	Art.	1.10.31(8)	3 6/12	1.4.28(2)	6 11/12	1.5.21(3)	. . .	. . .
Karlewski	Art.	1.10.31(9)	3 6/12	1.4.28(4)	4 9/12	1.7.23(2)	5 6/12	27.1.18(7)
Neumann-Neurode	Inf.	1.11.31	3 7/12	1.4.28(5)	4 6/12	1.10.23(1)	5 5/12	27.1.18(10)
F. v. Hammerstein-Equord	Inf.	1.12.31(1)	3 8/12	1.4.28(7)	4 6/12	1.10.23(3)	5 9/12	27.1.18(12)
v. Witzendorff	Inf.	1.12.31(2)	3 7/12	1.5.28(1)	4 7/12	1.10.23(4)	5 9/12	27.1.18(14)
Curtze	Art.	1.2.32(2)	3	1.2.29(8)	4 9/12	1.5.24(1)	6	18.5.18(6)
Bitthorn	Inf.	1.2.32(4)	3	1.2.29(10)	4 6/12	1.8.23	6 3/12	18.5.18(9)
Starke	Art.	1.3.32	3 1/12	1.2.29(11)	4 1/12	1.1.25	6 8/12	18.5.18(15)
Haenicke	Inf.	1.4.32(1)	3 2/12	1.2.29(13)	4	1.2.25(1a)	4 9/12	18.5.20(14)
F. v. Hirschberg	Kav.	1.4.32(2)	3 1/12	1.3.29(1)	4	1.3.25	6 8/12	15.7.18(17)
Roese	Inf.	1.4.32(3)	3 1/12	1.3.29(2)	3 11/12	1.4.25(1)	6 9/12	15.7.18(19)
v. Waldow	Kav.	1.4.32(4)		1.4.29(1)	4	1.4.25(2)	6 9/12	15.7.18(25)
v. Kleist	Kav.	(Char.) 1.1.32	2 9/12	1.4.29(4)	4	1.4.25(5)	6 7/12	20.9.18(6a)

SOURCE: Rangliste 1923-1932.

238

TABLE 11

BAVARIAN MAJORS WHO RECEIVED PREFERENTIAL PROMOTIONS

Name	Year of Promotion	Assignment When Promoted	Patent Advantage (Yrs)	Branch of Service	Gen.St. Officers	Non-Bavarian Officers	Wehrmacht Gens.
Wäger	1924	RWM	2	Inf.	X	...	X
Rüdel		Gen.St.					
	"	7.DIV.	2 1/2	Art.	X	...	X
Halder	"	A.R.7	"	Art.	X	...	X
Kesselring	1925	RWM	2	Art.	X	...	X
Wever	1926	I.R.4	"	Inf.	X	...	X
Krafft	"	RWM	"	Tech.	X	...	...
Hengen	1927	A.R.7	"	Art.	...	...	...
Müller(Franz)	"	RWM	"	Inf.	X	X	...
R. v. Speck	1928	RWM	"	Art.	X	...	...
Fahrmbacher	"	A.R.7	"	Art.	...	...	...
v. Arnim	"	St.7.DIV.	"	Inf.	X	X	X
Kübler	1929	St.1.DIV.	"	Inf.	X	...	X
Nissl	"	Inf.Sch.	2	Inf.	...	...	...
v. Fumetti	"	RWM	2	Inf.	X	X	...
Weisenberger	"	I.R.19	2	Inf.	X	...	...
Wimmer	1930	RWM	3	Inf.	...	...	X
Dietl	"	I.R.19	"	Inf.	...	...	X
Müller(Eugen)	1931	St.4.DIV.	"	Art.	X	...	X
Stapf	"	St.7.DIV.	"	Inf.	X	...	X
Konrad	"	RWM	"	Inf.	...	...	X
Jodl(Alfred)	"	St.7.DIV.	"	Art.	X	...	X
Jaenicke	1932	St.7.DIV.	"	Tech.	X	...	X
Zorn(Hans)	"	RWM	"	Inf.	X	...	X
Müller(Kurt)	"	St.7.DIV.	"	Inf.	X	...	...
Brandenberger	"	St.3.DIV.	"	Art.	X	...	X
R. v. Weber	"	RWM	"	Inf.	...	...	...

SOURCE: NA, 79, 83, pp. 1-120; Rangliste 1923-1932; Keilig, Generalität des Heeres im 2. Weltkrieg.

TABLE 1

CAREER PROFILES OF THIRTY-FIVE DISCHARGED BAVARIAN OFFICERS

Name	Grade	Patent	Assignment						
			1923	1924	1925	1926	1927	1928	1929
v. Beck	Brig.Gen.	1.4.26	Kdr.I.R.21	. . .	. . .	Kdt.Munich	a.D.	. . .	. . .
Zürn	"	1.2.27(3)	Kdr.R.R.17	. . .	. . .	. . .	Kdtr.Munich	a.D.	. . .
Selling	Gen.Artz	1.11.24	St.7.DIV.	. . .	. . .	. . .	a.D.	. . .	. . .
R. v. Schmidtler	Col.	1.10.23(6)	R.St./I.R.21	Kdr.I.R.20	. . .	. . .	a.D.	. . .	. . .
Feeser*	"	1.11.23(2)	Kdr.I/A.R.7	Kdtr.Munich	. . .	. . .	a.D.	. . .	. . .
Schrott	"	1.6.25(3)	St.Art.Kdr.7	St.GP.2	. . .	. . .	a.D.	. . .	. . .
R. v. Hörauf*	"	1.2.26(3)	Kdr.I/I.R.21	. . .	St.Art.Kdr.7	R.St./I.R.21	a.D.	. . .	. . .
Mack	Lt.Col.	1.3.21(2)	Kdr.II/A.R.7	. . .	. . .	a.D.	. . .	. . .	. . .
Glaser	"	1.4.22(1)	Kdr.A/I.R.21	. . .	. . .	a.D.	. . .	. . .	. . .
Hoffmann (J.)	"	1.4.22(2)	Kdt.Ingolstadt	. . .	. . .	a.D.	. . .	. . .	. . .
Kalbfus*	"	15.11.22(9b)	T7	. . .	Kdr.II/I.R.21	Kdt.Ingolstadt	. . .	a.D.	. . .
Fischer	"	1.2.23(12)	Kdr.A/I.R.20	St.GP.1	St.7.DIV.	St.7.DIV.	a.D.	. . .	. . .
Lüst*	"	1.2.23(17)	Inf.Sch.Instructor	Gen.St.7.DIV.	St.7.DIV.	R.St./I.R.20	a.D.	. . .	. . .
Haselmayr*	"	1.2.24(3)	Kdr.II/I.R.20	. . .	. . .	St./R.R.8	Kdtr.Munich	a.D.	. . .
Matthiess	"	1.2.25(1)	St.7.DIV.	. . .	. . .	a.D.	. . .	. . .	. . .
Gebendorfer	"	1.2.25(3)	In5	Kdtr.Ingolstadt	. . .	. . .	a.D.	. . .	. . .
Prügel	"	1.2.25(10)	St.Art.Sch.	Kdr.N.A.7	. . .	. . .	. . .	. . .	. . .
Baumann (O)*	Maj.	1.2.26(17)	Gen.St.7.DIV.	R.St./I.R.20	Kdr.I/I.R.20	. . .	a.D.	. . .	. . .
Tautkirch	"	1.10.20(47)	Kdr.8(M.G.)/I.R.20	Kdr.14/I.R.20	Kdr.5/R.R.17	St./R.R.17	a.D.	. . .	. . .
Koller	"	1.7.21(21)	St.7.DIV.	St.7.DIV.	. . .	Kdtr.Munich	. . .	. . .	. . .
v. Bally*	"	1.5.22(4)	St.A/I.R.20	. . .	Kdtr.Munich	a.D.	. . .	. . .	. . .
Woikard	"	1.5.22(18)	St.7.DIV.	. . .	. . .	St.A/I.R.20	a.D.	. . .	. . .
Thäter	"	1.10.22(4)	Kdr.15/I.R.21	. . .	. . .	a.D.	. . .	. . .	. . .
Schuster	"	1.2.25(10)	St.11/I.R.21	. . .	Kdr.7/I.R.21	St.II/I.R.21	a.D.	. . .	. . .
R. v. Schallern	"	1.2.26(11)	R.Adj./A.R.7	. . .	Kdtr.Ingolstadt	St.II/I.R.21	St.III/A.R.7	Kdtr.Ingolstadt	a.D.
Wallner	Capt.(W)	1.12.26(5)	Kdr.5/R.R.17	. . .	Kdr.1/R.R.17	. . .	. . .	St./R.R.17	a.D.
Beck	Capt.	18.11.14(86)	Ingolstadt	. . .	S.A.7	a.D.	. . .	. . .	. . .
Nüsslein	"	27.1.15(37)	Kdr.3/F.A.7	. . .	St.I/I.R.21	Kdr.1/I.R.21	a.D.	. . .	. . .
Lippmann	"	22.3.18(16)	Kdr.5/I.R.20	. . .	St.I/I.R.21	. . .	a.D.	. . .	. . .
Walther	"	18.10.18(46)	2/R.R.17	. . .	. . .	Kdr.2/R.R.17	a.D.	. . .	. . .
Wachter	"	1.1.23(2)	13(M.W.)/I.R.20	. . .	. . .	Kdr.14/I.R.20	a.D.	. . .	. . .
Finster	"	1.6.24(6)	1/R.R.17	6/R.R.17	. . .	. . .	a.D.	. . .	. . .
Kleyla	"	1.6.26(4)	3/F.A.7	. . .	. . .	4/A.R.7	a.D.	. . .	. . .
Veith	1Lt.	1.4.25(6)	1/I.R.13	2/N.A.7	. . .	a.D.	. . .	St.II/A.R.7	. . .
Munk	Lt.	1.1.16(12)	. . .	1/F.A.7	. . .	a.D.	. . .	. . .	. . .

SOURCE: Rangliste 1923-1929; NA, 79, 73, p. 600, passim.

*These officers were General Staff officers.

241

TABLE 2

NUMERICAL AND PERCENTAGE FIGURES FOR

DISMISSED REICHSWEHR OFFICERS, 1924-1932

Grade	1924	1925	1926	1927	1928	1929	1930	1931	1932
Lt. Gens.		2(2)		3(3)	2	1(1)	2(2)	1	1(1)
Maj. Gens.	4(2)	2	4(2)	4(2)	5(4)	6(4)	11(9)	6(2)	6(2)
Brig. Gens.	10(4)	3	6(2)	7(3)	11(6)	10(4)	8(4)	14(2)	15(6)
Cols.	22(6)	22(6)	19(4)	25(9)	26(6)	32(5)	45(16)	54(10)	33(10)
Lt. Cols.	13(2)	15(5)	19(6)	28(6)	32(11)	24(8)	19(4)	17(3)	16(2)
Majs.	12	27(13)	18(2)	22(8)	17(7)	16(7)	13(4)	21(4)	22(8)
Capts.	46(14)	47(3)	35(7)	39(6)	48(6)	44(6)	50(13)	22(6)	25(5)
1 Lts.	22(6)	20(1)	35(8)	20(2)	73(12)	47(8)	70(12)	28(3)	29(6)
Lts.	55(5)	57(11)	24(5)	14(3)	16(3)	6(1)	13(3)	13(3)	9(3)
TOTAL	184(39)	195(39)	160(36)	162(42)	230(55)	186(44)	231(67)	176(33)	156(43)

PERCENTAGE FIGURES FOR DISMISSED OFFICERS

Gens.	8%	4%	7%	8%	8%	9%	9%	11%	14%
Stabsoffz.	26%	31%	35%	44%	33%	37%	33%	50%	44%
Capts.	24%	24%	22%	39%	20%	23%	22%	14%	16%
1Lts./Lts.	42%	41%	36%	34%	39%	32%	37%	26%	27%
Nobles	22%	20%	22%	25%	23%	22%	28%	20%	27%

SOURCE: Rangliste 1924-1932

NOTE: The figures in parenthesis refer to the number of nobles in the particular group.

TABLE 3

TOTAL NUMBER OF DISMISSED REICHSWEHR

OFFICERS ACCORDING TO BRANCH OF SERVICE, 1924-1932

Year	Branch of Service			
	Inf.	Kav.	Art.	Tech.
1924	77	31	29	26
1925	85	46	34	28
1926	70	34	34	26
1927	70	34	34	19
1928	126	42	50	23
1929	99	31	39	29
1930	95	45	46	40
1931	86	19	40	32
1932	85	29	25	18
TOTAL	793	311	331	241

SOURCE: Rangliste 1924-1932.

243

TABLE 4

YEARLY NUMBER OF OFFICERS DISMISSED FROM THE INFANTRY REGIMENTS, 1924–1932

Year	I.R.1	I.R.2	I.R.3	I.R.4	I.R.5	I.R.6	I.R.7	I.R.8	I.R.9	I.R.10	I.R.11
1924	2 Capts. 3 Lts.	1 Capt. 1 Lt.	1 Lt.	1 Lt.Col. 1 Lt.	1 Lt.Col. 1 lLt.	1 Col. 1 Lt.Col. 1 Maj. 2 Capts. 1 lLt. 2 Lts.	1 Capt. 1 Lt.	1 Capt. 1 lLt. 4 Lts.	1 lLt.	1 Maj. 1 Capt.	1 Lt.
1925	1 Maj. 3 Capts. 2 lLts.	1 Col. 2 Lts.	1 Lt.	1 Maj. 1 Lt.	1 Col. 1 Capt. 2 Lts.	1 Maj. 1 Capt. 3 Lts.	1 Maj. 1 lLt.	1 Lt.Col. 2 Capts. 1 Lt.	1 Maj. 1 lLt.	2 Cols. 1 Capt.	1 Capt. 1 lLt. 1 Lt.
1926	2 Cols. 2 Lts.	2 Cols. 1 Capt. 2 lLts. 1 Lt.	1 Maj. 1 Capt. 1 lLt. 1 Lt.	1 Capt. 3 lLts. 1 Lt.	1 Lt.Col. 1 Capt.		1 Maj. 1 lLt.	1 Col. 1 lLt. 1 Lt.	1 Col. 1 lLt.		1 Maj. 2 Capt.
1927				2 Majs. 1 Lt.	1 Capt.	2 Cols. 2 Capts. 1 lLt.	1 Lt.Col. 2 Capts.	2 Capts. 1 lLt.	1 Col. 1 Capt.	1 lLt.	2 Lt.Cols. 1 Capt.
1928	1 Col. 1 Lt.Col. 2 Capts. 2 lLts.	5 lLts. 1 Lt.	1 Lt.Col. 1 Maj. 1 lLt.	1 Maj. 3 lLts.	1 Brig.Gen. 1 Lt.Col. 1 Maj. 1 Capt. 6 l Lts. 1 Lt.	1 Col. 1 Maj. 3 lLts. 1 Lt.	2 Lt.Cols. 3 Capts. 1 lLt.	2 Capts. 2 lLts.	1 Col. 1 Lt.Col. 3 Capts. 2 lLts.	1 Lt.Col. 1 Capt. 1 lLt.	1 Capt. 2 Lts.
1929	1 Maj. 1 Capt. 2 lLts.	1 Col. 1 Maj. 1 Capt. 2 lLts.	1 Lt.Col. 1 Capt. 2 lLts.	1 Lt.Col. 3 lLts. 1 lLt.	2 Lt.Cols. 2 Capts.	1 Lt.Col. 1 Capt.	1 lLt.	1 Lt.Col. 2 Capts. 1 Lt.	1 Col. 1 Lt.Col. 1 Capt.	1 Col. 1 Lt.Col. 2 Capts.	1 Capt. 2 lLts.
1930	2 Majs. 1 lLt.	1 Lt.Col. 1 lLt.	1 Maj. 3 lLts. 3 lLts.	1 Col. 2 lLts.	1 Col. 1 lLt.	1 Maj. 1 Lt.	1 Maj. 1 Capt. 1 lLt.	1 Maj. 1 Capt.		1 Capt. 3 lLts.	2 Lt.Cols. 2 Capts. 2 lLts.
1931	2 Cols. 1 Lt.Col.	1 Lt.Col. 1 Lt.	1 Brig.Gen. 1 Lt.Col. 1 Lt.		3 Cols. 1 Capt.	1 Col. 2 Lt.Cols. 1 Capt.	1 Brig.Gen. 1 Capt. 1 lLt.	1 Col. 2 Capts.	1 Col. 1 Capt.	1 Maj. 1 lLt.	1 Maj. 1 Capt. 1 lLt.
1932	2 Capts. 1 lLt.	2 Lt.Cols. 1 Maj. 1 Capt.	2 Majs. 1 Capt. 1 lLt.	1 Col. 1 Capt. 1 lLt.	1 Col. 1 Maj. 3 lLts.	1 Maj.	1 Lt.Col.	1 Brig.Gen.	1 Lt.Col. 1 lLt.	1 Lt.Col. 3 Capts. 1 lLt.	1 Lt.Col. 1 Maj. 1 lLt.
TOTAL	34	30	25	26	36	33	23	29	23	23	29

TABLE 4 - Continued

Year	I.R.12	I.R.13	I.R.14	I.R.15	I.R.16	I.R.17	I.R.18	I.R.19	I.R.20	I.R.21
1924	1 Lt.	1 1Lt. 1 Lt.	1 Capt. 2 Lts.	2 Cols. 2 Capts. 1 Lt.	1 Lt.Col. 1 1Lt. 2 Lts.	1 1Lt. 3 Lts.	1 Col. 3 Lts.	1 Lt.	1 Brig.Gen. 1 Capt. 2 Lts.	1 Capt. 6 Lts.
1925	2 Capts. 1 1Lt. 4 Lts.	2 Lts.	2 Capts. 1 1Lt. 2 Lts.	1 1Lt. 2 Lts.	1 Capt. 1 1Lt.	1 1Lt. 1 Lt.	2 Cols. 1 Lt.Col. 2 Capts.	1 Col. 1 Lt.Col. 1 Lt.	1 Col. 1 1Lt. 3 Lts.	1 Capt.
1926	1 Lt.Col. 1 1Lt. 2 Lts.	1 Lt.	1 Capt. 1 1Lt.	1 Lt.Col. 1 Capt.		1 Maj. 1 Lt.	1 Capt. 1 1Lt.	1 Lt.Col. 1 1Lt. 1 Lt.	1 Maj.	1 Lt.Col. 1 Maj.
1927	2 Capts. 1 1Lt.	2 1Lts.	1 Col. 1 Lt.Col. 1 Capt. 1 1Lt.	1 Capt. 1 1Lt.	2 Lt.Cols. 1 Capt.	1 Capt. 2 Lts.	1 Lt.Col. 1 Lt.	1 Maj.	1 Col. 1 Maj. 1 Capt. 1 1Lt.	
1928	1 Brig.Gen. 2 Lt.Cols. 1 Capt. 2 1Lts. 2 Lts.	1 Capt. 2 1Lts.	1 Lt.Col. 1 Capt. 1 1Lt.	1 Lt.Col. 1 Capt. 2 1Lts.	1 Brig.Gen. 1 Lt.Col. 3 1Lts.	1 Maj. 1 Capt.	1 Maj. 1 Capt. 2 1Lts. 1 Lt.	1 1Lt. 1 Lt.	2 Lt.Cols. 1 1Lt.	1 Col. 1 Maj. 1 Capt. 1 1Lt.
1929	1 Col. 2 Capts. 1 1Lt.		1 Lt.Col. 2 Majs. 2 1Lts.	1 Lt.Col. 2 Capts.	1 Col. 1 Lt.Col. 3 1Lts.	1 Col. 1 Lt.Col. 4 Capts. 1 1Lt.	1 Capt. 1 1Lt.	1 Capt. 1 1Lt.	1 Col. 1 Capt.	1 Brig.Gen. 1 Col.
1930	4 1Lts.		2 Capts. 1 1Lt. 1 Lt.	1 Brig.Gen. 1 Capt.	1 Brig.Gen. 1 1Lt.	1 Col. 2 Capts. 3 1Lts.	2 Capts. 1 Lt.	1 Col. 1 Capt. 2 1Lts.	2 Cols. 2 Capts. 2 1Lts.	1 Capt. 1 1Lt. 1 Lt.
1931	1 Col. 1 1Lt.	1 Col.	1 Maj.	1 Col. 1 Lt.	1 Col.	1 Brig.Gen. 2 Majs. 1 Capt. 1 1Lt. 1 Lt.	1 Col.	1 Maj. 1 1Lt.	1 Lt.Col.	1 Col. 1 Capt.
1932	1 Brig.Gen. 1 Capt.	1 Maj. 2 Capts. 3 1Lts.	1 1Lt.	1 Brig.Gen. 1 1Lt.	1 Lt.Col. 1 Maj. 1 Capt. 1 1Lt. 1 Lt.	2 Lt.Cols. 1 Capt.	1 Capt. 2 1Lts.	1 Maj. 1 1Lt. 1 Lt.	1 Lt.Col. 1 1Lt.	1 1Lt.
TOTAL	35	17	28	25	27	35	27	21	30	22

SOURCE: Rangliste 1924-1932

245

TABLE 5

TOP SECRET ROSTER OF FLYING OFFICERS AS OF 1.11.1930

Rank	Name	Patent	Assignment
Brig.Gen.	Ritter von Mittelberger	1. 3.30(1)	RWM
"	Streccius	1. 2.30(1)	I.R.17
Col.	Wilberg	1. 10.29(13)	Kdtr.Breslau
Lt.Col.	Hoth	1. 2.29(26)	St.GP.1
"	Quade	1. 4.30(9)	I.R.2
"	Schweickhard	1.11.30(16)	I.R.14
Major	Klepke	1. 7.26(4)	I.R.15
"	Sperrle	1.10.26(7)	I.R.8
"	Felmy	1. 1.27(3)	RWM
"	Mohr**	1. 2.27(26)	R.R.18
"	Kühl	1. 4.27(6)	I.R.1
"	Frhr. v. Freyberg Eisenberg-Allmendingen**	1. 5.27(4)	Kdtr. Döberitz
"	Holdermann	1. 2.28(8)	I.R.2
"	Grauert	1. 2.28(23a)	RWM
"	Volkmann	1. 2.28(28b)	Art.Kdr.2
"	Wimmer	1. 2.28(38a)	RWM
"	Bieneck**	1. 4.29(3)	R.R.14
"	v. Kotze	1.11.29	R.R.14
"	Student	1. 1.30(1)	I.R.2
"	Schubert	?	R.R.8
"	Cranz	1. 4.30(11)	R.R.14
"	Reinecke**	?	RWM
Capt.	Krocker	16. 9.17(2)	Kdtr.Breslau
"	Doerstling	20. 6.18(5)	I.R.10
"	Erdmann	15. 7.18(14)	N.A.6
"	Seldner	18. 8.18(8)	RWM
"	Pflugbeil*	18. 8.18(25)	R.R.11
"	Koch	18.10.18(5)	I.R.18
"	Sommé	18.10.18(6)	R.R.7
"	Dessloch	18.10.18(45)	R.R.17
"	Hartmann	1.12.21(1)	A.R.4
"	Behrla	1. 1.22(9)	St.GP.2
"	Martini	1. 6.22(3)	Kav.Sch.
"	Putzier*	1. 6.22(7)	A.R.2
"	Barlen	1.10.22(2)	R.R.18
"	Kieffer	1.12.22(10)	F.A.7
"	Müller (Kurt)	1. 1.23(1)	RWM
"	Müller (Angelo)	1. 2.23(7)	F.A.7
"	Gandert	1. 8.23(1)	I.R.1
"	Lorenz	1.11.23(4)	I.R.17
"	Zoch	1.12.23(2)	Kdtr.Döberitz
"	Hanesse	1. 1.24(5)	A.R.1
"	von Wühlisch	1. 2.24(2)	R.R.5
"	Ritter v. Pohl	1. 6.24(12)	A.R.5
"	Schultheiss	1.11.24(5)	R.R.3

TABLE 5 - Continued

Rank	Name	Patent	Assignment
Capt.	Krüger (Ehrhard)*	1.11.24(6)	I.R.1
"	Keiper**	1.11.24(8)	I.R.15
"Dipl.-Ing.	Hilgers	1. 2.25(17)	F.A.2
"	Sperling*	1. 2.25(18)	F.A.5
"	Frhr. v. Biedermann*	1. 2.25(19)	I.R.10
"	v. Harbou	1. 4.25(10)	I.R.2
"	Baumbach	1. 5.25(2)	A.R.2
"	Bonatz	1. 2.26(10)	R.R.7
"	Löb	1. 2.26(33)	P.B.6
"	Sturm*	1. 3.26(7)	I.R.8
"	Schläger	1. 4.26(11)	A.R.6
"	Speidel	1. 4.26(18)	RWM
"	Drum	1. 4.26(19)	RWM
"	Schroth**	1. 2.27(8)	R.R.11
"	Mai	1. 2.27(28)	K.A.5
"	Biwer	1. 4.27(7)	R.R.16
"	Fischer	1. 2.28(32)	I.R.2
"	Funcke**	1. 2.28(33)	I.R.18
"	Fink	1. 2.28(43)	R.R.1
"	Veith**	1. 2.28(50)	A.R.7
"	Schwabedissen	1. 3.28(2)	RWM
"	Friedel	1. 3.28(4)	I.R.15
"Dipl.-Ing.	Riesch	1. 4.28(14)	RWM
"	Tschoeltsch	1. 4.28(15)	I.R.10
"Dipl.-Ing.	Ploch	1. 4.28(31)	RWM
"	Seywald	1. 4.28(43)	K.A.4
"	Müller (Gottlob)	1. 5.28(5a)	K.A.7
"	v. Chamier-Gliscinski	1. 1.29(1a)	R.R.16
"	Fütterer*	1. 1.29(2a)	I.R.17
"	v. Heyking**	1. 1.29(5)	S.A.4
"	Pfeiffer	1. 2.29(24a)	F.A.6
"	Abernetty*	1. 2.29(33a)	I.R.5
"	Sattler*	1. 2.29(35)	Kdtr.Küstrin
"	Stapelberg	1. 2.29(40a)	I.R.15
"	Buchholz**	1. 2.29(42)	I.R.8
"	Frhr. v. Richthofen	1. 2.29(43)	A.R.5
"	Pistorius	1. 4.29(9a)	P.B.2
"	v. Gerlach**	1. 4.29(12)	R.R.11
"	Mälzer	1. 7.29(1)	A.R.4
"	Rieke**	?	I.R.16
"	Plaschke	1.10.29(14a)	R.R.3
"	Conrad	1. 2.30(17)	I.R.6
"	Fuchs	1. 2.30(22)	Kdtr.Berlin
"	Aschenbrenner	1. 2.30(32)	Kdtr.Küstrin
"	Baier	1. 5.25(11)	A.R.3
"	Weiner	1. 2.30(39)	K.A.2
"	Lohmann	1. 4.30(5)	A.R.1
"	Gaze	1. 4.30(13)	R.R.8

TABLE 5 - Continued

Rank	Name	Patent	Assignment
1Lt.	Berger	1. 4.25(175)	I.R.4
"	Kammhuber	1. 4.25(180)	RWM
ch.Capt.	v. Massow*	1. 2.31(22)	I.R.9
1Lt.	Reinshagen	1. 4.25(218)	I.R.5
"	Raithel	1. 4.25(226)	I.R.20
"	Meister*	1. 4.25(250)	I.R.4
"	Volkmann**	1. 4.25(256)	I.R.10
"	Korten	1. 4.25(280)	P.B.4
"	Weber	1. 4.25(281)	I.R.14
"	Becker	1. 4.25(289)	R.R.1
"	Schwartzkopff	1. 4.25(308)	I.R.6
"Dipl.-Ing.	Bassenge	1. 4.25(310)	I.R.6
"	Wieland	1. 4.25(325)	I.R.5
"	Cartun*	1. 4.25(327)	I.R.7
"	v. Oheimb	1. 4.25(354)	R.R.11
"	Jordan	1. 4.25(360)	A.R.5
"	Schimpf*	1. 4.25(373)	I.R.21
"	Meyer (Wilhelm)**	1. 4.25(380)	I.R.5
"	Jeschonnek	1. 4.25(386)	R.R.6
"	Heusinger	1.4.25(417)	St.Inf.Kdr.2
"	Ibel**	1. 4.25(436)	P.B.7
"	Pregler	1. 4.25(463)	A.R.7
"	Holle	1. 4.25(477)	I.R.16
"	Hoffmann v. Waldau	1. 4.25(487)	St.7.DIV.
"	Deichmann*	1. 4.25(524)	I.R.3
"	Notz	1. 4.25(589)	I.R.20
"	Krüger (Adolf-Friedrich)*	1. 4.25(616)	I.R.4
"	Macht	1. 4.25(656)	A.R.1
"	Boenicke*	1. 7.25(2)	F.A.5
"	Herhudt v. Rohden*	1.11.25(1)	F.A.6
"	Kösters	1. 2.26(12)	I.R.6
"	Kleinrath	1. 2.26(22)	A.R.2
"	Frhr. v. Houwald*	1. 2.26(41)	R.R.6
"	Kriesche	1. 3.26(3)	A.R.2
"	v. Scheel	1. 4.26(8)	I.R.11
"	Wilke	1. 8.26(1)	A.R.1
"	Knoke	1. 9.26(3)	I.R.16
"	Viek	1.10.26(4)	III./A.R.3
"	Platz**	1. 3.27(18)	P.B.4
"	Evers	1. 3.27(21)	I.R.18
"	Koester	1. 4.27(1)	S.A.2
"	Frhr. v. Wichtingen	1. 5.27(4)	R.R.11
"	de Salengre-Drabbe	1. 5.27(6)	I.R.12
"	Emminghaus	1. 6.27(9)	S.A.5
"	Plocher	1. 8.27(3)	I.R.13
"	Seidemann	1. 8.27(4)	I.R.9
"	v. Cramon**	1.11.27(11)	R.R.7

TABLE 5 - Continued

Rank	Name	Patent	Assignment
1Lt.	v. Wurmb	1. 1.28(1)	I.R.7
"	Schnarrenberger	1. 1.28(7)	I.R.14
"	Witt	1. 1.28(8)	I.R.5
"	Mehnert*	1. 1.28(10)	I.R.11
"	Schulz-Heyn*	1. 1.28(13)	A.R.1
"	Dinort	1. 2.28(9)	I.R.2
"	Meyer (Hans)*	1. 2.28(17)	I.R.1
"	Krahl*	1. 2.28(25)	I.R.10
"	Korte*	1. 2.28(51)	I.R.14
"	Berchtenbreiter*	1. 4.28(20)	I.R.20
"	Nielsen	1. 4.28(52a)	I.R.6
"	Boner	1. 4.28(62)	N.A.3
"	Pusinelli*	1. 4.28(75)	I.R.10
"	Hessel**	1. 8.28(14)	I.R.21
"	Hill*	1. 8.28(15)	I.R.3
"	Kreipe*	1. 9.28(6)	A.R.6
"	von Detten*	1.11.28(21)	R.R.3
"	Petzold*	1.11.28(26)	I.R.4
"	Schmidt v. Altenstadt*	1. 2.29(37)	R.R.4
"	v. Hoffmann*	1. 4.29(30)	R.R.4
"	Dybwad**	1. 7.29(6)	A.R.2
"	Doench*	1. 8.29(2)	III./A.R.3
ch."	Börner**	?	A.R.4
"	v. Koppelow**	?	R.R.11
"	Lerche	1. 4.30(5)	I.R.157
Lt.	Küster	1. 4.29(3)	R.R.14
"	Meinecke	1. 9.29(2)	A.R.3

SOURCE: Völker, Entwicklung der Militärischen Luftfahrt, pp. 255-259; Rangliste 1930-1931.

NOTE: In the case of certain Patents, indicated by a question mark, no record of the officer's rank could be determined from official sources.

*These officers are not listed in the 1930 Rangliste but appear in the 1931 Rangliste.

**These officers appear in neither the 1930 nor the 1931 Rangliste.

Appendix 8.
Operational Training

TABLE 1

REICHSWEHR TRAINING CLASSES (LEHRGÄNGE), 1925-1926

	Course Subject	Time and Place	Students
1.	General Staff Candidate Training	1.10.25-30.9.26 (Division Hq)	62 lLts., Lts. from all branches
2.	Technical General Staff Candidate Training	1.10.25-30.9.26 (Technical Colleges)	54 lLts., Lts. from all branches
3.	Officer Weapons School Class	1.10.25-15.2.26 1.4.26-15.8.26 (Dresden)	92 Stabsoffz. from all branches 92 Capts., lLts., Lts. from all branches
4.	Weapons School for Engineering, Signals, Artillery Offz.	1.11.25-31.8.26 (Munich) 1.12.25-30.9.26 (Jüterbog) 12.11.25-20.8.26 (Jüterbog)	7 lLts., Lts., from the Eng. Br. 4 lLts., Lts., from the Sig. Br. 22 lLts., Lts., from the Art. Br.
5.	Infantry School	1.3.-31.10.25 1.3.-15.10.26 (Ohrdruf)	70 Stabsoffz. from all branches 70 Capts., lLts., Lts. from all branches
6.	Training of Instructors in Physical Exercise	1) Jan-May 26 2) Jun-Oct 26 (Wünsdorf)	30 lLts., Lts. from all branches 30 lLts., Lts. from all branches
7.	Breaking in of Infantry Remounts	1.10.25-30.9.26 (Hannover)	32 lLts., Lts. from the Kav., Art., Supply and Sig. Branches
8.	Artillery for Non-Artilleriests	5.10.25-31.10.25 (Juterbog)	6 Gens., Stabsoffz. from all branches 58 Capts. from all branches
9.	Training and Marksmanship with Fortress-artillery and "Flak" Weapons	3.10.-3.11.25 (Königsberg)	34 Stabsoffz., Capts., Lts. from the Art. Branch
10.	Gas Attack Defense a) Gen. & Stabsoffz. b) Instructors at Schools c) Gas Defense Officers	Jan-Mar 4 classes, 4 da. ea. 4.1-8.1.26 Nov-Mar, 5 classes 11 days ea.	44 Gens. Stabsoffz. from all branches and the Navy 5 Medical Offz. from all branches and the Navy 45 Stabsoffz., Capts. from all branches and the Navy 44 Capts., Lts. from all branches and the Navy 5 Medical Offz. from all branches and the Navy
11.	Training Jr. Officers for Mortar Company	1.12.25-May 26 (Jüterbog)	23 Offz. from the Inf. Br.

TABLE 1 - Continued

	Course Subject	Time and Place	Students
12.	Combat School	20.10.-28.11 (Döberitz)	147 Stabsoffz., Capts., Lts. from the Inf., Kav., and Eng. Branches
13.	Artillery Reconnaissance	28.9-24.10.25 (Jüterbog)	26 Capts., Lts. from the Art. Br.
14.	Weather Instruments	Nov 25 (Jüterbog)	8 Capts. from the Art. Br.
15.	Motorized Transport for the Artillery	8.3-2.4.25 (Jüterbog)	11 Capts., Lts. from the Art. Br. (Mot.)
16.	Firing Course for Artillery Officers	6 weeks in period Apr-Jun 26 (Königsbrück)	67 Stabsoffz., Capts., Lts. from Art. Br.
17.	Engine and Machine Training	17.11.-19.12.25 (Munich)	18 Stabsoffz., Capts. from the Eng. Br.
18.	Searchlight and Equipment	Feb-Apr 26 10 weeks (Klausdorf)	7 1Lts., Lts. from the Eng. Br.
19.	Advanced Training for Supply Corps Instructors	a) 5.-31.10.25 b) Mar-May 26 9 wks c) May-July 26 9 wks (Hannover)	7 Stabsoffz., Capts. from the Supply Br. 7 Capts., Lts. from the Supply Br. 7 Capts., Lts. from the Supply Br.
20.	Advanced Training for Instructors in Pack Animal Service	8 days before or after High Mountain Exercise (7.DIV.area)	8 Capts., 1Lts., Lts. from the Supply Branch
21.	Special Motorized Supply Training for Berlin	from 1.10.25 3 courses, 3 months each (Berlin)	10 Stabsoffz., Capts. Lts. from Mot. Transport Br. 5 Stabsoffz., Capts., Lts. from other Br.
22.	Examination as Military Motorized Equipment Inspectors	14 days in May 26 (Berlin)	28 Capts., Lts. from Mot. Transport and Art. Br.
23.	Training in Communications Intelligence	14 days in Mar 26 (Berlin)	7 Capts., 1Lts., Lts. from the Sig. Br.
24.	Training in Signals Service	12.10-12.12.25 (Jüterbog)	10 Capts., Lts. from the Supply Branch
25.	Training in Messenger Pigeon Service	12.-22.1.26 (Spandau)	4 Capts., 1Lts., Lts. from the Supply Br.
26.	Instruction in Dog Handling	2-15.1.26/17-31.1.26 (Sperenberg)	14 (ea.) Capts., 1Lts., Lts. from Inf. and Art. Branches
27.	Tracking with Dogs	Feb-Apr 26 (Sperenberg)	3 Inf. Offz. who are leaders of the DIV. messenger dog schools from 2., 3., 4., divisions

SOURCE: NA, 79, 56, pp. 1088-1091.

TABLE 2

REICHSWEHR TACTICAL RIDES (REISEN), 1924

	Type of Ride	Leader	Participants
1.	Commanders	Chef der Heeresleitung	Gens. and Senior Stabsoffz.
2.	General Staff Offz.	Kdr. Truppenamt	General Staff Stabsoffz. Assigned to Field and Staff Posts
3.	District	C.St.DIV.	Senior Capts. and Stabsoffz.
4.	District Air Defense	Div. Air Defense Specialist	Stabsoffz.
5.	General Staff Candidates	Kdr. T4	lLts., Capts.
6.	Junior Officers Assigned to the Defense Ministry	Senior General Staff Officer	lLts., Capts.
7.	Lehrgang R General Staff Trainees	Kdr. T4	lLts., Capts.
8.	Practical Year General Staff Trainees	Kdr. T4	lLts., Capts.
9.	Second Year General Staff Trainees	C.St.DIV.	lLts., Capts.
10.	Supply	C.St.GP.	Capts., Stabsoffz.
11.	Air Defense	Defense Ministry Air Defense Specialist	Capts., Stabsoffz.
12.	District Area	DIV. Inf. Kdr.	Stabsoffz., Capts.
13.	Garrison Terrain	---	---
14.	Troop Terrain	---	---
15.	Artillery*	Kdr. In4	Stabsoffz., Capts.
16.	Cavalry*	Kdr. In3	Stabsoffz., Capts.
17.	Signals*	Kdr. In7	Stabsoffz., Capts.
18.	Engineering*	Kdr. In5	Stabsoffz., Capts.

SOURCE: NA, 79, 65, pp. 150-153.

*These rides would occur only if sufficient funds were available.

TABLE 3

REICHSWEHR TRAINING CLASSES (LEHRGÄNGE), 1928-1929

	Course Subject	Time	Students
1.	Supply Orientation	1 week Oct 28	1 Gen. Staff Offz. from ea. Group and Division
2.	Motorization	1 week Mar 29	Weapons School Instructors
3.	Cavalry	1 week Oct 28	30 Stabsoffz. and Capts. of Kav.; also Stabsoffz. from other Weapons
4.	Requirements for Horse-manship in Units	1 week Oct 28	30 Stabsoffz. from Branches using Horse-Drawn Weapons
5.	Breaking in Infantry Remounts	1 year	32 Offz. from Branches using Horse-drawn Weapons
6.	Artillery for non-artilleriests	2 weeks Oct 28	60 Stabsoffz.
7.	Gas Defense	2 times, each 1 week Mar 29	80 Offz. each
8.	Use of Smoke	1 week Oct 28	Offz. from ea. Division's Smoke Section
9.	Munitions	1 week Jan 29	35 Offz. from Unit Staffs
10.	Fortification and "Flak" Weapons	4 weeks Oct-Nov 28	3 Offz. from ea. Division
11.	Survey Equipment	4-5 weeks Sep.Oct 28	7 Art. Offz.
12.	Motorization for Artilleriests	2 months Oct.Nov 28	1 Offz. from ea. Art. Regiment
13.	Quadrant and Sighting for Artilleriests	4 weeks Oct 28	25 Art. Offz.
14.	Engineering for Gen. and Stabsoffz.	10.6-23.6.28	20 Gen. or Senior Stabsoffz.
15.	Motorized Transport	2.5-30.7.28 2.10.28-15.2.29	15 Offz. each
16.	Supply for Supply Corps Offz.	3.10.-16.11.28	Capts. and Senior 1Lts. from Supply Branch
17.	Equipment Instruction for Supply Corps Stabsoffz.	26.11.-1.12.28	Supply Branch Stabsoffz. Assigned to Group and Division
18.	Signals for Stabsoffz.	28.1.29-9.2.29	12 Sig. Offz.
19.	Signals for Lts.	5.10.28-26.1.29	10 Sig. Offz.
20.	Communications Intelli-gence	1 week Mar 29	7 Offz.

TABLE 3 – <u>Continued</u>

	Course Subject	Time	Students
21.	Communications for Motor Transport Officers	16.4.28–14.7.28	---
22.	Communications for Instructors in Signals	30.7.–18.8.28	---
23.	Weapons Handling	1 week Mar 29	---

SOURCE: NA, 79, 64, pp. 1187-1195.

NOTE: Not listed are yearly classes for General Staff candidates, including officers assigned to technical colleges, and officers scheduled for weapons school refresher courses.

TABLE 4

REICHSWEHR TACTICAL RIDES (REISEN), 1928-1929

	Type of Ride	Authority
1.	Commanders'	Chef der Heeresleitung
2.	Truppenamt Kdr.'s	Truppenamt
3.	Preferential Promotion	Truppenamt
4.	Supply	Truppenamt
5.	General Staff Instructors	Truppenamt
6.	General Staff Candidates	Truppenamt
7.	Weapons Branch Officers	Truppenamt
8.	Weapons School Instructors	Infantry Inspector
9.	Engineer Officers	Engineer Inspector
10.	Cavalry Officers	Group Command
11.	Artillery Officers	Group Command
12.	Engineer Officers	Group Command
13.	Supply Officers	Group Command
14.	Signals Officers	Group Command
15.	Medical Officers	Group Command
16.	Veterinary Officers	Group Command
17.	District Tactical	Division/District Command
18.	District Supply	Division/District Command
19.	First and Second Year General Staff Candidates	Division/District Command
20.	District Air Defense	Division/District Command
21.	District Area	Division/District Command
22.	Garrison Terrain	Division/District Command
23.	Troop Terrain	Division/District Command

SOURCE: NA, 79, 64, pp. 1196-1197.

Index

About the Author

DAVID N. SPIRES, a Major in the United States Air Force and formerly an Associate Professor at the U.S. Air Force Academy, is currently on active duty in Europe. A specialist in the military history of the Weimar Republic and Third Reich, his writings have appeared in *The Citadel Proceedings of the Symposium on Hitler and the Nazi Era*.